PATH FOR
THE PERPLE

Towards Knowledge and Certainty

A Year Course on the Spiritual Path in 313 Steps
Drawn from *100 Stages of the Wayfarers* by ʿAbdullah al-Anṣārī

Compiled, edited and expanded upon by Julia A. Katarina
Original text translation and commentary by Ali A. Allawi

CLAIRVIEW

For Munya

Clairview Books Ltd.,
Russet, Sandy Lane,
West Hoathly,
W. Sussex RH19 4QQ

www.clairviewbooks.com

Published by Clairview Books 2026

A CIP catalogue record for this book is available from the British Library

ISBN 978 1 912992 81 2

Cover by Morgan Creative
Typeset by Symbiosys Technologies, Visakhapatnam, India
Printed and bound by 4Edge Ltd, Essex

Contents

Translator's Note

The modern person, not only in the West but in most of the world nowadays, has effectively abandoned the notion of a theocentric world. The process of decoupling knowledge and personal and societal ethics from its base in a revealed religion is most advanced in the West, but its consequences are encountered to a greater or lesser extent everywhere. Even in the remnants of traditional societies, the chipping away of the spiritual foundational bases of ethical and personal conduct is well advanced. The bookstores are groaning with books on self-help and self-knowledge; psychotherapies abound; spiritual retreats and movements are ubiquitous; but it is the human being—not God, Allāh, the Absolute or however the Ultimate Deity is named—that is the measure of all things.

In the process, the great spiritual traditions of mankind and the classical works of inner Awareness that emerged from them, have been banished from popular consciousness. The perspectives and values of a theocentric world have little purchase in these postmodern times. Echoes of them persist nonetheless, but they are garbed in the world-view of the sceptical, doubting and angst-ridden individual. This is a terrible loss. By ignoring, dismissing or trivialising the traditional pathways to self-knowledge, simply because the postmodern mind refuses to acknowledge their foundational basis, the human being is alienated from the experiences and openings that came from adherence to a spiritual path that is rooted in the great religious traditions of mankind. These were designed and honed over centuries of practice as a way to improve, uplift and energise human beings in the service of their own well-being, their societies, and in their understanding of the Divine.

Each of the religious traditions of mankind has its own inner dimensions, its esoteric aspects, as it were. The rituals, practices and forms of worship define the outer aspects of the religion, but it is through the inner aspects, where the individual seeks, through a systematic process of spiritual practices and states, to rise in consciousness and self-knowledge. The ultimate purpose of these exercises is to search, given each individual's capacities, as much as possible for the understanding of the Divine Will. By bringing oneself closer and closer to the Presence of the Sacred Reality, an individual ascends to higher understandings of their own self. The self in turn, experiences radical changes in its own awareness and its inner life can become infused with Sacred Grace. The self then, almost inevitably, shifts from earlier preoccupations and engrossments with its own needs and desires, to one that can reverberate with ever more subtle signals from the unseen. And belief and certainty in the reality of the unseen, however defined or experienced, is a universal feature of all traditional spiritual systems.

Ethical conduct thus becomes a natural outcome of a self that has renounced its worldly desires and has been freed from its imprisonment in a lower form of consciousness. The spiritually realised individual cannot but behave ethically, driven by the need of the self to fulfil its purpose towards the Divine through service and love to mankind.

In *Islām*, the path of inner knowledge and certainty, rooted in the pursuit of the sacred, has been associated with Sufism, or *taṣawwuf*, to use the Arabic term. Sufism is not the only spiritual path in Islam, and it has had an often contentious relationship with orthodoxy, preoccupied, as that would normally have to be, with legal, doctrinal and formal aspects of the religion. Sufism has also been severely criticised, even defamed, by Islamic modernists, who see in its practices and doctrines troubling, even sacrilegious, deviations from some of the core teachings of Islam.

Nevertheless, Sufism has bequeathed a massive legacy to the world of Islam. It is even seen by some as the original religion of the early centuries, with chains of teachers and guides, *silsilāt,* traceable back to Alī ibn Abi Tālib, the cousin and son-in-law of the Prophet Muhammad. Sufism has coloured the practice of the religion in profound ways. It was organised through religious orders, known as *ṭuruq*, each established around a saintly figure who drew his spiritual authority through a chain of Masters reaching back to the Prophet Muhammad. At the dawn of the modern era, Sufism was widespread in the world of Islam, with its centres, kitchens, teaching institutions, hospitals and orphanages ubiquitous throughout the Islamic world.

With the encroachment of Western imperial powers into the Islamic world, the Ṣūfi orders gradually began to lose their power and influence. They were in full retreat by the twentieth century. In recent times, Sufism has had a partial renaissance, partly driven by the inability of materialist ideologies to fill the spiritual wildernesses of the postmodern world, unmoored as this world is from any sense of the Sacred.

The religious, literary and artistic output of Sufis across the ages has been prodigious. It ranges over the entire landscape of Islamic life and civilization, girdled by the Sufis' quest for signs of the Eternal in the world and in the cosmos. Several classical works discuss the attributes of the path of the Sufis: the ethical deportment of the *murīd* (adept); their devotions, supplications and good works; and their relationships with each other, with their *murshid* or *shaykh* (spiritual directors), and their engagement with society at large.

Many of these books, such as the *Risāla* of al-Qushayri, the *Luma*ʿ of as-Sarrāj, the *Ḥikām* of Ibn ʿAtā Allāh, and the *Tabaqāt* of as-Sulāmi, continue to be widely read to this day, and form an important part of the education of the Ṣūfi novice. These works encapsulate the Ṣūfi worldview and experience, rooting it in the Qur'anic revelation and reconciling it with the requirements of Islamic law. They provide the foundations for the possibility of an engaged and active spiritual life. Other treatises deal with the various stages of the spiritual evolution of a person, within the ways of the Ṣūfi path. These can be a general description of stages on the path to full self-realisation. It could also be considered a detailed manual of practice that identifies spiritual states, *aḥwāl,* that accompany the serious adept in their journey. It was almost an article of faith that no adept could seriously advance on the path through these stages without the tutelage of a realised spiritual master.

In making a sequential review of these works, one can easily surmise that they are an early form of self-analysis. However, these are works that stand alone in their deep understanding of the human soul, seen through the prism of a world defined by signs of God in creation. Their premise is fundamentally different from contemporary understandings of psychology, even those schools that postulate that human life and action ultimately seek a purpose and meaning. A central tenet of this Ṣūfi cosmology of the *nafs* (self or ego), is that the self offers a range of possibilities activating, or with the potential of being activated towards a higher purpose. This model draws its inspiration from the *Qur'ān*, which describes various types of selves.

The animal self is driven solely or mainly by material wants and physical desires. This is the so-called commanding self (*an-Nafs al-Ammāra*)—the lowest form of self, base and childlike, that seeks only to gratify its desires and needs. This self can migrate to a higher form of consciousness, towards the blaming self (*an-Nafs al-Lawwāma*). This is a self that has awakened to its obligations to others, accepting responsibility for previous faults and empty desires—one that tries to act ethically and with scruples. The next stage is a higher level of awareness, towards the inspired self (*al-Nafs al-Mulhama*), which becomes more aware of the actions of the Divine within itself. The human being recognises that the self has developed the capability of reflecting the qualities of the Divine.

At this point, there is a decisive shift in consciousness within the person, where events, ideas, beliefs and experiences are filtered through the primal certainty that is the Divine Will. This is a significant shift that may elicit rapture. It requires careful management before the self advances to the next stage, the settled self (*an-Nafs al-Mutma'inna*). The settled or stable self is one that responds with equanimity and serenity to the forces that direct its actions and responses, knowing that the source and end of all lies with the Divine. At this point the self's spectrum becomes established and the self can move onto a yet higher plane, which is acceptance and acknowledgement of its condition.

This is the contented or absolutely serene self (*an-Nafs ar-Rāḍiya*) that opens the possibility of dialogue with the spiritual realms. The adept begins to experience an effacement of character, a recognition that one does not 'own' one's actions or their consequences. The final stages in this Ṣūfi model of the human self is one where the actions and conditions of the self are affirmed by a higher, guarding authority within the person. This is the self that is pleasing to its Guardian (*al-Nafs al-Marḍīya*). At this point the Ṣūfi is aligned along an arc of ascent, where the self dissolves in an ocean of unity. This is the stage of annihilation or *fanā'*. Fortified by the unfolding of the full spectrum of the self's possibilities, the fully realised Ṣūfi does not withdraw into isolation but returns to the world of mortals, filled with love and the drive to serve others. This is the Stage of Continuity of Being, *baqāʾ* or Eternal Presence, that continues to work with humanity throughout earthly life and beyond the threshold of death.

The passage of the self's evolution to higher levels is not something that can be realised on the basis of individual efforts, unguided by a teacher and supported by like-minded and like-hearted seekers. The institutional forms of Sufism are integral to the process and in the past the *ṭuruq* provided the scaffolding for the genuine seeker's spiritual ascent by providing guidance, companionship, discipline and a rigorous programme of instruction and practices. However, very few traditional *ṭuruq* have successfully navigated the pathways of the modern world, and many have become only vestiges of their former reality. Their outer structures have been maintained, but their ultimate purpose, namely to guide the individual seeker along the path of self-realisation, relegated to a lesser role.

Nevertheless, the classical manuals of instruction and guidance hold great reservoirs of spiritual wisdom, and have stood the test of time. But they need to be updated, their language made more accessible to a contemporary audience, and their practices more attuned to present-day circumstances. The same has been true for other great world religions, where classical texts of spiritual journeying have been represented and continue to be used as important aids and instruction manuals for adepts. Or for those who simply want to polish their conduct, empathy and understanding of the human condition, and their experience of the sacred. One thinks of the *Spiritual Exercises* of Ignatius Loyola, which still provide important guidance for lay people in the Catholic tradition.

Amongst this magnificent spiritual legacy of Islam stands out the work of the great Ṣūfi teacher, *Khwāja* ʿAbdullah al-Anṣārī (1006–1089) and his masterwork of *Manāzil As-Sāʾirīn*, or The Station of the Wayfarers. Anṣārī was born in the fortress of Qahandaz in Herāt in 396 AH (1006 CE), a city that is now in western Afghanistan. Herāt was an important town in the region of Khorasān, a province then of the far-flung Abbasid Empire. The empire was nominally run from its capital, Baghdad, but the period saw the decomposition of the empire into contending factions which struggled for supremacy in the empire's varied provinces. It was also a time of great religious disputations between various legal and theological schools of Islam. Anṣārī was a descendant of one of the prominent companions of the Prophet Muḥammad, Abū Ayyūb al-Anṣārī, who was killed while laying siege to Constantinople.

Abū Ayyūb was buried near the gates of the great city, and his burial site became an important shrine. One of Abū Ayyūb's sons participated in the capture of Khorasān in the first century of the hijra, and settled in the city of Herāt. ʿAbdullah Anṣārī's father, Abū Mansūr, was a learned sage and practised Sufism, which he seemed to have adopted while on an extensive stay in the city of Balkh. Thus, Anṣārī's early years were infused with the spirituality of Islam and its inner core of Sufism, both in his home life and the company that his family kept. His father's early death plunged Anṣārī and his family into dire need, but they were supported by a wide circle of friends, teachers and companions of the family. Anṣārī was tutored in the traditional Islamic curriculum and continued his advanced education in the nearby city of Nishapūr, before returning to Herāt permanently.

He completed the hajj once, but his second pilgrimage was cut short enroute. He tarried in the town of Rāyy, where he met the well-known ecstatic Ṣūfi, an illiterate villager, Abul-Ḥassan Al-Kharaqāni. This encounter left a profound impression on Anṣārī, reinforced further by a meeting with another well-known Ṣūfi master, Abū Saʾīd abul-Khayr, in Nishapūr. Ansari remained grounded in his Sufism, a so-called 'sober' Sufi, even though he had experienced ecstatic states. These were so profound that they prompted a rapturous reception of his exalted status by other participants in such gatherings. But Anṣārī remained a 'sober' Ṣūfi, rather than an ecstatic, fearing that such recognition of his status would corrupt his ego, *nafs*. Returning to Herāt, Anṣārī began to teach traditional Islamic sciences, but infused with the spirit of *Taṣawwuf* or Sufism. However, his adherence to a strict form of outer *Islām*, the narrowly doctrinaire Ḥanbali school, made him a contentious figure and he was involved in many disputations with other legal and theological adversaries whose doctrines were then prevalent.

This led to Anṣārī being frequently called to defend his position by the authorities and even exiled from Herāt several times. But in time, his reputation grew and his students and followers multiplied. His students compiled his spiritual discourses into yet another important devotional work of Anṣārī's, a mixture of prose and poetry in Persian, his *Munājāt* or Intimate Utterances. Anṣārī died in Herāt in 481 AH (1089 CE), loaded with honours, and thousands attended his funeral rites. He was buried in Kazerkah, in north Herāt. His tomb was embellished and expanded over the centuries, and it has become one of the most important shrines in the city of Herāt and a destination for all his followers and admirers of his works and his legacy.

Manāzil was not Anṣārī's first handbook on the spiritual path. It was preceded by *Sad Meydān* or 'the One Hundred Fields', a short treatise in Persian on the stages of the Ṣūfi path. However, it was written more as a summary and addendum to his lectures. Twenty- seven years later, his main adepts encouraged Anṣārī to elaborate on this short work and render it in Arabic, the lingua franca of the Islamic world, to ensure as wide a readership as possible. Anṣārī then dictated the *Manāzil* in 475 AH, to three of his core disciples. The earlier work could now be built upon, benefitting from Anṣārī's maturity and experience, and *Manāzil* is a more rounded, more developed and helpful pedagogical work than *Sad Maydān*. Many entries in the earlier work were omitted in the *Manāzil* and vice versa. Anṣārī could now define the genuine spiritual seeker into three categories: the first are those who seek the Divine Presence through a mix of spiritual concern and hope; the second category are those who have left the world of duality and see only Oneness; the third category are those in between. The journey is thus divided into three overarching stages.

The first leg is for those who have committed to the rigours and pitfalls of the path; the second leg is for those who have entered the path and accept the unfamiliarity and isolation that might ensue; the third leg is for those who are reaching the state of self-effacement and begin to see only oneness in all of existence. Structurally, the *Manāzil* is divided into ten stages, with each stage having ten doors, ranging from the first Door of *yaqḍa* or Awakening to the hundredth Door of Unity, *tawḥīd,* via *fanā'*, Annihilation and Total Self-effacement. The wide-ranging influence of the *Manāzil* in the world of Sufism as well as amongst traditional but spiritually-minded Muslims can be attested by the number of commentaries and glosses written on it. One scholar noted a total of 18 commentaries on the *Manāzil* over the ages. It has been an undoubted core teaching manual for Sufis and other Muslim spiritual adepts over the centuries.

Context of the Current Book

In 2012, I discussed with my spiritual teacher and guide, *Shaykh* Fadhlalla al-Haeri, the possibility and desirability of giving a series of talks on *Manāzil.* The talks were to be in London, where I was then based, and were to be given to a core of the *Shaykh*'s followers in the UK, as well as to friends from related Ṣūfi groups. These included, in particular, the *Mawlawīya* of London, followers of the *ṭarīqa* of *Mawlāna* Jalāl ud-Dīn ar-Rūmi. The London *Mawlawīya* were led by Sīdi Mahmoud Mustafa, whose authority came from an acknowledged master of the *ṭarīqa, Shaykh* Kabir Helminski. The logistics for the talks were expertly organised by the late Mustafa Moussawi, and were held at various venues in London, but mostly at the Royal Asiatic Society. There was a dual purpose to these talks, as outlined by *Shaykh* Fadhlalla, which I had attempted to follow.

The first was to introduce the listeners to a masterwork of writing on spiritual journeying, using classical commentaries as a tool, but adding insights from contemporary masters. The other purpose was to ascertain whether the *Manāzil* can be 'modernised' in the sense that it could make sense as a guide for contemporary seekers. Here, I noticed that many of the givens that *Khwāja* Anṣārī and all pre-modern commentators took for granted, were now seriously deficient or absent. The traditional seeker would approach the *Manāzil* with a grounding of certainty in the reality of the unseen. This could not be assumed for the modern seeker, who might be far more influenced by the doubts, scepticism and uncertainties that bedevil modern societies, even supposedly ones rooted in an Islamic worldview. The effects of Islamic modernist thought has seriously eroded the realisation of knowledge of the ineffable in the minds of many modern Muslims, not to mention seekers from a non-Islamic background, or those with no religion.

I chose to address this conundrum directly, by prefacing the *Manāzil* with a list of 10 preliminaries, conditions and states that the genuine modern seeker must acquire if he or she was to proceed with and benefit from the *Manāzil* proper. Although the discourses were recorded and subsequently circulated to a relatively wide spectrum of people, they languished for over a decade without further work on them. I had accepted a position at the National University of Singapore in 2013, and I was absent for prolonged periods in Iraq later. It was not possible for me therefore, to build the case for an updated and expanded *Manāzil.*

However, this situation changed after an eventful summer retreat of the *Mawlawīya* held in 2022 in the Yorkshire countryside. I was then introduced to Julia Katarina, a talented musician and music psychologist, with an MA in Islamic Law. She aspires to combine all three subjects in a PhD. Julia is steeped in the *Ṣūfi/ʿirfāni* tradition, with fluent Arabic (written and spoken). Although studying at *Ḥawza*, a traditional Shiʿī seminary, she is a person who is deeply familiar with the Western European mindset and experience, having been born into it and educated at Michael Hall Steiner School. We discussed the *Manāzil* and their significance for genuine seekers on the path of *taṣawwuf.* Julia also believes in the possibility and desirability of making the *Manāzil* more accessible and appealing to the contemporary mind. She agreed to take on the task of transcribing the 2012 discourses and using them as a platform to expand and elaborate on their importance, as well as to render them as a workable manual for spiritual seekers.

The resultant work is not a simple translation or commentary on the *Manāzil.* Rather, it is a re-imagination of the *Manāzil* in ways that are meaningful to a postmodern mind as well as to the traditionally minded, without losing the imperative of rooting it inside the spiritual universe of Islam. In this sense, the work is a composite of several themes: an expanded preliminaries section, bringing the stages from 10 to 11; a new translation that is more impactful; a redefinition of some of the gateways; and a manual of spiritual exercises and *adhkār* (litanies) for seekers and to aid teachers and guides. The work is therefore a new rendering of a classic, and fully reflects the remarkable effort and time that Julia has devoted to this noble task.

Ali A. Allawi
London, 2025

Editor's Note

A Brief Explanation of the Seven Stages of Soul as Understood in Islamic Tradition

The *Manāzil* of Ansari is predicated on a basic model of the self that was well established in the world where Islam and Islamic perspectives prevailed. This model has been well explicated in the Seven Stages of Soul by *Shaykh* ash-Shabrāwi. He describes the different levels of transformation, named in the *Qur'ān*, through which the human soul has to work its way, in order to reach the level of *Insān al-Kāmil*, the complete or whole human being. The first, lowest stage, the default setting of the majority of people, is the lower ego (*an-Nafs al-Ammāra*), which could be described as the commanding self or even the animal self. In some cases or instances people can even resemble or identify with a particular animal. This can be in displaying certain positive and negative characteristics of that animal, being particularly fond of it; or through the potent animal symbolism of some ancient doctrines, such as the Chinese Zodiac or Native American, Hindu or African mythologies.

This stage is also called the instinctive self and, although there is nothing inherently wrong with it, the uniquely human element of free will and independent thought are at their weakest in this stage. It is all about following desires, sympathies and antipathies, and succumbing to physical appetites. On the other hand, it can also be the driving force behind worldly achievements and material success. This phenomenon should be quite clearly observable once you have passed through the preliminary stages, first seeing it in others and then in one's self. At this point, self-scrutiny gives rise to the second level of soul, namely *an-Nafs al-Lawwāma,* the blaming or remorseful self. This self is so termed as it reproaches itself for its mistakes and shortcomings, instead of merely reacting to those of others. Eventually we see that our reaction to the terrible events of this world is actually a form of self-reproach, remorse and guilt. We recognise that we share responsibility for human atrocities and injustices; not directly, but because as human beings we also carry the potential to perpetuate similar acts.

Once this painful process has been worked through and, to a certain extent, cleared out through shedding the light of consciousness on the darker contents of the psyche, a space appears within the chalice of the heart to receive inspiration. This is *an-Nafs al-Mulhama,* the inspired self mentioned in the previous section and at the end of the Preliminary Stage of the *Manāzil.* Once the soul is inspired by the Divine Light it connects with the life force itself, with the spirit that breathes into it, and experiences overwhelming feelings of joy and contentment, *an-Nafs al-Mutma'inna.* This is seen by many as the ultimate outcome of the first four of Shabrawi's stages. The fifth and sixth stage being further levels of refinement of the self, as they are called *an-Nafs ar-Rāḍiya,* the pleased self, and *an-Nafs al-Marḍīya,* the pleasing self, respectively.

The final stage of the evolution of the self is not static but continues apace, as the process of completion or *kamāl* of the individuated soul never actually stops. The soul ever strives for perfection as it mimics the Perfection of its Creator. Needless to say, very few people have reached the elusive seventh stage of the 'perfect man' or complete human being. Among those who have are the prophets and prophetesses, Imams and some saints and *awliyā* throughout human history, and from various religious and spiritual traditions globally. Only a relatively small number of them are known and a smaller minority still confirmed in their high station. *Imām* Abū Ḥāmid āl-Ghazālī, the great medieval Islamic theologian and Ṣūfi, describes this group as those veiled only by pure light, in his *Mishkāt al-Anwār*—Niche of Lights, while other groups are veiled in varying ratios of light and darkness.

In Defence of the Use of Arabic Terms and Qur'anic *Āyāt*

Given that this text is based on a translation of the original, it continues to hold many of the original Arabic terms, as well as Arabic script and there is good reason for this. In the case of the *āyāt*, or verses, it is out of respect for the *Qur'ān* for the benefit of Arabic speakers and reciters and for the beauty and meaning of the shapes of the letters. As for the key terms, either in common use or related to the stages and doors of the *Mānāzil*—the Singular of which, 'Manzal' will be used instead of 'Qisim' as in the original Arabic text قِسِم—there is often no exact

English equivalent. Translation is always a compromise as all languages are complex and have their own subtleties. Arabic is especially nuanced, with a particularly broad vocabulary, much of which is beyond the knowledge of even native speakers. In fact, in order to fully grasp the language and all its grammatical rules and vast vocabulary, you would have to study it for your entire life, irrespective whether it is your first language and you have spent years in formal schooling.

The academic transliterations are to help with pronunciation, accoding to the rules of recitation (*tajwīd*).

The original script is to help with further research into their meanings in different contexts and to establish their related words.

Speakers of Arabic might baulk at seeing translations of words and terms with which they think they are familiar. At the same time, non-Arabic speakers might question the use of Arabic terms and names, even in transliteration, as it becomes a struggle to learn them or even to grasp the necessary terms. But if Arabic is seen as a sacred language because of its breadth, structure and form, then it makes a lot more sense. Sacred Arabic is not the same as colloquial spoken Arabic. It is a way in which human beings dialogue with the unseen. There are other traditions that use different languages to communicate with what is seen as the ineffable, such as Sanskrit, Russian, biblical Hebrew, Greek and Latin. But we believe that Arabic is the one that best approximates the language of the primordial religion. There are of course other paths and traditions, but if one were to choose the path of Islam as the gateway to the primordial religion, then knowledge of Arabic, and especially the odd hundreds of words of Quranic Arabic, is essential.

Think of Arabic as a language that lends itself to understanding the subtler realities. One may hold that the way the mind is wired differs from the way European languages are structured. Indeed this is also the case with Classical and modern Arabic, and few latter-day Arabic speakers have any connection with the potential of Classical Arabic to unlock the spiritual dimension of existence. If you make a choice based on the conviction that this path is most proximate, or the least adulterated of the paths in its present, as well as original form, then a commitment is required to understanding the subtler meanings of the language. Not to compare Christianity and Greek or Latin, although

Latin also is a language that is no longer spoken and neither is classical Greek; however, it is the way the spiritual tradition of Christendom was expressed in the Middle Ages. You cannot avoid Arabic in its sacred form. It is not that onerous to repeat a certain set of words. The repetition of the words, the way the words sound to you, may play a part in raising your spiritual consciousness.

The Arabs were sole custodians of the religion of Islam for a very short period of time, only a century or so before other races and nations took it on. Arabic became an almost universal language in its sacred form. Islam and the Qur'anic phenomenon by its very nature are non-racial and transnational. Otherwise, it would not have spread the way it did and continues to do. What you need to do on a spiritual level is to connect with a sacred Arabic, try to enhance your condition and take it as a core of the ritual forms, drawing on insightful experiences by masters of the time. The act of remembrance, *dhikr*, is a good way of learning the Divine Names in Arabic through repetition. It is a whole universe of possibilities. This work is for people who have the taste and resolution, *himma*, for it.

The *Qur'ān* begins, in the first revelation, with the word 'recite', *iqra'*, the imperative of the verb 'to read', from which the noun '*Qur'ān*' derives. Reading the *Qur'ān* in translation, then perhaps in the original Arabic, and eventually even learning to recite it, can result in enormous insights and spiritual conditions. This could lead to memorising a few short chapters and verses of the *Qur'ān*, which is a step higher than simply reading them. It is also necessary to conduct the formal prayers of Islam. In the formal prayer, *salah*, it is recommended to recite full *sūrāt,* the self-contained chapters of the *Qur'ān,* which are made up of *āyāt*, or verses. There are five formal daily prayers which divide the 24 hours of a day into natural pauses. They coincide with dawn, midday, the afternoon, the setting sun and night. At these moments, a person drops his or her immersion in the matters of the world and turns their attention to God. The rules of prayer are essentially the same for all the various jurisprudential schools of Islam, with minor variations as to posture and recitation patterns. When the time for prayer beckons, the face of the praying person is turned in the direction of the Holy Sanctuary in Mecca, a universal expression of the levelling of all individuals in front of their Creator.

There is a courtesy when approaching or engaging with sacred scripture. A genuine seeker following in the primordial path of Islam, must believe, or at least acknowledge, that the words of the *Qur'ān* are sacred and emanate from a Sacred Source. The words have remained unaltered and intact ever since they were revealed, in time, to the Prophet Muhammad. When we repeat them in reflection, remembrance, or prayer, we must remain acutely conscious of their sacred nature and endeavour to recite them as accurately as we possibly can. Although perfectionism is to be avoided, as it is a preoccupation of the ego, practice, study and application of the appropriate effort is a sign of care and respect. This necessitates the search for companions on a similar path to act as reflectors and supporters. The guidance of a teacher, who has the appropriate skills and background, is critical in this matter.

One of the first rules of correct pronunciation is the assimilation of the article, *al* (ال) into the first letter of a noun when it is a sun letter. The Arabic alphabet is divided equally into sun letters and moon letters, which must be memorised to enable correct articulation of *al* (ال), in the case of moon letters, for example *al-qamar* (the moon), *al-balad* (the land) or *al-kitāb* (the book). When the first letter of a noun is a sun letter, the *al* (ال) is not articulated but mirrors the first letter so that it is pronounced twice or emphasised with double the weight (*shadda*), for example *ash-shams* (the sun), *as-samā'* (the sky) or *an-nafs* (the self). So far, the writing out of sun sounds as they are spoken has not yet caught on in the literature, but it will be done throughout this book to aid proper pronunciation for non-native speakers. The following are the emphasised sun letters, before which the letter l of the article *al* (ال) is silent:

ن	ل	ظ	ط	ض	ص	ش	س	ز	ر	ذ	د	ث	ت
n	*l*	*ẓ*	*ṭ*	*ḍ*	*ṣ*	*sh*	*s*	*z*	*r*	*dh*	*d*	*th*	*t*

Julia A. Katarina
London, 2025

Introduction

This book is based on the classic work of *Khwāja* ʿAbdullah al-Anṣārī's *Manāzil as-Sāʾirīn ila al-Maʿārifa wal-Yaqīn* (hereon referred to as *Manāzil*). Anṣārī wrote mostly in Farsi but *Manāzil* was written in Arabic, evidently to reach a wider audience. The title means 'the Path of the Wayfarers Towards Knowledge and Certainty' and it is a highly structured exposition of the Islamic path of spiritual development. This book is an attempt to bring *Manāzil* into the modern context and render it more accessible by utilising contemporary language.

The original purpose of the *Manāzil* was to act as a guide and companion to seekers on a spiritual path, and this book emphatically reconfirms this intention. This book could be read by a wide spectrum of readers, and it should be especially useful to those who may benefit from it in their own spiritual development. The book before you is designed as a companion tool in the form of a structured course. The original meaning and structure of the *Manāzil* has thus been maintained, with added commentaries, examples, and explanations. A scientific numbering system to ease navigation and orientation through the course has also been introduced. The 'spines' of the book are the Stages and Doors into which the *Manāzil* is divided. Although they follow a linear path of progression, a reader need not strictly adhere to the linear structure if their experience or predisposition suggests otherwise.

This book rests on the masterpiece of *Shaykh* ʿAbdullah al-Anṣārī. Professor Ali A. ʿAllāwi has translated the work and added his commentaries and explanations. Julia A. Katarina has summarised or expanded upon the work and structured it into a one-year course. An entire new stage has been added to the original *Manāzil*, bringing the number of stages to eleven. This was deemed necessary as a preliminary stage to Anṣārī's *Manāzil*, to meet the sensibilities of modern readers and seekers. Julia Katarina also added examples and background to some of the terms, in order to render the steps along the path more relatable and practicable in daily life. Each chapter is one of the eleven stages. The ten doors within each chapter are numbered according to their place in the hundred steps outlined by *Shaykh* al-Anṣārī. Whichever page you open the book to, it will be obvious where you are in the whole process.

The three degrees of each doorway are translated from Anṣārī's original text and the names of the stages and doors also transliterated and given in Arabic script, as are the *Qur'ān* quotes he gave for each doorway. Most of the quotes contain the name of the door they introduce and all are followed by chapter and verse numbers for ease of reference and contextualisation.

The *Manāzil* is one of the most important books of 'spiritual wayfaring' in the Ṣūfi tradition. Anṣārī wrote it specifically to be a usable manual to help people along the path of faith and practice. Anṣārī's age, the fourth century of the *hijri* calendar or eleventh century of the CE, was a significant period in Islamic religious life. According to later pre-eminent Sufis, it was a time when Sufism was a living reality without a name, before it subsequently became a name without much reality. The *Manāzil* was written with the state and condition of the 'wayfarer' clearly in mind. There are few other manuals like it; works in the literature that deal with journeying, or passing from one condition, one state, one stage to another on the spiritual path. One such work is the famous epic poem by ʿAttār, 'The Conference of the Birds'. Although written decades after the *Manāzil*, ʿAttar's poem is a literary classic of Islamic religiosity that reflects the *Manāzil's* spiritual journeying.

The path of a present-day wayfarer does not necessarily have to go through identical stages, nor does it have to incorporate experiences of the very same states and conditions as the earlier masters had previously traversed and described them. But the beginning and end are one, and it is the enabling and facilitating of the experience of this reality that is the purpose behind this book. By bringing an eleventh century spiritual classic into a twenty-first century context, the book can act as a fulcrum for developing a usable manual and map for the modern wayfarer. The book draws on the concepts and conditions embedded in the *Manāzil*, with reference to some other texts, while moulding them in a way that can facilitate reaching the desired goal of self-knowledge.

Nearly all the great works on spiritual journeying were written by masters for people who were already committed to the path of Inner Enlightenment. They were teaching aids for a diverse group of people around the master, ranging from the most proximate and realised to the curious listener. They were intended to provide some coherence and order to the often lifelong struggle to gain knowledge of the self and to open the pathways of spiritual insights. The language employed assumed that the reader was at least aware of the fundamentals of the Ṣūfi path and the tenets of faith. The pre-modern world was infused with a sense of the sacred which made for easy familiarity with the terms and expressions used. The formal structures of these works might appear somewhat rigid to the modern mind through their use of strict categories and hierarchies when describing the stations or stages of the journey.

There are also a number of early classic works of Sufism which dealt more with the forms and contents of the inner world, the life of the relationship between the adepts and masters. The *Manāzil* was one of the first detailed instruction manuals. In many ways it has a modern feel to it, but in other ways it is also a product of its time and place and may not translate very well if you use and follow it verbatim. What is important is to take it in the form in which it appears and try to distil it into the modern context, knowing that a modern readership does not necessarily have the same sensibilities as readers of 1,000 years ago. One cannot read these books and expect within a matter of days to imbibe all the knowledge, all the circumstances of all these states, stations and stages that they embody. One has to live with and apply them gradually over time. The other aspect of it is more to do with the individuals themselves and their preparedness and predisposition.

These works were written at a time we tend to call the pre-modern era, in which the certainty of people regarding the realm of the unseen, and the certainty of would-be seekers regarding these subtler realities, was far greater than it is now. It is not that the times were necessarily better than they are now. In many ways, there is great advantage to the expansion of the quantitative aspects of life, but certainly not to the level of detracting from the qualitative aspects. The pre-modern world, not only the Islamic world, was one where religion and the daily encounter with the sacred and with the unseen was an aspect of ordinary life. It was not an add-on to an otherwise secular world, as it is in some contexts now.

When we approach these texts, it is helpful to start by trying to identify what the purpose was behind them and how they can be of use to us now and also to recognise that we are not the same spiritual species as people were in pre-modern times. However, this does not imply that we should write ourselves off because we are unable to achieve the level of perception and recognition of the subtler realities of our antecedents. What it does mean is that we have to work that extra bit harder. We have to accept that we might have to start, not at level zero, but even a level below that, in order to acquire the presumed knowledge and understanding with which these texts were approached. The *Manāzil* are a very clear example of this, as they make certain assumptions about the spiritual state and condition of the wayfarer. They assume that the wayfarer's encounter with the sacred, with the divine, is a given, rather than a long striven for goal. In a world infused with the sacred, such a possibility was never questioned.

We have to accept that the material 'quantitativeness' which prevails in our outer world affects one's inner condition. It diminishes the faculties which intuitively or instinctively are able to relate to the unseen. As such, it would be best to examine ourselves and see whether we are in a condition to be able to launch ourselves on this journey. If such a possibility in one's inner capacities is accepted, then we can take full advantage of, and benefit from, our immersion in the *Manāzil*. The original *Manāzil* text makes certain implicit assumptions about the preparedness of the wayfarer. They may appear formidable and very spiritually advanced to a contemporary readership. This book works on the basis that those embarking on such a journey in present times will benefit from guidance to lay the spiritual foundations.

To this end, the authors identified the need for a preparatory stage, before the wayfarer actually enters Anṣārī's stages. We have therefore begun with what we have termed the 'Pre-Stages', where wayfarers can explore whether they are able to genuinely, consciously and honestly resonate with the unseen.

A Pre-Stage: Stirrings and the Very Preliminaries (*al-bashā'ir wat-tamhīdiyāt*) البشائر والتمهيديات

Why is there a need for a pre-stage? Why can we not start directly with the Stage of the Beginnings, as Anṣārī's *Manāzil* calls for? The answer is relatively simple. The contemporary world has mainly driven the sense of the sacred outside the realm of a person's daily experience. The loss of the qualities and faculties needed to recognise the subtler realms is a universal phenomenon and the recovery of these abilities is an essential element for the modern wayfarer. But first, a person must sense and then desire to know the reality that underpins all realities. It is these stirrings that are the first steps on the path of the latter-day wayfarer, who starts as a spiritual wanderer, not yet a wayfarer.

The first stirrings generally arise as a reaction to the inversion of vices into virtues and vice versa. Doubt is displaced by certainty; aggression turns to co-operation; self-regard to selflessness; greed to sharing; envy to contentedness; excess to frugality; noise to silence; anger to serenity; grasping to letting go; and so on. These stirrings are transmuted to a permanent condition that seeks to find redress. This is the beginning of the beginning: the Door of Agitation. That is where spiritual wandering first commences. In order to facilitate this commencement, it is important to become aware of our sometimes subconsciously held beliefs and assumptions about ourselves and those we encounter. It is a very deeply ingrained and automatic reflex to judge others and stems from our evolutionary survival compass—the notion that others pose a potential threat, and those who appear different from ourselves a possible existential one. Fixed ideas about our own limitations are also taught from a young age, in order to keep us safe.

Challenging Assumptions (*taḥaddī al-iftirāḍāt*) تحدي الافتراضات

These safety 'mechanisms' are precisely what arrest our spiritual development. What has been described in social psychology as the 'fixed' mindset as opposed to the 'growth' mindset in worldly terms, could be likened to what in spiritual terms happens when we challenge, 'get over' or push ourselves out of the 'comfort zone'. This could be by simply questioning an instant judgement that comes up when encountering another person, especially when they seem very different from ourselves. Sometimes, however, we take issue with someone because they possess a trait we abhor in ourselves; on some level we recognise it, consciously or otherwise, and flinch at the reflection we see in them. Other times we may catch ourselves treating others as obstacles in our way or, conversely, as a means to an end. Assumptions arise when we forget that appearances can be deceptive and think we can know something about a person from the way they look or behave.

It takes extensive, and intensive training to be able to deduce in any meaningful way, even to hone one's intuition to the point of being able to analyse someone and comprehend their situation would take years of focused self-study, as every individual is utterly unique, as are their paths and biographies. Stereotypes, you may argue, come from somewhere and usually have some foundation in observable realities and repetitive behavioural patterns of certain group constructs, but they may only occur because we subconsciously choose to conform to them in order to belong to some false collective, 'fit in' and not 'stick out', and find some 'safety in numbers'. Like all of reality, humanity is heterogeneous and complex for a reason, and we are required to try and understand each other, so the more 'other' they are, the better. As Goethe said, '*Dich in Unendlichen zu finden musst unterscheiden und dann verbinden*'. 'In order to find yourself in the infinite, you must differentiate and reintegrate.'

The Overarching Divine Names (*asmā' al-ḥusna*) for the Stages أسماء الحُسنة الشاملة للمنازل

At the beginning of each stage, a pair of Divine Names are selected to give the overall theme and aim of the stage. Some pairs are seemingly opposing polarities, while others re-emphasise each other. Either way, they are all from the 99 *asmā' al-ḥusnā* in the *Qur'ān*—God's supremely Beautiful Names—and are therefore Divine in origin and represent the superlative form of each Essence or Action. We can aspire to embody a limited human version of these attributes and are encouraged to personify as many of them as possible in order to strive towards the ideal of the *insān al-kāmil*, the complete, realised human being. As we work our way through the stages, we can bear in mind and heart these overarching Names while reading and as *dhikr* during times of quiet contemplation, as well as in daily activities, while walking, before sleep; or upon waking.

The overarching Names for the Preliminary Stage are The Hidden, *Al-Bāṭin* الباطن and The Manifest *Aẓ-Ẓāhir* الظاهر.

Suggested mantra (*adhkār*) commensurate with the Stages (*Manāzil*) اذكار للمنازل

The 100 doorways are the expository constructs of the ten stages of the *Manāzil*. In and of themselves they do not constitute a practical programme of exercises and litanies for the wayfarer. That has to be developed separately and in a manner that need not necessarily follow the strict order of the doorway, but may evolve naturally as an accumulation of the individual three Names *adhkār* of the stages (see Appendix 1)*;* they nevertheless have to be true to their purpose. A plan that has evolved calls for grouping the stages around three Names of Allāh that appear to be most pertinent for the wayfarer at that particular stage and condition of spiritual development. These are simply indicators, and those who follow the prescriptions of a particular *Shaykh* should seek sanction from their *Shaykh*. The wayfarer should then start at the first stage and combine the *dhikr* with reflections on the Qur'ānic *āyāt* that start each of the doorways of that stage. The *dhikr* for each stage will be given at the end of its description and should be repeated regularly and joined with the times of *salah,* prayer.

Timeframe

It may be useful for some seekers to plan work over a certain timeframe and the exercises are designed to be divided into weekly sections over the course of a year. As it is widely used to coordinate the global community in the modern world and for the sake of convenience and ease of understanding, we will use the Gregorian calendar here, acknowledging that there are other calendars which would work just as well. The Hijri calendar might have been a more obvious choice, given the period and Islamic context of the original manuscript; however, it is a lunar calendar and migrates through the seasons, which would cause inconsistency in the event of repetition of the course, which may or may not be problematic, and it also does not have the right number of days for our purposes. The Hijri calendar months vary in length and follow a specific hierarchy. This may be appropriate and it would be interesting to compare its application to the two calendars, the latter starting in Muḥarram.

For our purposes here, particularly the first reading of the book over the course of a year, the numbers are calculated thus: 365–313=52. The structure therefore fits perfectly into the 52 weeks of the year, working through two doors per week, focusing on understanding one degree a day. During the first two weeks of reading through the Preliminaries, which do not have three degrees, you will focus on one door per day. Each week ends with a day of reflection on the doors and degrees of that week and with a recommended, independently chosen or prescribed *dhikr.* Following this plan will guide the reading of the book within a specific timeframe and keep the momentum of working through it consistent, which will also help maintain motivation. The timeframe is designed to help you get a coherent mental picture of the path by giving you time to read through the commentaries—neither too quickly nor too slowly—so that any insights that may come to you will be allowed sufficient time for absorption, experience and response. Actual mastery of the steps may take longer and cannot be forced or rushed.

Practical Application

The *Manāzil* can constitute a practical path, but if you just read them you are not likely to become a realised being. You could probably learn them by heart and nothing would happen to you. They have to be part of a practical programme that includes spiritual exercises, devotions and litanies. However, they do lend themselves to groupings around each Stage or *Manzal.* The Divine Qualities of Essence and Attributes of Action that seem to be pertinent for each stage can form a mantrum, or *dhikr,* for individuals who want to use the forms of the *Manāzil* as part of their regular practice. For example, at the Preliminary Stage of Stirrings you could call upon Allāh as The Opener, *Al-Fattāḥ*. 'May Allāh open this door for me, *yā Fattāḥ* enable and help me in this quest.' It is for that particular purpose; you can change it, but it is to call upon Allāh as the Source of that Quality through the Names.

When you enter into the Stage of Beginnings, you have just started and should call upon *Al-Mubdi'*, the One Who Originates all things. You start with a clean slate, calling for God's forgiveness. You call upon Him thus, '*yā Mubdi', yā Tawwāb, yā Samī'*.' Then the third stage will be the Stage of the Gateways. When you call on Allāh the response comes from *Al-Mujīb* and the doors of subtler realities are generously opened. So you call on *Al-Mujīb, Al-Laṭīf, Al-Karīm*. If you want to follow this route in conjunction with revisiting these *Manāzil* on a regular basis, it may be helpful to recite them quietly maybe 10, 33 or 100 times during the day after prayer, *ṣalāh*. In the Stage of Deeds you want the Actions of Allāh Who bestows benefits, to Whom you deputise your affairs; Who Keeps Watch and Guard so you call on *Al-Raqīb, Al-Wakīl, An-Nāfiʿ*.

In the Stage of Ethics you call upon Allāh the All-Patient, *Aṣ-Ṣabbūr, Ash-Shakūr, Al-Ḥalīm* and as you go through the various groupings, until the last stage, when you call upon *Al-Bāqi,* The Remaining, Eternally Subsisting, *Al-Wāhid*, The One, *Al-Jāmiʾ*. If you find them useful for your own purposes, by all means do them regularly, singly or combined as a long *dhikr*. You can also use different permutations, or if you follow a *shaykh* you must ask his permission and advice on the correct way of doing it or for a personalised *dhikr*. It can concentrate your mind and help you focus. It can also remind you of the condition that you are in or the Stage you are at, so that when you move from one to the other, you progress from differential reliance— you always rely on Allāh—on one set of Names to another set of Names that may be more pertinent for that particular Stage.*

J.K. & A.A.

---

*Working with the Names is extremely powerful and an explanation of their meaning can be found in books by Daniel Dyer, Rosina-Fawzia Al-Rawi and Sayyid Fadhel Milani, among others and further reading on ʿAbdullah al-Anṣārī and his predecessors, contemporaries and successors, on Islamic Mysticism and the spiritual path in the bibliography. Al-Rawi, R-F., (2015) *Divine Names: 99 Healing Names of the One Love.* Calligraphy by Majed Seif, translation by Monique Arav. Northampton MA: Interlink Books. Al-Rawi, R-F., (2017) *Göttliche Namen: Die 99 Heilenden Namen der Einen Liebe.* Kalligraphie von Majed Seif. Neu Isenburg: Cosmics Verlag. Dyer, D. T. (2016) *The 99 names of God.* Calligraphy by Azim Rehmat Din. Kendal: Chickpea Press. Milani, S.F.H. & Hegedüs, A. (2004) *The source of Islamic spirituality: comment on Surah 17 The Night Journey—Surah Isra'a / Bani Isra'il.* London: Islam in English Press.

Stirrings and the Very Preliminaries
(*al-bashā'ir wat-tamhīdiyāt*) البشائر والتمهيدات

Overarching Names: The Hidden *Al-Bāṭin* الباطن
The Manifest *al-Ẓāhir* الظاهر

WEEK ONE

1. The Door of Agitation (*Bāb al-Iḍṭirāb*) باب الإضطراب

وَكَذَٰلِكَ نُرِي إِبْرَاهِيمَ مَلَكُوتَ السَّمَاوَاتِ وَالْأَرْضِ وَلِيَكُونَ مِنَ الْمُوقِنِينَ

Wa kadhālika nurī Ibrāhīma malakūt as-samāwāti wa al-arḍi wa liyakūna min al-mūqinīn

'...This is how We made Abraham see the kingdom of the heavens and the earth, so that he would have certain faith.' *(*Qur'ān*: 6:75)

Agitation is a disturbance that troubles the heart. It is a sense of imbalance, disproportion and inappropriateness between the outer world and a person's inner reality, and a difficulty in reconciling the two. Agitation is generated spontaneously, triggered by an event or chain of events, or comes about as a product of continuing reflection. It is a reassertion of the existence of innate qualities that have lain dormant. Agitation on the outer level is the drive to increase or expand quantitative knowledge. Agitation of the inner world is the drive to experience qualitative knowledge. Either Agitation demands to be quelled. It is a spur to mental or spiritual action. Without Agitation there is no beginning. Agitation is the first door. It is a disturbance that troubles one. It is the sense that comes when a person feels that the outer world, the world of measurement, the world of observation, in itself is insufficient to describe reality; it creates an inner sense of disquiet, imbalance and disproportion and it is this Agitation that is the first step in which a person knows that there is something beyond the material.

There is no point in simply talking about the world of the unseen; you actually have to be experientially related to it. Agitation can be triggered by anything: by sitting on the number nine bus, by a terrible

*From Tarif Khalidi's translation: Khalidi, T. (2008) *The Qur'an*. London: Penguin Classics.

event, or even a wonderful event. It is a disturbance, a tingling, for those who are more inclined to reflection and introspection; it can be a product of continuing reflection. But what it does is, it tells you that there is something beyond sight, sound, feeling, touching, beyond the psyche, beyond the mind, beyond the realm of the physical and the psychological. Psychology, in the contemporary sense, is a mental measure of the outer world and is, inasmuch as it is based on the perception and ordering of sensory information, therefore quantitative and positivistic. In the classical sense, however, it is understood as the study of the soul, which would encompass the subtle senses and spiritual perception.

This Agitation is when a person's inner faculties—entirely different from the outer faculties—suddenly come to life, or you become aware of them and that there is something there that you have to cultivate in order to be able to relate to the unseen. This Agitation, energetic disturbance, or turbulence has two possible outcomes, stemming from an outer Agitation or an inner one. Outer agitation is a disturbance that leads one to accumulate knowledge and information from the outer world—an automatic reflex of people who have been immersed in the world of the material and the quantitative—and understand the world at large according to that paradigm. They may think that by reading about the experiences of others, delving into books and texts, and by meeting with certain people, they will be able to quench this Agitation.

This outer Agitation ultimately has to do with expanding knowledge as it relates to the outer world, in the hope that this expansion will somehow awaken inner faculties. Although reading and research are commendable and can lead towards greater understanding, inner Agitation, on the other hand, is the Agitation for the qualitative, intuitive knowledge that you sense you have inside you, waiting to be tapped into. Both forms of Agitation require quenching. It is a kind of constant sense of tingling, a sense of imbalance; you need to either read more and find out more about it, meet people who are disturbed by it, or talk to people who have been there. Starting from a very low base, in both cases, the impulse is to quench it. Without experiencing this Agitation, knowledge of the unseen is only theoretical, inherited, second-hand—something that you hope to feel or experience through ritual repetition.

2. The Door of Perplexity (*Bāb al-Ḥayra*) باب الحيرة

إِنَّ الَّذِينَ لَا يُؤْمِنُونَ بِالْآخِرَةِ زَيَّنَّا لَهُمْ أَعْمَالَهُمْ فَهُمْ يَعْمَهُونَ

Innalladhīna lā yu'minūna bil-'ākhirati zayyannā lahum a'mālahum fahum ya'mahūn

'... As for those who do not believe in the Hereafter, We have made their deeds appear attractive to them so they stumble around in Perplexity'. (*Qur'ān*: 27:4)

Perplexity is a puzzlement born of the rise of long-dormant inner senses that confront or question long-ascendant outer senses. It is an unaccustomed light that sits uneasily with conventional perceptions. Perplexity is a fragile state. It can be smothered by a rampant rationality reasserting the authority of the outer senses. It can veer into sentimentality and spiritualism or, on the other hand, it can concede to the reality and growing authority of the inner qualities. Perplexity can be both expansive and contractive. Expansive Perplexity is the delight in discovering the possibilities of a new dimension of perception. Contractive perplexity is the anguish that arises from questioning the false certitude that comes solely from the outer senses. Both expansive and contractive perplexities are valid pathways to the spiritual wanderer. Spiritual wandering is similar to being in a dark room, perplexed as to which senses to use to quench this Agitation to move to the next Door, that of Awareness.

The next door is for those who want to continue, as opposed to giving up, going back to outer life, and denying that there is any truth to these subtle faculties. If you want to move on, you move through the Door of Perplexity, recognising that outer knowledge is deficient, insufficient and inadequate. It is really a puzzlement because you know that outer knowledge is insufficient to manage your relationship with the unseen, but at the same time, you know that you have not yet recognised the mechanisms within you that allow you to question the dominance of the outer senses. You have spent your life measuring things, thinking about things, rationalising, assessing, weighing things, and feeling in control of things. These are the faculties that you know. If these faculties cannot resonate with the agitation or the agitation is not quenched by them, you will become perplexed.

Why is this continuing? Why can it not be quenched by reason, repetition, or observance of certain rituals? Perplexity arises when you know that there is this unaccustomed light inside you, of faculties that have been lying dormant for so long. They clash with conventional perceptions. Now, this is the most dangerous state for people who have begun to sense the unseen because it is a very fragile state. It can be easily smothered because you cannot control it and do not know how to deal with it. The easiest way to deal with it is to rationalize or try to encapsulate it, or categorize it in ways that you can understand. If you do not deal with it appropriately, it can veer into something quite poor for the passage of the spiritual wayfarer; that is, sentimentality and spiritualism, which is part of the dead end to which Perplexity can reach without conscious intervention.

Perplexity—or *ḥayra*, as Anṣārī called it in Arabic—is both progressive and retrogressive. Progressive Perplexity is that which recognises that there is a new world out there to be discovered and you are aroused by a burning desire to discover it. You are willing to go through the struggle of discovering it. Retrogressive Perplexity, which is another possible outcome, is a retreat or withdrawal in which you end up questioning the certitude that comes from your outer senses. Not knowing what to do about it, you pull back rather than trying to go to the next step. You are satisfied with these faculties, without knowing what they are, where they are, or why they are there; without any idea how to evolve or develop them. They are recognisably there in reserve, against a uni-dimensional perspective on truth.

3. The Door of Awareness (*Bāb al-Waʿī*) باب الوعي

الَّذِينَ آمَنُوا وَتَطْمَئِنُّ قُلُوبُهُم بِذِكْرِ اللَّهِ ۗ أَلَا بِذِكْرِ اللَّهِ تَطْمَئِنُّ الْقُلُوبُ

Alladhīna āmanū wa taṭmaʾinnu qulūbuhum bidhikri Illāhi alā bidhikrillāhi taṭmaʾinn ul-qulūb

'...They who believe and whose hearts feel secure in the remembrance of Allāh, indeed, let hearts feel secure in the remembrance of Allāh.'

(*Qurʾān*: 13:28)

Awareness is the recognition of the presence of subtler realities within the self. It is the first step in understanding that the self has a spectrum that ranges from the most gross to the most sublime. Awareness is the verification that there is a higher reality and purpose to existence. It is the irrevocable unmooring of the self from the apparent certitudes of material or mental processes and their construct of realities. Active Awareness propels the person towards a journey of discovery of the inner, latent faculties of knowledge. Passive Awareness leaves the person content only with certainty of the existence of another dimension to knowledge without the desire to map the contours of such knowledge.

These might seem to be rather modular ways of looking at it, and they do not necessarily follow in this order, for some it might be slightly different.* Awareness is a basic recognition and confirmation that you have subtle realities and senses inside you. It is an early sign that your self-knowledge is beginning to become more refined. The self begins to assume a rainbow shape. It has different hues to it within a spectrum of colours and various states and conditions. This is a form of verification. This Awareness verifies to you again that there is a higher reality and purpose to existence. There are two forms of Awareness:

> Active Awareness, in which a person journeys, on the discovery of the inner faculties of knowledge, trying to understand what they are, who they are, why they are, what their functions and capabilities are, and what they are there for.
>
> Passive Awareness is the acceptance that these faculties exist, that there is another dimension of knowledge, but without any particular desire to experience them fully or alter your sense of reality. You just stop at that point.

Awareness then leads to Inquiry. You want to investigate the contours of this Awareness, to verify its source and nature; it is affected by listening, exchanging, observing and reflecting. You end up verifying the knowledge and experience of others when your Inquiry leads to individuals who have been there and have obviously risen in terms of their spiritual understanding and Awareness. They in turn verify your Inquiry.

*For example, Junayd al-Baghdadi is said to have been unable to complete a stage before moving to the next one. He looked at the lower levels from the higher levels in order to correct and complete the previous levels.

4. The Door of Inquiry (*Bāb at-Tasāʾul*) باب التساؤل

وَيَتَفَكَّرُونَ فِي خَلْقِ السَّمَاوَاتِ وَالْأَرْضِ

Wa yatafakkarūna fī khalqis-samāwāti wal-ʾarḍ

'...Who reflect upon the creations of the heavens and earth.

(*Qurʾān*: 3:191)

The mutual verification of one another's Inquiry is still only the outer form of Inquiry through triangulation. The inner form of Inquiry is to verify the knowledge, in one's heart, of the experiences of the self. You start using different measurements. Both levels of Inquiry, that is trying to find the right vehicle, venue, and person, to confirm the contours of this inner knowledge, awareness and Inquiry, are necessary for the wayfarer. Inquiry of the mind without the heart is a barren knowledge, and Inquiry of the heart without the mind is a formless knowledge. Both are necessary to formulate the contours of the faculties of inner knowledge that allow you to understand the unseen and to verify the source, nature and direction of awareness. Inquiry is to experience self-in-awareness by listening, sharing, observing and reflecting. Inquiry of the mind is to verify the knowledge and experience of others. Inquiry of the heart is to verify the knowledge and experiences of the self; balanced, thorough and useful knowledge requires both the subtle, intuitive faculties of the heart and the analytical, detailed, perceptive faculties of the mind to be fully co-operational without competing for dominance.

5. The Door of Guidance (*Bāb al-Hidāya*) باب الهداية

إهْدِنَا الصِّرَاطَ الْمُسْتَقِيمَ

Ihdina aṣ-ṣirāṭ al-mustaqīm

'...Guide us to the straight path.' (*Qurʾān*, 1:6)

Guidance is the acknowledgement that the self lacks an understanding of where it stands, where it is going and how it will get there. It is the confirmation that the terrain of the wanderer can be a bleak wilderness full of perils, pitfalls and mirages. A guide is therefore necessary. Providers of Guidance must themselves be familiar with the terrain of the wanderer and provide Guidance that is manifestly true. The Door of Guidance for the spiritual wanderer in the Stage of Stirrings is not the same as the attachment to a spiritual master. This comes later, when the Stage of Stirrings has given way to the first Stage of Beginnings. The provider of Guidance in this stage may not be the spiritual master of later times. This path is not yet the first Stage of the *Manāzil*, and you have to differentiate between true and false Guidance. This is a very important measure needed to differentiate between the two. Any guide who points to themselves, rather than leading you to the One Reality, is a false guide:

> True Guidance leads the wanderer along the paths that arouse the latent faculties within the self that can unite the two levels of Inquiry. True Guidance focuses the self on the Sole Reality behind all realities.
>
> False Guidance leads the wanderer along the paths of dependence and false comfort on only one of the two levels of Inquiry. False Guidance focuses the wanderer on the provider of Guidance.

Guidance may take the form of a physical guide whom you know, see, resonate with, and can exchange with, or it can be an unseen guide. It is ultimately both. These days, many people who are chosen as guides are realised masters who have crossed the threshold into the unseen worlds and are represented in this world by their descendants, followers and students. However, there are also many who pose as guides but in reality have neither the lineage, legitimacy or the quality and substance of Guidance. The knowledge of the guide is necessary when you reach the Door of Seeking Guidance. It is an acknowledgement that you yourself are deficient in knowledge and understanding of where the contours of Awareness lie within you, where they are going, and how to make use of them. Without that guide, the terrain of the spiritual wanderer you have become by reaching the fifth door, becomes a wilderness with pitfalls, perils, mirages, and shadowy states and conditions.

The terrain for a lone spiritual wanderer is fraught with perils. A guide will help you navigate through encounters and tell you how to avoid dangers, misunderstandings, and the wrong paths. Your guide at this stage need not be a great master and may not be the guide you will need when you are more spiritually advanced. Someone who has undergone a spiritual journey, perhaps without elevating their own spiritual status, yet with sufficient experience to impart their knowledge, can act as your guide—a teacher, a friend, or a counsellor, for example, or anyone whose qualities can aid your progress. You are still at the stage of wandering and trying to discover the sacred. Guidance is of benefit if one feels its absence and overlooks the faults of the guide.

Many people want to flee from the next door; it is the Door of Selection, where the wanderer has to commit to a formal spiritual path.

6. The Door of Selection (*Bāb al-Ikhtiyār*) باب الإختيار

وَاخْتَارَ مُوسَىٰ قَوْمَهُ سَبْعِينَ رَجُلًا

Wa akhtār Mūsā qawmahu saba'īna rajulan

'...Moses then selected seventy men from his people.' (*Qur'ān*, 7:155)

Selection is to consciously choose a path or stream that emerges from true guidance and that flows from the One Reality and returns to the One Reality. It is the pathway of Prophets and Messengers and is bounded by the banks of the Primordial Contract—the original covenant between the forms of creation and the essence of creation. All true religions have elements of the Primordial Contract—what Islam calls the *Dīn al-Ḥanīf*—but although all streams begin and end in the same reality, the selection of a stream is vital. Selection is a method, a programme and a consciousness that one has to commit to, for without it the necessary discipline for the spiritual wanderer is lost. The craft upon which you launch your quest must be fit for the type of currents that you will experience. In our pathway, the Door of Selection has opened to Islam as the *Dīn al-Ḥanīf* (religion or spiritual path of monotheistic universalism—i.e. unity in diversity or multiplicity).

The closest and most authentic expression of the Primordial Contract within Islam is the pathway of *Taṣawwuf* (Sufism), the inner dimensions of Islam that share a great deal with other authentic faiths and ancient esoteric streams. Religions are above all spiritual disciplines that require you to abide by certain rules and commit to a formal spiritual practice. All formal, authentic spiritual paths start and end at the same point. There are a lot of steps in between, which you may or may not accept, acknowledge, or find useful, but humanity has been at this since the dawn of intellect and consciousness and there are many formal schools of religion, most of which have been through various reformations and renewals. You need to commit to a structure, mainly because you need to constrain yourself as you move along. The Selection of a school or pathway ultimately must relate to the original unfolding of the spiritual path to human beings, or what one would call the primordial covenant between created entities and their Creator.

Within these overarching structures and prescribed ritual practices, each individual's path is utterly unique, and no aspect of its finer details, personal experiences, or convictions can be generalized or prescribed to anyone else's. The Universal Religion is the path of *Islām*, but it can be any other path that has the same level of discipline and has the same beginning and end—in unity. However, the doorway has to be the confirmation of the existence of the Primordial Religion, *ad-Dīn al-Ḥanīf*, and the Selection of the Stream that you are going to choose. That Selection requires discipline, which means that you must abide by the laws and by-laws of this practice. Selection of the pathway involves a method, a programme, and the consciousness that one path is not necessarily the same as the other.

There is no point dabbling in different disciplines in your own way. It is not like a smorgasbord; you have to select one and stick with it. Recognise that the disciplines and constraints that are embedded in that path are necessary. To allow you to unchain yourself in the inner world, you must bind and constrain yourself in the outer world. In the inner dimension all the authentic pathways are the same—there is very little doubt about that. As you rise in your spiritual realisation, the differences begin to merge, but they are very real at the point where you enter. If one thinks that one can do bits and pieces here and combine them there, it will not work; it has not worked. Ultimately, selecting a discipline is the only choice.

First Reflection Day:

The first overarching Name and first half of the recommended *Dhikr* for the Preliminary Stage of the Stirrings may be repeated 33 times each in order to focus the mind and allow any insights, which you should take a note of and perhaps write down or otherwise record. Once you reach the *Manāzil* of *Shaykh* Anṣārī, you will only have two doors a week to read, while reflecting on the three subtle degrees of each door in between. On the reflection days you may ponder the overarching Names but they are not intended for repetitive *dhikr,* as many of them are *Jalāli* or Majestic Names and caution is recommended in evoking them emphatically, rather you are encouraged to focus more on the *Jamāli* Names of a gentler way of beauty. It is highly recommended to add the three Names of the recommended *dhikr* for each stage to your daily and/or weekly remembrance practice as you progress along the path:

Al-Bāṭin (The Hidden) *Al-Fattāḥ* (The Opener) *Al-Qādir* (The Enabler)

Yā Bāṭin ~ Yā Fattāḥ ~ Yā Qādir يا باطن ~ يا فتاح ~ يا قادر

WEEK TWO

7. The Door of Perseverance (*Bāb al-Muthābara*) باب المثابرة

اصْبِرُوا وَصَابِرُوا وَرَابِطُوا

Uṣburū wa ṣābirū wa rābiṭū

'...Bear in patience, persevere and remain steadfast.' (*Qur'ān*, 3:200)

Once you select that discipline, you have to persevere in it, and launch your craft on the stream. Now, this stream that you have launched your craft upon will meet other streams later on, as they return back to the Reality of One, but you should not jump from one stream to the next. You can, but you have to change your craft if you want to do that; you cannot expect the boat that you launched yourself onto a particular spiritual path on to be useful on all streams. When you start, the requirements are very simple; at the early stages, the discipline required is not necessarily to submit entirely to the discipline but to accept that there is a discipline. Perseverance is the discipline to persist in the selected pathways. In the metaphor of the stream and the pathway, it is the tributary of the tributary that leads to the main river. It is to recognise that the tributary is not the main pathway and to have the confidence that it will ultimately lead to it. The smallest tributaries are the easiest to navigate, with the narrowest banks, the shallowest waters, and the slowest flows. The Stirrings are the smallest tributaries.

> Perseverance in the outer realm is to abide by the rules of spiritual 'navigation' as the necessary discipline of the selected pathway.

> Perseverance in the inner realm is to maintain a state of preparedness for the eventual, inevitable openings of the latent faculties.

8. The Door of Companionship (*Bāb ar-Rifqa*) باب الرفقة

وَحَسُنَ أُولَٰئِكَ رَفِيقًا

Wa ḥasuna ulāʾika rafīqā

... [Prophets, men of righteousness, martyrs and the virtuous]—'and what splendid company they are!' (*Qurʾān*, 4:69)

Companionship is the in-gathering of like-minded, like-hearted spiritual wanderers. Companionship reinforces and amplifies the steadfastness of wanderers. It makes Perseverance simple and agreeable, lightens the burdens, and smooths the pathway. With Companionship, the wanderer becomes more determined; without it, the wanderer can lose heart and direction. Companionship is Reflection of the self onto the other person; it is the other person's reflection on your self. Where openness, trust, loyalty, and sincerity are present, the Mirror of Companionship reflects well. Where narrow-mindedness, suspicion, doubt, pride and competitiveness are present, the mirror of Companionship reflects dully or not at all. Choose your companions as you choose all that is most valuable to you, but take care to choose those who challenge you, not those who flatter you. Most of all, choose companions who do not necessarily agree with you, as they may loosen your grip on your opinions in light of fresh knowledge and perspectives. Then, from Companionship, Discipline, Perseverance and Inquiry, you develop Inner Sight, the verification of the existence and reality of your inner senses and faculties. From this Inner Sight comes insight.

9. The Door of Inner Sight (*Bāb al-Idrāk*) باب الإدراك

ثُمَّ مَا أَدْرَاكَ مَا يَوْمُ الدِّينِ

Thumma mā adrāka mā yawm ud-Dīn

'...Indeed, how can you know what is the Day of Judgement?'

(*Qur'ān*, 82:18)

Inner Sight is the verification of the inner faculties. There are many definitions of the inner senses that combine to give Inner Sight. At the Stage of Stirrings, the wanderer can only grant their existence without determining their properties. The full range of the powers of Inner Sight unfolds much later. Here we are only given glimpses of it, but enough to confirm their truth. They appear as flashes or glimpses that encompass entire horizons. They can be frequent or rare, but they will astonish the wanderer with their potency for revealing what is true and meaningful. Inner Sight is the first step in ascribing value and recognising meaning. With Inner Sight the wanderer finally puts to rest the preponderance of the material and the gross. With Inner Sight the subtler realities become perceptible. The task becomes adding to these subtler realities until they balance the outer world with the inner. Quality rises to balance quantity. The exercises described in Steiner's book, *Knowledge of Higher Worlds*, can be helpful in this endeavour.*

The Austrian architect and physicist (natural philosopher), polymath and educator, Rudolf Steiner (1861–1925) devised a three-phase form of meditation and a set of six spiritual exercises in order to develop the subtle faculties of Inner Sight through conscious development of

*Steiner, R. & Collison, H. (1937) *Knowledge of the Higher Worlds and its Attainment: a Revised and Enlarged Edition of 'The Way of Initiation' with 'Initiation and its Results'*. 3rd. ed. / Authorized English translation by G. Metaxa / Edited by H. Collison. S.l: Rudolf Steiner Publishing Co.; Zajonc. A. (1993). *Catching the Light: The Entwined History of Light and Mind*. Oxford University Press.

what he viewed as the threefold nature of the human being: Thinking, Feeling and Willing. Steiner's three stages of meditation are Imaginative Cognition, Inspiration and Intuition. The goals of meditation include remembering past lives and accessing universal knowledge via the 'Akashic Records', a kind of global collective consciousness. The six basic exercises include focusing on one simple man-made object, such as a pencil or a paperclip, exclusively for at least five minutes a day, doing the same deed freely at the same time each day, reserving judgement and focusing on the positive aspects and outcomes of every situation. They are all towards activating the subtle faculties by developing a healthy, balanced, conscious approach to the three main areas of Thinking, Feeling and Willing.

With Inner Sight, you begin to ascribe value to things, recognise meaning and finally lay to rest the preponderance of the material over the subtle, of quantity over quality. It does not mean that you substitute them but with Inner Sight, the subtler realities emerge and begin to balance the outer side and it is balance that we are seeking. You cannot smother quantity with quality; it is very difficult. You need both. What we have is a preponderance of one over the other or a complete smothering of one by the other. One of the main tasks of the Preliminary Stirrings is to rebalance this. Once this is done, you become a traveller, no longer a wanderer. You know where you are going, you are not simply wandering around but have an aim and purpose.

10. The Door of Travelling (*Bāb as-Siyāḥa*) باب السياحة

قُلْ سِيرُوا فِي الْأَرْضِ ثُمَّ انظُرُوا كَيْفَ كَانَ عَاقِبَةُ الْمُكَذِّبِينَ

Qul sīrū fīl-arḍ thumma anẓurū kayfa kāna ʿāqibat ul-mukādhibīna

'...Say: Travel the earth and see what was the destiny of liars.'

(*Qurʾān*, 6:11)

Travelling is the process by which the wanderer ceases to be a wanderer and instead becomes a seeker. The goal is now clear. The tremors of agitation at the beginning of the stirrings are replaced by the decisiveness of journeying towards the end of stirrings. The person now travels as a seeker for the One Reality, driven by the One Reality.

You have now successfully progressed from the Stage of the semi-dormant inner realities to the Stage where these realities are recognised as true indicators and verifiers of truth. Travelling does not necessarily mean in the literal, physical sense, although it can stem from it or also lead to it. It could be inspired by wandering in and exploring beautiful new places, walking in familiar places and visiting 'holy' places or anywhere of emotional or spiritual significance. It may lead to major pilgrimage, but could equally happen at home. Beware of attaching too much significance to a particular destination or physical place, lest it become an idol, detrimental to your development, a decoy to your true aim.

11. The Door of Idols (*Bāb al-Asnām*) باب الأصنام

قَالَ بَلْ فَعَلَهُ كَبِيرُهُمْ هَٰذَا فَاسْأَلُوهُمْ إِن كَانُوا يَنطِقُونَ

Qāla bal fa'alahu kabīruhoum in kānū yanṭiqūna.

'...He said: Rather, it was the greatest among them [idols] who did it, ask them, if they can speak.' (*Qur'ān,* 21:6)

In order to start out on the true path of spiritual transformation of the self in earnest, the heart must begin to be cleared of its natural attachments to that which is created, in order to make ample space for the Divine Light of its Creator. Things to which we attach importance and feel desire for, other than Allāh, could be termed Idols, although it sounds somewhat archaic, that is, things which are created by human hands. Although some things may be useful aids in everyday life, they cannot in and of themselves help or harm us without our wielding them. Idolising things like fashion, instruments, money, power, technology or even weaponry is the most basic level of idolatry and is relatively easy to let go even in the early stages of spiritual development. In the intermediate stages it becomes necessary to weed out the less material attachment to which we devote a disproportionate level of attachment, such as other beings, emotions, such as fears and phobias, and at a higher level even more subtle aspects of earthly life with which we may become obsessed. Even the pillars of our spiritual practice can become Idols, if taken to extremes.

12. The Door of Mirrors (*Bāb al-Marāyāt*) باب المرايات

قَالَ قَائِلٌ مِّنْهُمْ إِنِّي كَانَ لِي قَرِينٌ

Qāla qā'ilum minhoum innī kāna lī qarīnun

'...And one of them shall say: I had a close friend....' (*Qur'ān,* 37:51)

With the exception of the prophets of old and certain scholars and saints of the intermediary period, the path is not a monastic one of seclusion from the world. Retreat is also a military strategy and serves a particular purpose. Equally isolating oneself for limited periods can be beneficial when necessary to recover, refocus, and regroup but ought not to be a long-term pattern, as we need the reflections of other human beings to mirror our psychological and spiritual processes and keep them moving forward. It is easy to hide from the self or to suppress many shadowy, unfavourable aspects of the self when secluded from others. They then stagnate through denial or become volatile under the pressure of repression while hidden from others and can erupt in their presence, rather than being transformed by a gentle emergence into conscious awareness through repeated encounters in relationships of every kind. The principle and premise of this door is projection: qualities we see in others, both positive and negative, are often aspects of ourselves.

13. The Door of Reproachfulness (*Bāb al-Lawm*) باب اللوم

وَلَا أُقْسِمُ بِالنَّفْسِ اللَّوَّامَةِ

Walā uqsimu bin-nafs il-lawwāma

'...And by the self-reproaching soul.' (*Qur'ān,* 75:2)

Reproachfulness is aimed towards the self rather than the other. Self-blame can become self-flagellation in extreme cases, but as extremes tend to be avoided on the Ṣūfi path, self-reproach refers more to self-scrutiny than self-blame, which is an essential part of the process at all stages. The premise is that self-development starts when blaming others stops, as the assumption that any problem is someone else's fault renders one powerless to improve the situation at all. As soon as self-responsibility is assumed, you are immediately empowered to change yourself in any way necessary in order to improve your situation. This works on any scale or level, in subtle, internal ways as well as more obvious, outward manifestations. As soon as we get over the self's need to be right at the expense of others or the truth, and adopt the humility of healthy self-critique, we remove a significant obstacle from our own path.

You are now fit to pass from the Preliminary Stage of Stirrings to Anṣārī's Stage, *Manzal* of Beginnings (*bidāyāt*). You now have the internal faculties. The commanding self (*an-Nafs al-Ammāra*), or lower self, that was the only expression of the 'rainbow' self, at the time when inspiration first struck you, has changed its nature. Through the process of self-scrutiny it experienced, having attained the second level of the reproachful self (*an-Nafs al-Lawwāma*), it is now becoming an inspired self (*an-Nafs al-Mulhama*). It is necessary for the seeker to reach this Stage of self, or level of soul, in order to move you to the Stage of Beginnings. These first three levels of the soul can be compared in the context of Goethe's Colour Theory* or Newton's Optics** as the red to yellow border phenomenon of the lower end of the spectrum, and the next three levels with the higher frequencies or the blue end of the spectrum. It is also somewhat analogous to the Chakra system in Buddhism and Hinduism.

Second Reflection Day:

Add the twin overarching Names and second half of the recommended *dhikr* for the Preliminary Stage of the Stirrings:

Aẓ-ẓāhir (The Manifest) *Al-Muqaddim* (The Advancer/Progressor) *al-Mu'akhir* (The Delayer)

Yā ẓahir ~ Yā Muqaddim ~ Yā Mu'akhir يا ظاهر ~ يا مقدم ~ يا مؤخر

*Goethe, J. W. von (1967) *Goethe's Theory of Colours. Translated by Charles Lock Eastlake.* London: Frank Cass & Co.

**Newton, I. (2003) *Opticks*. Amherst, N.Y.; Prometheus Books.

Stages of the Wayfarers Towards Knowledge and Certainty

Manāzil as-Sā'irīn ila al-Ma'rifa wal-Yaqīn

The Hundred Step Path of 'Abdullah Anṣārī Within Ten Stages

'Abdullah Anṣārī lived in Herāt, which is in modern-day western Afghanistan. In those days it was part of the Greater Khorasān area of the Persianate world. His lineage is traceable to the family of the Prophet. For a person of such subtle instincts and insights, he was also a very rigorous and, in many ways, dry scholar. So he balanced this dryness with his ecstatic state. He wrote mainly in Persian, including some wonderful poems, exhortations—*Munājāt*—some examples of which will appear in English translation in the 'Reflection Day' sections. This book was written in classical Arabic, *Manāzil as-Sā'irīn*, The Stages of the Wayfarer, although he had written a Persian (*farsī*) version some 30 years earlier. The first stage of Anṣārī's *Manāzil* is the Stage of Beginnings. Attempts have been made to make the Stages more accessible and user friendly by modernising some of the wording, while maintaining the content and meaning.

They should not necessarily be thought of in very structured, hierarchical forms, but there is a definite structure in the layout, which follows Anṣārī's original ordering of the Stages, doorways and degrees, and there is a hierarchy, just not in the rigid sense of the pre-modern writers. The word 'hierarchy' itself is of Greek origin and there is no equivalent in Arabic. The word used in Islamic texts is *tartīb*, which is more akin to ordering in an appropriate way. It is not value-laden, nor does it imply preference, as hierarchy does. The idea of ordering in Islām is unrelated to the power differentials in hierarchy and shows the fundamental difference in worldviews between *Islām* and the Greco-Roman heritage misappropriated by Western civilisation.

The words God, Allāh, Truth, Reality, the One, the Infinite, the Eternal, as well as the All-Merciful, the All-Powerful, Sustainer, Creator, Bestower and other references to the Divine Names and Attributes will be used interchangeably throughout this book. Reflections on some of these *asmā' al-ḥusnā*—the Beautiful Names—will be suggested at regular intervals, particularly at the beginning and end of each stage.

1. The Stage of Beginnings *(Manzal al-Bidāyāt)*

منزل البدايات

Overarching Names: The Lifegiver *Al-Muḥyī* المحي
The Lifetaker *Al-Mumīt* المميت

WEEK THREE

This is the stage where the self, after it has awoken to reality, struggles to find its newfound expression in individual and social matters. The Stage of the Beginnings has ten doorways:

1.1. The Door of Awakening *(Bāb al-Yaqẓa)* باب اليقظة

Anṣārī's first Stage is the Door of Awakening. Unlike the Door of Awareness—the preliminary door that opens when you are beginning to rediscover your subtle spiritual faculties, Awakening is when you have already recognised them. It is literally like a person who has been asleep, and you wake them. The first onrush of being awakened is what the spiritual wanderer experiences. Anṣārī introduces all of these doors with an appropriate Qur'anic verse, or *āya*, and the one he starts with at the Door of Awakening is:

قُلْ إِنَّمَا أَعِظُكُم بِوَاحِدَةٍ ۖ أَن تَقُومُوا لِلَّهِ مَثْنَىٰ وَفُرَادَىٰ ثُمَّ تَتَفَكَّرُوا

Qul innamā a'ẓukum biwaḥdatin an taqūmū lillāhi mathnā wa furādā thumma tatafakkarū

'I offer you a single counsel: draw close to God, in twos and ones, and then reflect...'. (*Qur'ān*, 34:46)

Anṣārī says that Awakening is to arise from a condition of absent-mindedness and heedlessness, *ghaflah,* and is the first stage of enlivening the heart by the raising of awareness. Awakening manifests itself by seeing the bounties that you have been given, with your inner eye, and despairing from counting them. You begin to see the world from its inner realities, and what was a condition of outer constraints or conditions of restrictiveness are seen with inner sight as innumerable bounties, *ni'ām,* you despair of counting. And you recognise that their bestower is not human. The Bestower lies elsewhere. The knowledge that bounties are infinite and that you are the recipient of these bounties comes from the light of inspired reason, spiritually recharged, the spark of inspiration and the example of those guides who have been transported to these realms before. It is not just counting your blessings but recognising that all of reality, all of the manifestations of everything, are a form of bounty, and their Source lies beyond human beings.

Awakening also requires that you recognise that you can slip out of it and that you can fall into states and conditions where you go back to sleep again. To avoid that, you have to constantly remind yourself of the Bestower, the Truth. You have to know that your self, when it is awakened, begins to recognise that behind all the manifestations of all kinds of realities lies only One and very importantly, to stay awake, to be continually reawakened, and to use that as a platform to move on to the next Stage. This requires that you are willing to break habits as an essential element in any spiritual wayfaring. You have to be prepared to leave your comfort zone. These habits can be anything—the way you sleep, eat, study, the way you do your devotions, anything which gives you a regular, familiar comfort zone that is false needs to be broken. It works wonders. Breaking habits that are restrictive to the spiritual path are an essential requirement for Awakening.

The Stage of Awakening is in three degrees and you are invited to contemplate one each day:

1. Seeing innumerable bounties with the inner eye and recognising their Bestower. This knowledge is attained through the light of reason, a spark of Inspiration, and the example of those who have been transported to these realms beforehand.
2. Recognising the dangerous signs of slippage, and earnestness in avoiding their pitfalls. This is assisted by glorifying the Truth and knowing the self.
3. Awareness of the passage of time and resolving not to waste the time left. This is achieved by adding to one's spiritual knowledge, recognising the boundaries, seeking the company of, and maintaining good relations with, fellow wayfarers.

Above all, Awakening requires the willingness to break habits.

The increase in and sharpening of consciousness implied by Awakening necessitates the forming of new modus operandi and the falling away of unconscious habits formed over time which, however deeply ingrained and regardless of their origin, may no longer be compatible with the increase in spiritual Awareness and practice experienced and cultivated by the aspiring wayfarer. Mannerisms, defensive ways of communicating, which sometimes manifest in a particular tone or use of the voice will gradually reach conscious awareness as something incongruent with the growing sense of openness and sensitivity to the subtleties of one's being and surroundings. It will no longer be necessary to keep people at bay with the superficial layers of personality or fill silences with small talk, as you become increasingly comfortable with the depth of self, the complexity of humanness and the intensity of calm, honest, intense interactions.

1.2. The Door of Recognising Error *(Bāb at-Tawba)* باب التوبة

وَمَن لَّمْ يَتُبْ فَأُولَٰئِكَ هُمُ الظَّالِمُونَ

… *Wa man lam yatub fa'ūlā'ika hum aẓ-ẓālimūn*

'And those who are unrepentant are surely the oppressors.' (*Qur'ān*, 49:11)

Once the wanderer has become a traveller and the traveller has become a wayfarer, after the Awakening comes recognition that you have erred in the way that you have conducted yourself and have lived in the past. Allāh says in the *Qur'ān* that those who are unrepentant are surely the oppressors, that is, they oppress themselves by not recognising the error of their ways. But you cannot really seek redress for error unless you know what you have transgressed. This becomes a reality, the categorisations of transgressions that require you to recognise them and to rectify them and resolve not to repeat them. It is by knowing that Reality, the One, is in a state of constant Interchange and Exchange with created beings that a person becomes truly regretful and remorseful regarding the transgression towards oneself or towards others. There is also fear of the possibility of regression, that you might go back to committing these errors. That is why the knowledge of your inner Realities that allow you to deal with these errors becomes vital.

Recognising Error is not possible unless one identifies the contravention. This becomes possible after the wayfarer is immediately aware of the transgression when it occurs, is content after the condition is rectified, and resolves not to repeat it, knowing that the Truth is observing them. A person must be regretful and remorseful regarding the transgression both towards self and others, and always aware that their remorse is conditional. Before this state is reached, the wayfarer becomes aware of the subtler realities behind it: that God is The Ultimate Arbiter and Bestower of Forgiveness, and that when forgiveness is bestowed, it is simply the manifestation of the Names of The All-Forgiver, *Al-Ghafūr* الغفور, *Al-Ghaffār* الغفار, *Al-'Afū* العفو and The All-Just, *Āl-'Adl* العادل

Recognition of Error is in three degrees, one of which may be contemplated on each day of the rest of the week:

1. Seeking redress from the consequences of error becomes therefore a pathway towards understanding the Divine Names behind all actions and states.
2. There is no arbiter but The Arbiter. This doorway becomes established when the wayfarer recognises that there is no way to seek redress outside the redress that comes from the Truth.
3. In the third degree the wayfarer repents from the idea of seeking repentance, leaving the matter entirely to Allāh as The Arbiter.

Third Reflection Day:

Repeat 99 times:

أستغفر الله العظيم واتوب اليه

Astaghfir Allāh al-'aẓīm wa atūbu ilayh

I ask God's forgiveness and turn towards Him.

WEEK FOUR

1.3. The Door of Accountability *(Bāb al-Muḥāsaba)*

باب المحاسبة

يَا أَيُّهَا الَّذِينَ آمَنُوا اتَّقُوا اللَّهَ وَلْتَنظُرْ نَفْسٌ مَّا قَدَّمَتْ لِغَدٍ

Yā ayyuhalladhīna āminū, attaqū Allāha waltanẓur nafsummā qaddamat lighadin...

'O those who are secure in their knowledge, fear God, and let each self consider what it has laid in stock for the morrow....' (*Qur'ān*, 59:18)

From the Door of Recognising Error, you move to the Door of Accountability, or *muḥāsaba*. The pathway of Accountability, *muḥāsaba,* is measurement. What is your measure of inner Accountability? It is to measure the huge chasm that exists between the infinite gifts of the Creator, God, the Truth and your transgressions. This is the measure of Accountability. For you to have appropriate and proper Accountability, there has to be a degree of inner Wisdom and you have to know the tricky ways of your lower self, so that you recognise that your transgressions are real, because the bounties are infinite and if you are not in constant thankfulness for being within the reality of these bounties, then transgression is inevitable. You must also recognise and confirm, in a State of Accountability, that bounties do not come from human beings, and whatever goodness you receive comes from Reality, from the Truth, from Allāh. It may be manifested through individuals, through societies, but its source is One.

The Stage of Accountability is built on that of Recognising Error, think of one part each day:

1. First, to measure the chasm between God's gifts and your transgressions. This requires the light of wisdom, disbelief in the ways of the lower self, and the ability to distinguish between the bounties from God and counterfeit bounties from men.
2. Second, to differentiate the obligations that God has upon you from what you think you own or possess. Fulfilling your duties thus becomes a gift bestowed on you, and whatever sentence is meted out to you can only be just.
3. Third, to know that fulfilling your duties is always to your advantage, while transgressions against yourself or others are always to your detri-

ment. Do not lose the scale by which you gauge the way in which you spend your time.

1.4. The Door of Deputization *(Bāb al-Ināba)* باب الإنابة

وَأَنِيبُوا إِلَىٰ رَبِّكُمْ وَأَسْلِمُوا لَهُ

'Wa 'anībū 'ilā Rabbikum wa aslimū lahu.'

'And refer your affairs to your Sustainer.' (*Qur'ān*, 39:54)

From Accountability you move to the next door, the fourth door in the Stage of Beginnings, which is the Door of Deputization. Deputization is to refer your entire affairs, outer and inner, back to God, back to Allāh. Referring your affairs is a higher station than recognition of and seeking redress for errors, because you move from being in a state of defiance by maintaining errors, to a state of concurrence. The former requires that you act through your self. The latter refers the entire affair to a Higher Authority and the act of removing errors becomes subsumed under the Deputization of Allāh, the Higher Authority. The act of deputizing or referring, even your outer affairs, to a Higher Power, removes the self from the equation and inhibits you from believing that it is somehow independent and able to do, achieve and realise things through independent action.

Independent action is, in many ways, a mirage, and by deputizing your affairs to a Higher Authority, you realise that the outcomes are not due only to your actions. You act, as you are able and to the best of your knowledge, at a point in time, but the ways in which outcomes manifest themselves are outside your control. If you have already deputized the outcomes to the Highest Authority, then your actions must be error free. In sum, seeking redress for errors is to move from defiance to concurrence, while deputizing your affairs to Allāh Most High is a higher station as your concurrence becomes total. The self then recognises the deceptiveness of 'independent' action and that outcomes are entirely ordained by an Absolute Authority.

Deputization is of three parts; please work towards integrating one part each day:

1. First, to appeal to the Truth for redress as the wayfarer would, after duly apologising for seeking redress elsewhere.

2. Second, to return to God by recognising the Primordial Contract and affirming your intention to abide by it.
3. Third, to spontaneously turn to God with no involvement of your will. The wayfarer reaches this condition after despairing of the self's inability to achieve anything without referral to God, and basks in the delights of referring the matter entirely to the Source of Action and Command.

> Fourth Reflection Day:
>
> مراقبة ومحاسبة
>
> *Murāqiba wa muhāsaba*
>
> Vigilance, self-scrutiny and taking account of your actions, morning and evening.

WEEK FIVE

1.5. The Door of Contemplation *(Bāb at-Tafakkur)* باب التفكّر

وَأَنزَلْنَا إِلَيْكَ الذِّكْرَ لِتُبَيِّنَ لِلنَّاسِ مَا نُزِّلَ إِلَيْهِمْ وَلَعَلَّهُمْ يَتَفَكَّرُونَ

Wa anzalnā ilayka 'dh-dhikr litubayyina lin-nāsi mā nuzzila ilayhim wa laʿallahum yatafakkarūn

'Upon you We sent down the Remembrance, to make clear to mankind what has been sent down to them—that they may contemplate.' (*Qurʾān*, 16:44)

The next door that Anṣārī talks about is the Door of Contemplation, or *tafakkur*, as he calls it. He defines Contemplation as the recourse to inner sight in order to become aware of what you truly desire. You may think that you truly desire wealth, prestige or something to do with the outer world, but your inner desires, if you are on the path of spiritual travel, cannot have the same measure as the outer quantitative desires. Inner sight that is agitated or moved by Contemplation makes you aware of what it is that you truly value, truly desire, and Contemplation becomes a true measure of knowing what you long for and desire in the inner world. It also requires that you reflect on the nature of oneness, on the nature of reality. This is necessary to overcome the disturbances that will always be there to deflect a person from the path, create false turns and missteps. If you reflect on any condition with the principle of *tawḥīd*, oneness, then any pitfalls and traps will be smoothed out and you will no longer be subject to deflection or be waylaid on your journey.

Contemplation also requires you to reflect on the subtleties of creation, the linkages between all manifest and unmanifest states and conditions, and how they all interrelate, link, amplify and add to each other, and that in their totality, they all point to the One. The appropriate end of Contemplation is to see the interconnectedness of things, behind which stands One Reality. It is also to know that the outer faculties in themselves have limitations that make it impossible for them to establish the subtle interlinkages that exist between seen and unseen, various hierarchies of being of creation and Contemplation of this kind begins to hone your inner qualities, as if you are polishing or sharpening them, putting an edge to them so that you can see and recognise the signs of inner, unseen, higher realities, in all kinds of places. They begin to crystallise and become, in themselves, a reality.

Contemplation is a very important stage to pass through on the travels of the wayfarer, and it has three degrees, as do all of the stages, one for each day:

1. Contemplation is the recourse to inner sight to become aware of what is truly desired.
2. There is Contemplation on the nature of oneness, which is to overcome the ocean of disturbances. This can only be done through reliance on the light of unveiling while abiding by the outer rules and constraints.
3. There is also Contemplation of the subtleties of creation; and Contemplation on the meaning of acts and states. These forms of Contemplation ease the pathways to understanding realities.

Contemplation requires that one acknowledges the limitations of the intellect and the chain of cause and effect. Understanding subtleties requires that a person hones the ability to recognise signs and indicators of higher realities, and their foundation in the Acts of the Bestower.

1.6. The Door of Reflection *(Bāb at-Tadhakkur)* باب التذكر

وَمَا يَتَذَكَّرُ إِلَّا مَن يُنِيبُ

Wa mā yatadhakkaru illā man yunīb

'And none remembers except those who delegate [to God].'

(*Qur'ān*, 40:13)

From Contemplation you progress to the Door of Reflection. Personal experiences are useful for Reflection if the intellect is enlivened, and if the person becomes aware of the slippage of time. The Fruits of Reflection are effective if the person moves from simply hoping for change to its realisation. Recourse to the *Qur'ān*, limiting relations only to persons of quality, reducing outer commitments and excessive physical demands are all essential for the Reflection that leads to recollection. *Shaykh* Anṣārī says Reflection is higher than Contemplation as a State. The reason is that Contemplation is to seek what is lost to you. You contemplate something because you are trying to extract something from it, while Reflection is to find what is already there. When you remember something, you draw on your memory bank. It is already there. When you contemplate something, you are not sure exactly what you are looking for. You contemplate an issue or an event or a condition, but you are trying to find it.

Reflection, apart from having the guide to focus and establish the forms of your remembrance, also benefits from the experiences of other people and from the Fruits of your own Reflection. Your own personal experiences become an important element in Reflections, but now they have to be seen in a different context. You recall, not so much the life events of your past, thereby trying to recreate your state at that point, but instead recollect things in relation to a much deeper base and how they all link to the One. You remember things if they enhance your Awareness and knowledge of higher realities. Reflection as a conscious spiritual effort, for the wayfarer has a different objective than regurgitating your physical, psychological experiences of the past in ethereal form. When you choose the guide who helps you on your spiritual path, the guide is of benefit only when you recognise their utility by their absence.

Reflection, for *Shaykh* al-Anṣārī, also comprises three degrees; think of one per day:

1. *Dhikr* or *tadhakkur* becomes much facilitated by a guide. This is the spiritual guide, the *shuyūkh*, the realised beings who are the necessary aids and assistants on the path.
2. Reflection benefitting from the experiences of others and on your own experiences and observations in the spiritual context.
3. Reflection emanating from the fruits of contemplation on the interconnectedness of events along the path, the guidance inherent in their symbols and how they relate to higher realms.

> Fifth Reflection Day:
>
> توحيد—لا اله الا الله
>
> Silent Dhikr: There is no god but God—Exhale '*Lā ilāha*', inhale '*illallāh*'. Repeat 99 times.

WEEK SIX

1.7. The Door of Steadfastness *(Bāb al-I'tiṣām)* باب الاعتصام

وَاعْتَصِمُوا بِحَبْلِ اللَّهِ جَمِيعًا وَلَا تَفَرَّقُوا

Wa a'taṣimu biḥabli llāhi jamī'an wa lā tafarraqū

'And hold fast, all of you, to the rope of God and do not fall into dissension.' (*Qur'ān*, 3:103)

وَاعْتَصِمُوا بِاللَّهِ هُوَ مَوْلَاكُمْ

Wa a'taṣimu billāhi huwa mawlākum

'...And hold fast to God, He is your Protector…' (*Qur'ān*, 22:78)

From Reflection, we move to the Door of Steadfastness. Holding fast to the Rope of God is a form of commitment to the contours of the spiritual pathway that you have selected and vigilance in meeting its commands. This is the spiritual confirmation of the earlier preliminary Door of Selection. You have to not only confirm the veracity of the pathway and its promises, hopes and consequences, but you also have to commit yourself to only be bound by the Commands of a Higher Authority and to see the existence of creation in the prism through which creation is manifest. This will lead you to seeing only Truth, *ḥaqq*, and allow you to yield to the Power of this Reality, and push you to bring yourself nearer to the Source of that Power. That is what holding onto the Rope of Allāh means. You want to be near to the Source of Power, the engine that moves, enlivens and enlightens the world. It means vigilance and obedience to the Commands. Steadfastness by the Power of God is to stand above all concerns and to be rid of all hesitancy.

It has three degrees to endeavour to pledge a firm commitment to each day:

1. The First Degree of Steadfastness is to accept the veracity of the message and the promises of rewards and consequences.
2. The Second Degree of Steadfastness is to refuse to be bound by any power save that of God, to see creation through the prism of the Creator, and to reject any other encumbrances.
3. The Third Degree of Steadfastness is to only see Truth alone, after succumbing to Truth's Power and seeks to bring yourself nearer to the Source of Power, which is, in effect, holding fast to the Rope of God.

1.8. The Door of Fleeing *(Bāb al-Firār)* باب الفرار

فَفِرُّوا إِلَى اللَّه

Fa firrū ila Allāh

'And flee to God.' (*Qur'ān,* 51:50)

The next door is the Door of Fleeing, or the word in Arabic is *firār.* It can also mean evading. *Shaykh* Anṣārī says Fleeing is to Flee from what never was to what is always present. Here we Flee from what is illusory, ephemeral, transient and transitional and impermanent to what is permanent, real and everlasting. You move from only hearing about things to witnessing them and experiencing them directly. We come to this metaphor of being told about a fire, then seeing the fire, then feeling the fire, and then being in the fire. You Flee from hearing about conditions and states to actually witnessing them, to being in them, from experimentation to realisation, from the form of things to their content and inner meaning. The Flight of those who are most advanced on this path is from what is not real to the Only Reality. And then you flee from Fleeing. You do not need to flee anymore. It becomes something that you pass through and move beyond in three degrees:

1. Fleeing of the First Degree is to move from ignorance to knowledge; from lassitude to fortitude; from constrictiveness to expansiveness.
2. Fleeing of the Second Degree is from hearing of a state to actually Witnessing it; from experimentation to actually realising; from the forms to the contents.
3. The Fleeing of the Third Degree is from what is not real to the Only Real; and then Fleeing from Fleeing and towards Truth.

Sixth Reflection Day:

Dhikr Ash-Shiblī:

The Qutb Abū Bakr ash-Shiblī (861–946) was born in Sāmarrā, Iraq and died in Baghdād but was of Persian descent, and a disciple of Junayd al-Baghdādī, or perhaps Junayd was a disciple of his (or both)? There is a charming anecdote of a novice approaching him and asking him why he was always heard repeating the *Ism Al-Jalāla*—Name of God—'Allāh'. Surely, they thought, he should be repeating the declaration of faith, *shahāda,* 'there is no god but God' *lā ilāhā illa Allāh* and not just continuously saying '*Allāh, Allāh'*.

Shiblī reportedly replied to the young scholar that he was afraid that he might expire between the statement of negation *lā ilāhā* and that of affirmation *illa Allāh* and thus die an apostate or unbeliever (*kāfir*) having said 'there is no god' and not having had the chance to complete the sentence with '...but God'. The student was so overwhelmed by this answer that he fell down in a dead faint, or possibly even actually died, unable to withstand the intensity of Shiblī's expression of utter Devotion.

الله الله

Repeat the Name of Allāh a thousand times today and daily as many times as you can.

The world cannot end as long as at least one person is saying Allāh Allāh.*

*Quote attributed to Socrates.

WEEK SEVEN

1.9. The Door of Spiritual Exercises *(Bāb ar-Riyāḍa)* باب الرياضة

وَالَّذِينَ يُؤْتُونَ مَا آتَوا وَّقُلُوبُهُمْ وَجِلَةٌ أَنَّهُمْ إِلَىٰ رَبِّهِمْ رَاجِعُونَ

Wa alladhīna yu'tūna mā ātū wa qulūbuhum wajilatun annahum ilā rabbihim rāji'ūn

'Those who expend what they expend with hearts anxious for acceptance.' (*Qur'ān*, 23:60)

Spiritual Exercises are the training of the self to accept truthfulness. A person has to accustom themselves to truthfulness through speech, actions and intentions, and to testify to what has come to them from Truth itself. Their existence then becomes reconciled to what is true in existence. We understand Spiritual Exercises to mean prayers, *dhikr*, collective remembrance, recitations, *du'a*, but Anṣārī defines them collectively as the training of the self to accept truthfulness. Truthfulness here is the True Reality that underlies all manifestations. That is the point of all of outer and inner Spiritual Exercises: to train the self to see and accept only what is true and to discard what is not.

That leads to a person becoming accustomed and intuitively attuned to Truthfulness, through speech, actions and intentions, and to becoming reconciled with even the most unpleasant of things and circumstances, as in them there is a certain truth and reality. There are various kinds of Spiritual Exercises, with different objectives and purposes. In the early stages, they are to grow oneself and refine one's manner of conduct and ethics, through knowledge, and to purify all actions by acting sincerely and appropriately to account for the rights of others over you. For those who are higher on the ladder of spiritual awareness, you transcend seeing diversity. You see the multiplicity that exists only in reference to their ingathering by and into the One. You would not entertain any obstacles or deviations or ways which would deflect you from this knowledge.

Spiritual Exercises are made up of three degrees, one to be done each day:

1. Spiritual Exercises of the First Level are to cultivate one's ethics through knowledge, to purify all actions through sincerity of intention and to appropriately account for the rights of others in all dealings.

2. Spiritual Exercises of the Second Level are to close the variability in one's condition, not lapsing back to any stations previously occupied, turning back only to correct and improve them, and to persevere in moving up the hierarchy of the Stages of the Wayfarers.
3. Spiritual Exercises of the Third Level are to transcend towards seeing only the One, rising to the ingathering of all in the One, refusing to entertain any obstacles or deviations from this vision.

1.10. The Door of Listening *(bab-as-Sama')* باب السمع

وَلَوْ عَلِمَ اللَّهُ فِيهِمْ خَيْرًا لَّأَسْمَعَهُمْ

Wa law 'alima Allāhu fīhim khayran la'asma'ahum

'Had God known of any good in them, he would have made them hear.' (*Qur'ān*, 8:23)

The last door of the first Stage of Beginning Anṣārī calls the Door of Audition. The word in Arabic is *Sama'*. It is not so much the spiritual chanting that one may hear or do that is meant here, it is resonating with the Sound that originates from the Divine. The first Primordial Sound that came out of nothing and commanded things to 'Be' and they came into being, *kun fa yakūn*. That is the audition, the sound sense that you need to have in this stage of spiritual wayfaring. It is to understand sound in its primordial, creative sense, as being one of the first manifestations of Allāh. There was a sound and a response to that sound. Allāh Names Himself as *As-Samī'*, the All Hearing, or All Listener. To listen, a sound has to originate, its meaning be deciphered, its emanation from the Originator established and its connection with all other manifestations understood.

The first act of creation was not bringing matter into being, or bringing the ideals or principles into reality, it was a sound that came from the Command 'Be' (*kun*) that came from the crack that opened out of which existence emerged. This is the sound that Anṣārī talks about. Recognising the primordial cry and its echoes in creation. The echoes of the cry is existence. It helps the wayfarer to erase the traces of all that is mundane and transient, in interpreting the Truth behind all manifestations. He says it connects the Eternal, *Al-Bāqī* (الباقي), with the everlasting/Infinite, *Al-Bāri'* (البارئ). Sound brought things into being, and sound draws back being into the Bosom of the Creator. The subtle purpose of Listening, the first sense to develop in the foetus, is to achieve the reality of awareness of the creative potentiality of sound and word. Listening is of three degrees:

1. The Listening of the First Degree is to respond with care to the echo of the promise; to respond with perseverance to the call of the promise, and to see with inner sight the bounties of the One.
2. The Listening of the Second Degree is to see the traces of what is desired in all situations and symbols; and to ponder over each whisper from the unseen and to free oneself from enjoying the illusion of independence.
3. The Listening of the Third Degree is to wipe out any traces of mundane causes of unveiling when it has occurred; to connect the Infinite with the Eternal and Everlasting; and to return the end to the beginning.

These are the ten Doors of the Stage of Beginnings. Each one requires in itself a great deal of pondering and reflection. For this to be of practical use to people, other than as an academic or scholarly discourse, it is useful to try to relate them to your own personal experiences and see where you stand in this hierarchy, in this medley of doors that have opened. Where are you really? Are you at the Stage of Stirrings? Maybe you are already beyond these stages. Each person must assess their true condition. You have to be true to yourself, otherwise all this is useless. The tendency is to want to be further along than one is and to project oneself to a higher level and then get lost in the complexities of that Stage due to having neglected to pass through the doorways leading up to it. Or in the name of modesty to assume a lower position and remain in the early stages long after achieving readiness to ascend the hierarchy, thus causing unnecessary delay and running late.

Like learning a language, revision is required, as is honesty with your current level, knowledge of grammar and vocabulary, in order to know where to start, how to continue and what you need to make good progress. This is something that needs to be measured carefully. How do you use that? What use is it to you? You have to ask yourself if you are, for example, at the Door of Awakening or the Door of Deputization, what do you need to do to be established in one of these conditions. You may be in a different condition that Anṣārī has not mentioned. This might be something you can ask and is very important if you are going to persevere. Most people do not and they become exhausted by it, or it is so easy that they just want to move on. We are now in Door Ten. There are 90 other doors to come, each with three degrees. You can imagine the effort required to continue to the highest stage, so orientation is very important for those who want to use this guide as a tool to help them on their pathway.

Seventh Reflection Day:

Dhikr for the Stage of Beginnings:

Al-Mubdi' (The Originator) *At-Tawwāb* (The All-Forgiver) *As-Samī'* (The All-Hearer)

Yā Mubdi' ~ Yā Tawwāb ~ Yā Samī' يا مُبدئ—يا تَوّاب—يا سَميع

2. The Stage of Gateways (*Manzal al-Abwāb*)

Overarching Names: The Ennobler *Al-Mu'iz* المُعِز
The Humiliator *Al-Mudhil* المُذِل

This is the Stage of the true Gateways to the inner world. The previous Stage of Beginnings are for those who are in a preparatory stage, where most people are content to remain indefinitely. This is no criticism, as it contains some beautiful and powerful doorways and experiences, which require of the seeker an enormous amount of long-term work toward self-knowledge. For the few to whom glimpses of the inner world are vouchsafed, the Gateways beckon them to pass through the doors and continue on to higher Stages. The Stage of the Gateways has ten doors: the Door of Sorrow, *ḥuzun*, the Door of Apprehension, *khawf*, the Door of Concern, *ishfāq,* the Door of Reverence or *khushū'*, the Door of Quietening, which is *ikhbāt*, the Door of Asceticism, *zuhd*, the Door of Self-Discipline, *wara'*, the Door of Devotion, *tabattul*, the Door of *raja'*, which is Hope or Confident Belief and the Door of *raghba*, translated as Inclination.

WEEK EIGHT

2.11. The Door of Sorrow *(Bāb al-Ḥuzn)* باب الحزن

تَوَلَّوا وَّأَعْيُنُهُمْ تَفِيضُ مِنَ الدَّمْعِ حَزَنًا

Tawallū wa a'yunuhum tafīḍu min ad-dam'i ḥazanan

'Whereupon they left, their eyes overflowing with tears, in sorrow.'

(*Qur'ān,* 9:92)

As in all of his stages, Anṣārī starts with a Qur'anic *āya.* This āya shows that what God is implying in the *Qur'ān* is that those who have a sense of Sorrow are in a high station. Sorrow is a commendable state in the *Qur'ān.* The first door is *ḥuzn*, which *Shaykh* Anṣārī defines as pain for what has passed you by or regret for what has been denied you. The Door of Sorrow is one that, if you approach it with sincerity, suffering from anguish at missed opportunities, of which you did not avail yourself, or you were availed of openings and given access to secrets, but did nothing about it. If these are what drives one's Sorrow, then that Sorrow can be a door to these gateways. It could also mean having become entangled in undertaking barren deeds that have little effect or purpose on your journey. All this is a form of negligence in doing what is obliged of you. You may have a sense of deep regret at the loss of the days that you did not take opportunities for spiritual advancement when they appeared to you and chose ease, rather than hearing and paying attention to what was being asked of you and doing what was required.

As is his custom, Anṣārī divides each of these doors into three degrees:

1. The First Degree of general practice, called the *amma*, which he defines as coming from neglect of doing what one is obliged to do, or negligence in service.
2. The Second Degree in this Door of Sorrow is the Sorrow of those who he calls *Ahl al-Irāda,* those of will. Here he defines those who are of the Second Degree 'their sorrow is one in which the heart is connected to separation'. This is the degree of those who see their connectedness with all the manifestations of Allāh, but do not see beyond that.
3. The Third Degree of those who experience Sorrow is the Sorrow of seeing the oneness behind all creation, all manifestations of Existence, and at this Stage your Sorrow is really not regarding you but regarding others, 'why can they not see beyond the Sorrow that comes from separation?'

The *nafs* or ego is absorbed in witnessing, which means that the heart becomes obsessed with separation and becomes connected with created things, to which you apply your love and longing, rather than joining them all into Love for the Truth—*al-Ḥaqq*. The Sorrow of those of will, is a Sorrow which comes from seeing separation and one's inability to derive True Love from separation, only because the *nafs* is not focusing, not zeroing in on and witnessing what is beyond or behind the manifestations of creation. It is not really a Sorrow for yourself, as much as it is a grief for those who are unable to see *al-ḥaqq*, the Truth behind all truths and manifestations of existence. It is a projected form of Sorrow. These three degrees, if sincerely felt, can open up the gateways towards the seeker.

2.12. The Door of Apprehensiveness (*Bāb al-Khawf*) باب الخوف

يَخَافُونَ رَبَّهُم مِّن فَوْقِهِمْ

yakhāfūna rabbahum min fawqihim…

'They fear their Lord above them.' (*Qur'ān*, 16:50)

The Second Door is *bāb al-khawf*, which can be translated as fear, but Apprehensiveness is more accurate. Anṣārī describes this fear or alert apprehension as pulling yourself away from a sense of security by examining the Divine utterances that come from Allāh via His chosen messengers. It is Apprehensiveness that makes you secure in your actions and thoughts, but once you open up to what Allāh is saying, through His messengers, you receive this onrush from above. It is not so much the desire for heaven or fear of hell, the main cause of Apprehensiveness is the fear that one may not be able to see or witness the Lord. The Second Degree of Apprehensiveness is the fear or alert Apprehensiveness that a kind of trick, *makar,* might afflict the *anfas,* the selves who are confirmed in their Apprehension. They are fearful that, because they are immersed in this alertness, something untoward will happen that may separate them and remove this Presence from them. It is a fear of losing a state of great ease and sweetness as one of God's plans.

Once again, this doorway has three degrees, one to be done daily:

1. The First Degree is the Apprehensiveness that one has of being punished, *al-khawf min al-'uquba.* And then he goes on to say, '*al-khawf alladhi aṣ-ṣaḥb al-īmān wa hu al-khawf al-amma.*' This apprehension comes from the fear of chastisement because of one's faith in the scriptures, in angels, in *ḥisāb wa 'iqāb* (*accountability and retribution*).
2. In the Second Degree you are not so much concerned about chastisement and punishment, but are perhaps more concerned about being veiled from Allāh when the Day of Reckoning comes.
3. The Third Degree in this doorway is the highest form of fear or Apprehensiveness. If the fear of chastisement is the station of the *nafs,* the alert soul, and the fear of losing the sweetness of witnessing manifestation, the concern of those with heart and presence, then for

those who are already confirmed in the State of Witnessing, it has to do with the fear of seeing the *jalāl* or Majesty of God's Presence.

This is the highest degree of alert Apprehensiveness; it is fear that your constant witnessing and adoration of the One may actually lead you to witness the Attributes of *Jalāl*, Majesty, that can obliterate you. These are the three degrees, depending on one's state and condition, whether one is of those with faith, *īmān* or those who have witnessed through their heart, the Presence of Allāh or those who see Allāh alone and therefore are fearful of seeing one of His manifestations of Majesty.

Eighth Reflection Day:

Read, recite and reflect on the Verses of the Quraysh, which translates as: 'In the Name of God the Compassionate, The Merciful, for the covenants of the Quraysh, (1) Their covenants for journeys by winter and summer, (2) Let them serve the Lord of this House, (3) Who feeds them against hunger and keeps them safe from fear. (4)'

Bissmlllah ir-raḥmān ir-raḥīm li'īlāfi Quraysh (1) *īlāfihim riḥlat ash-shitā'i wa aṣ-ṣayfi* (2) *falya'budū rabba hadha al-bayt* (3) *alladhī aṭa'amahum min jū'īu āmanahum min khawf* (4)	بِسْمِ اللَّهِ الرَّحْمَٰنِ الرَّحِيمِ لِإِيلَافِ قُرَيْشٍ (١) إِيلَافِهِمْ رِحْلَةَ الشِّتَاءِ وَالصَّيْفِ (٢) فَلْيَعْبُدُوا رَبَّ هَٰذَا الْبَيْتِ (٣) الَّذِي أَطْعَمَهُم مِّن جُوعٍ وَآمَنَهُم مِّنْ خَوْفٍ (٤)

WEEK NINE

2.13. The Door of Concern *(Bāb al-Ishfāq)* باب الإشفاق

قَالُوا إِنَّا كُنَّا قَبْلُ فِي أَهْلِنَا مُشْفِقِينَ

Qalū innā kunnā qablu fī ahlinā mushfiqīn

'We had once been fearful for our families.' (*Qur'ān*, 52:26)

The Third Doorway is the Door of *ishfāq*, or Concern as it is translated. The *Shaykh* defines *ishfāq* or Concern as 'the perpetuation of caution that is informed by mercy [*Al-Ishfāq dawām al-ḥadhar maqrūnan bit-taraḥum.* الإشفاق دوام الحذر مقروناً بالترحم]'. The person who is Concerned about their station and status is cautious about that condition and seeks God's Mercy in the direction their soul, or heightened self can accept. Again, this door has three degrees. At the First Degree you are Concerned that your work will be dissipated, because it is not accepted by Allāh. You are Concerned about creation, because their excuse for not doing the right acts comes from ignorance and may lead to their loss. It is the Concern of those driven by a high degree of self-realisation. As it relates to them, it is the loss of their works. As it relates to others, they will lose their works, or the rewards for their works and their excuses will be unacceptable.

The Second Degree of this Door of Concern is that as one's heart becomes polished, something will come and tarnish it, or crowd out all the efforts that one has put in to only reflect reality. Once a form of certainty is achieved, it is tested by cause and effect, rather than by *tawakkul,* Reliance on Allāh. If you are in the Doorway of Certainty, you could feel that it might be shaken by subjecting your Certainty to ratiocinations and the laws of cause and effect that drive one away from pure *tawakkul* which cannot be based on causality. The Third Degree of this doorway is Concern that, at some point, you may attribute that causality to acts by created entities and become surprised or astonished at certain things that happened through human agency, without seeing the One behind it. This prompts you to thank the agent, then Allāh rather than the other way around.

1. The First Degree is Concern for the self as it continues in its stubbornness and inclination towards meeting its own whims. The *nafs* is compared to a wild horse that you have to constantly bridle so that it does not charge off in any direction.
2. The Second Degree of this Doorway of Concern is about the use of time, its manifestation and that time is wasted because one is concerned with other things, other activities, other relations, that distance one from the Truth, *al-ḥaqq*.
3. The Third Degree of this doorway is the awareness that all that has happened is from Allāh and cannot carry any other explanation or justification.

2.14. The Door of Reverence *(Bāb al-Khushū')* باب الخشوع

أَلَمْ يَأْنِ لِلَّذِينَ آمَنُوا أَن تَخْشَعَ قُلُوبُهُمْ لِذِكْرِ اللَّهِ وَمَا نَزَلَ مِنَ الْحَقِّ

Alam ya'ni lilladhīna āmanū an takhsha' qulūbluhum lidhikr Illah wamā nazala min al-Ḥaqq

'Is it not time for those who believe that their hearts should grow reverent at the mention of God and the Truth that has been revealed?' (*Qur'ān*, 57:16)

The Fourth Door is *Bāb al-khushū'*, which is translated as the Door of Reverence. Reverence is in essence a kind of submission that is touched by concern and Love. It comes from a broken self and the way it manifests itself is in the form of surrender. Once again, Anṣārī divides this door into three degrees, which are as follows:

1. The First Degree is acceptance of the Decrees of Allāh and submission to the requirements that emanate from these de facto realities. Submission is a form of worship that is an acknowledgement of the Divine Decree, together with a confirmation of one's inability to counter it and consequent acceptance of its reality.
2. The Second Degree of Reverence is to take account, *taḥassub* or *taraqqub*, of the vices of the self and to make sure that you do not just witness them, but you plan to actively stop them, to ambush them even, when they raise their heads.
3. The Third Degree of Reverence is to protect what you have witnessed from any unveiling of what you have seen and to purify all you are witnessing from seeing anything but Allāh.

Ninth Reflection Day:

Fast for all or part of the day, according to your capacity. The aim is to feel hunger, emptiness and calm. An unaccustomed quietude and slight detachment from the world of normal multisensory experience. A stillness and slowing down, and a lessening of distractions.

WEEK TEN

2.15. The Door of Quietening *(Bāb al-Ikhtibāt)* باب الإختبات

بَشِّرِ الْمُخْبِتِينَ

...bashshir al-mukhbitīn...

'And give glad tidings to those who find rest in God.'

(*Qur'ān*, 22:34)

The Fifth Door is *bāb al-ikhtibāt*, translated as the Door of Quietening. Anṣārī starts with the above *āya* and the *Shaykh* defines Quietening as tranquillity towards what has drawn you and to what you have been drawn by the power of ardour or longing. The highest form of attraction is the Divine Attraction by which you allow yourself to be carried in a state of tranquillity. This Quietening is the first station of tranquillity and it is one of the great states of the true *mu'min* (believer). It protects the true *mu'min* from any ambivalence or threat of regression as it is a confirmed door. In this condition you burn your bridges towards seeing, in creation and in all existence, alternative explanations and you substitute inauthentic realities and worldviews for the True Reality *al-wāqi' al-ḥaqīqī*. Its three degrees are:

1. The First Degree is that the infallibility or permanence of your state of Quietening drowns out any desires. The light of *Ḥaqq* takes over the self, enlightens it, destroying any other desire.
2. The other definition of it is that the will, or *irāda* connects the heart with the Truth, *al-ḥaqq* and you respond to all of its commands and prompts voluntarily. It requires presence with *Ḥaqq* and nonacceptance of any distractions from it. The sweetness of being in this condition separates you and keeps you away from those who do not see the Reality behind and before every action.
3. A Third Degree of this door is that you do not allow cause and effect to increase or decrease your desire. Your condition is one that is defined by your yielding to the commands of Allāh and nothing could allow you to be distracted from *Al-Ḥaqq*.

This door that you are in is not affected by any sense of despair or conflict. You are established in that tranquillity and the Third Degree of this Door of Quietening is also that you become indifferent to praise or condemnation because you no longer concern yourself with the creation, *al-khalq*. You begin to see with the eye of *fanā'*; creation melts away in the Eye of Annihilation and you are ecstatic that the *nafs* is now tilting permanently towards witnessing the True Reality.

2.16. The Door of Asceticism *(Bāb az-Zuhd)* باب الزهد

بَقِيَّتُ اللهِ خَيْرٌ لَّكُمْ إِن كُنتُم مُّؤْمِنِينَ

Baqīyat Ullāhi khayrun lakum in kuntum mu'minīn

'What remains from God is better for you if you were true believers.'

(*Qur'ān*, 11:86)

The Sixth Door is the Door of Asceticism, *zuhd*. What this *āya* means is that what you will receive from Allāh in Goodness is far better for you than all the wealth of the world, so leave what is impermanent and perishable for what is Permanent. He defines *zuhd* or Asceticism in the following way: *Az-zuhd* or Asceticism is to eliminate all desire for anything completely. When the desire for something is obliterated, the self becomes distant or no longer has any tendency towards anything. He says for most people this is a door of proximity to Allāh and for seekers, *zuhd* is absolutely necessary, in the sense of losing desire for created things or beings, because if you concentrate your heart on Unity, *tawḥīd*, there is no possibility of you doing without in the *dunya*, in this world. It is a necessity for the seeker to be an ascetic.

Anṣārī goes on to say that for the *muḥaqqiq* (verifier) it is an irrelevance, because they do not see anything but Reality, only *al-Ḥaqq*. A verifier or *muḥaqqiq* can verify the experiences of the seeker, in that they have gone through many of the doors and achieved the relevant level of self-realisation, experience and spiritual development to be able to guide a seeker and answer some of their questions. Asceticism is not really a true station because it gives the world weights and measures, when there is really nothing but Allāh. How can you be a *zāhid* (ascetic) to Reality? It is a kind of rejection of Asceticism. '*zuhd 'an az-zuhd*' means you are Ascetic from Asceticism. This Asceticism has again three degrees:

1. The First Degree is to stay away from what is doubtful, after you leave what is unlawful, *az-zuhd fi ish-shubah*. Always go for what is less problematic. If it is problematic, you err on the side of caution and avoid it.

2. The Second Degree is *az-zuhd fil-fudūl*. This means you do without the bounties that are given to you. You thank Allāh for them but anything beyond your absolute necessity becomes a kind of *fudūl*, something that is extra.
3. The Third Degree of Asceticism is *az-zuhd fiz-zuhd*, to do without doing without. That is achieved in three aspects. One is by demeaning what you have done without, while the second is to be indifferent to it, whether you are in a state of riches or poverty. The third way of doing without doing without is not even considering how this has come about.

Why should you reflect on it? If you suddenly win the lottery, you do not ruminate over it, it just happened. It is not for you to look for reasons or rationale behind God's bounties. You thank Allāh and are grateful for it but in no way affected by it in terms of your lifestyle, choices or attitude to and treatment of the people. Anything that you achieve or receive that is more than what is needed carries the danger of making you somehow connected to that extra; you become used to it. This can lead to complacency and inertia. The challenge is to live a God-conscious life regardless of its outer nature. Until that is achieved or within reach, it is in the doing without anything beyond the bare necessities which is the recommended self-training and is the Second Degree of Asceticism.

Tenth Reflection Day:

Try a slightly longer fast. Make notes of any unusual thoughts or emotions that arise, however subtle and unintrusive. Compare it with last week's experience of fasting. Write down your physical, mental and emotional experiences, what you struggle to do without, which bounties were brought to your attention that you may have previously taken for granted. Note ways in which doing without certain things helped, for example with focus, and ways in which it hindered. List the essential things you need in order to optimise your work and what you can do without, which may optimise it or focus you more on your spiritual practice. Work out how to balance abstinence with indulgence in a more constructive and disciplined way, in order to achieve your desired results or better.

WEEK 11

2.17. The Door of Self-Discipline *(Bāb al-Wara')* باب الورع

وَثِيَابَكَ فَطَهِّرْ

Wa thiyābaka faṭahhir

'And purify your garments.' (*Qur'ān*, 74:4)

The Seventh Doorway is the Door of Self-Discipline, *wara'*. The *Shaykh* starts with the above *āya*. Garments referred to can be anything: the earthly life (*dunya*), your clothes, money, possessions; they can be any of your attachments. All of these are considered by the *sālik* or the *sā'ir* (wayfarer) as *najis*, impure and you have to purify yourself from such attachments, cut off from all of these and your heart has to discipline itself to do only what is right and correct. Anṣārī himself defines *wara'* or Self-Discipline in the following way: Self-Discipline or Abstinence is deep caution over everything that may be considered suspicious or impure so that you do not fall into the pit of what is unacceptable. He quotes the Qur'ānic *āya*, 'these are the limits of Allāh. Do not come near them.' *Wara'* is part of the Ascetic Stage and the last Stage of Asceticism for the layperson. However, it is the First Stage of Asceticism for the seeker, and it is again divided into three degrees to be pondered over the next three days:

1. The First Degree is to avoid horrible things or activities, because of the predilection of the self and surround oneself with all that is good and fortify one's faith.
2. The Second Degree of Self-Discipline is to guard the boundaries, the frontiers, strengthen them, build them, lift them higher and ensure that they protect the borders and boundaries of the *nafs*.
3. The Third Degree is to stay away, to abstain from anyone or anything that leads to fragmentation, wasting of time, seeing separation, and being connected to what is separate. The seeker has to oppose anything that fragments *tawḥīd* or Unity.

2.18. The Door of Devotion *(at-Tabattul)* باب التبتل

وَاذْكُرِ اسْمَ رَبِّكَ وَتَبَتَّلْ إِلَيْهِ تَبْتِيلًا

Wa'dhkur isma rabbika wa tabattal ilayhi tabtīlan

'And devote yourself [to the Truth] in consummate devotion.'

(*Qur'ān*, 73:8)

The Eighth Door is the Door of ardour, longing, yearning or Devotion. Devotion (*tabattul*) he defines as a complete rupture from all except Allāh. You separate yourself completely from anything but the *ḥaqq* and you respond to the call of the *Ḥaqq* to worship Him, and none but Him. The devotee (*al-mutabattul*) who is cut off from the world from the *dunya*, for the sake of the afterlife, has separated themselves from all but the *ḥaqq*. It is a form of voluntary sequestration, as it were, in the presence of Allāh—ecstatic sequestration.

These are its three degrees:

1. The First Degree is to cut off any chances or glances that may connect you with creation with created existence. You see it, you engage with it, but you do not give it any reality beyond its created status as an outcome of Allāh's actions.
2. The Second Degree is where the self is separated completely from its whims. You detect the scent of proximity to Allāh and you begin to soar from the wonders of unveiling so it is a state of heightened awareness, of the Presence of Allāh through the Doorway of Devotion.
3. The Third Degree is one in which you are cut off from the past. You perfect your upright posture in the Presence of Allāh and you hasten to reach your goal. And you witness the beginnings of gatheredness in Allāh.

Eleventh Reflection Day:

Wake yourself up for night prayers before *fajr* time, the darkest hour before dawn, which is the most powerful time to pray and often the quietest, most still time, with the freshest air.

WEEK TWELVE

2.19. The Door of Confident Expectancy (*ar-Rajā'*) باب الرجاء

لَّقَدْ كَانَ لَكُمْ فِي رَسُولِ اللَّهِ أُسْوَةٌ حَسَنَةٌ لِّمَن كَانَ يَرْجُو اللَّهَ وَالْيَوْمَ الْآخِرَ وَذَكَرَ اللَّهَ كَثِيرًا

Laqad kāna lakum fī rasūl Illāhi uswatun ḥasanatul-liman
kāna yarjū Allaha wal-yawm al-ākhira wa dhakar
Allaha kathīran

'In the Prophet of God you have an excellent example to follow for one who seeks God and the Last Day...' (*Qur'ān*, 33:21)

The Ninth Doorway is the Door of Confident Expectancy, *bāb ar-rajā'*; it could also be translated as belief or hope, but Confident Expectancy through invocation is more appropriate. The *Shaykh* says that *rajā'*, or Confident Expectancy, is the weakest station of the seeker because, from one point of view, it is a kind of opposition. Why would you oppose God's Will? You are seeking, hoping, and are confident in the outcome but you know that Allāh Owns all outcomes and that an owner can act in any way they see fit. So if you become confident with what to expect from Allāh, in some ways, you are opposing His Will. The other side is that Allāh has no need of His servants, and he can forgive them and do anything He Wills with them, but what He Does with them is always for the best and according to what each individual's needs.

So why would this doorway have any deep significance if the entire affair belongs to Allāh? This doorway is one that is commended and required by the *Sunnah* (practice) of the Prophet (Pbuh) and it is stated in the Book that you are to seek God's approval if you are to seek His Presence. This is why you do it, not because you are in some way or another able to influence God's decree. It is not your decree. He is not influenced by the actions of human beings, but it is incumbent upon you to supplicate—this is written in the Book and in reports of prophetic conduct. If the prophet did *du'ā* (supplication), you do *du'ā*. You do not sit and question what is the point of *du'ā*? How am I going to change God's decree? He Is, of course, Able to change His decrees, not according to our wishes and whims, but according to the deeds *mu'āmalāt* and *'ibadāt* of His servants and complete the work they start or intend.

Rajā', Confident Expectancy, has three degrees, one to be practised each day for the next three days:

1. The First Degree pushes the seeker to bring themselves to sincere requesting and the request in itself is more important than the outcome. If you are in a state of calling on Allāh, that in itself is more significant than getting what you call for.
2. The Second Degree of *rajā'* is to call for the desire to strengthen your devotions, spiritual exercises and commitment to the pathway of the Prophet (Pbuh). It is a desire to perpetuate the state of servanthood, the state of dependence on God's Commands, Decrees and Bounties.
3. The Third and highest Degree of this confident belief, is the *rajā'* of the heart, which is ardent desire and expectation to meet your Creator. The seeker seeks The Beloved and becomes distant from creation. People whose hearts have been purified through spiritual exercises are now seeking Allāh's Grace through constant *du'ā*, supplication.

2.20. The Door of Inclination *(ar-Raghba)* باب الرغبة

وَيَدْعُونَنَا رَغَبًا وَرَهَبًا ۖ وَكَانُوا لَنَا خَاشِعِينَ

Wa yad'ūnanā raghbataw wa rahbataw wakānū lanā khāshi'īna

'And they call upon Us in hope as well as in apprehension.' (*Qur'ān*, 21:90)

The Tenth Door of the second Stage of Gateways is the *bāb ar-raghba*, or the Door of Inclination. *Shaykh* Anṣārī says that this Doorway of Inclination is of a higher quality than the Doorway of Confident Expectancy or *rajā'*. Confident Expectancy is a form of yearning that seeks fulfilment, not knowing what that fulfilment will look like, but Inclination is an action towards that fulfilment with a clearer idea of its contours and what the outcome might be. It is further along the pathway to Allāh as there is a strong feeling of His Presence and an imagination of that ultimate meeting. The end of the Door of Confident Expectancy is the Door of Inclination, that is why this Door of *raghba* is higher than the Door of *rajā'*. He divides *raghba* into three degrees, as is his custom—consider one per day:

1. The First Degree is the Inclination of those who seek knowledge from the Divine Texts. This kind of knowledge is strengthened by witnessing and this Inclination blocks its proponent from retrogression.
2. The Second Degree is the *raghba* or Inclination of those who are already in a state of witnessing and already proximate to the Divine Presence. These people seek only more experience and have an exposure to the breeze that comes from the Divine Presence, this is their Inclination; they call upon Allāh so that they can experience this Divine Breeze more intensely, which makes them focus only on this goal.
3. The Third Degree of Inclination is that of the people of witnessing, *raghbat ahl ash-shuhūd*, the people who have witnessed the *Ḥaqīqa* or the Truth, Reality, and have arrived in nearer proximity to the Divine Presence.

He calls the people of the First Degree *ahl al-khabr,* those who believe in the unseen and in the reports from the books, the Divine Texts and the *sunnah* of the Prophet. Their Inclination is to deepen their knowledge of the Divine Scriptures and the *sīra* (biography) and *sunnah* of the Prophet (Pbuh). Their faith and their path are strengthened by witnessing. In particular, the witnessing that comes from worshipping Allāh as if you see Him. This is the *raghba* of those who are immersed in the Divine Texts and in the prophetic way. The Second and Third Degrees of Inclination represent the tender beginnings of the obliteration of the self. Once you have reached that station, it is one of the highest and most honourable stations, the beginning of *fanā'*, annihilation of the self, before duality is finally vanquished.

Twelfth Reflection Day:

Suggested *Dhikr* for the Stage of Gateways:

Al-Mujīb (The One who Responds) *Al-Latīf* (The Most Subtle) *Al-Karīm* (The Most Generous

Yā Mujīb ~ Yā Latīf ~ Yā Karīm

يا مجيب ~ يا لطيف ~ يا كريم

3. The Stage of Deeds (*Manzal al-Mu'āmalāt*) منزل المعاملات

On the Stage of Deeds Anṣārī wrote:

> When the gateways of the unseen open up from afar and the light of truth descends on the heart and then reflects on the self, the heart perceives the Divine Presence through inner sight. The self becomes trained through acts of obedience. The heart in turn deals with the truth through the power of certainty. The signs of intimacy [with the Truth] appear with the lights of sanctity. The tranquil self accompanies the heart and takes on its colouration as it ascends to the higher levels and gains access to their particularities.

This is the state which the adept experiences at the Stage of Deeds or transactions. The purpose of this stage is to nurture the inner qualities that govern the wayfarer in their dealings with the world that is beginning to open up for them. This is the world of the unseen, of subtler realities—the world of the qualitative rather than the quantitative—where matter recedes and meanings emerge. The outer forms melt and the inner meanings begin to emerge. The Stage of Deeds is about how you deal with the inner meanings. It starts where all things start, with yourself, the *nafs*, which has moved from suddenly waking up to this universe, this realm, or dealing with how to nurture it. How do you groom the *nafs* so that it can deal with a subtler world? Think of it in terms of a baby learning to walk, or a child who is being weaned from liquids to solid food. It is not that different. We are now learning what to do to deal with a world that has different parameters, rules and shades to the outer world.

We also need to grow ourselves when we are dealing with a world or universe that has a completely different access to the one that we are used to. Just as a child or adolescent youth or adult learns to deal with the demands of the outer world, so too do we have to learn to deal with the demands of the inner world and these have stages and steps. You cannot jump these stages; you have to be true to yourself. The core of all of this is the self. It is important that we ourselves acknowledge that we sometimes jump in the deep end, but we must understand that the outer world cannot be a way into the inner world, by itself. Outer worship may give us a small, spiritual high, but what we want to do is to sustain it, to continue, maintain it and to grow with it and make sure that it grows to its proper potential, rather than snuff it out at the beginning. The way to do it, the key to dealing successfully with the unseen, assuming we have a desire for it, is to refine our virtues.

Virtue is a heavy word, like piety—it can be too cumbersome and burdensome. But once they become virtues of the inner way, it is more like the courtesy, or *adab,* of deeds. Once you have the courtesy of dealing with the signs and signals that come from the unseen, you reach the heart of the *Qur'ān*—or any divinely inspired Book. This stage involves nurturing the inner qualities that govern the wayfarer in their deeds in uncovering the realm of the unseen and the effects of that on their dealings with the world. It starts naturally with developing the quality of care and concern—or nurturing itself—for those defining aspects of the 'transacting self"; in other words, the ten doorways of this stage. The goal of this stage is to bring the self to the point where its dealings with the unseen are determined by a set of refined virtues that culminate in a total yielding to an inner light that reflects the Truth. This naturally manifests itself also in dealing with the world in all its outer forms.

WEEK THIRTEEN

3.21. The Door of Protection *(Bāb ar-Ri'āya)* باب الرعاية

فَمَا رَعَوْهَا حَقَّ رِعَايَتِهَا

Famāra'awhā ḥaqqa ri'āyatihā

'But they did not give it [Allāh's pleasure] due.' (*Qur'ān,* 57:27)

The first door of the third Stage, and the twenty-first overall, is the Door of Protection, which is about giving due to others, in the spiritual sense, is to understand that they share with you an immutable quality—namely humanness. They may be the most despicable person on earth, horrible things can be attributed to them, but they share with you that immutable quality, which is the soul. When you have reached the third Stage of Deeds, you see the other in their outer form, but you have to give due to the fact that they share with you these immutable qualities and you see their actions in two ways: there are actions that are driven by their self, and their actions behind which is the Only Actor, the Truth or Reality, *al-Ḥaqq, ar-Raḥman* as Allāh calls Himself the Merciful. Giving Due has three levels. One is to the outer world, the second is to yourself and the third is to Reality, to Allāh.

Giving Due to yourself is to know that your self has the potential to rise to the highest levels. You must believe that these qualities are within you. They may not be noticeable or discernible now, but they are there. Therefore courtesy (*ri'āya*) of yourself is to glorify yourself. That does not mean beating your chest and saying how great you are, like Tarzan, but rather saying that you have within you *an-Nafs al-Mutma'inna, an-Nafs ar-Rāḍiya, an-Nafs al-Marḍīya* and that itself is a very luminous and precious quality. The final Stage of Protection is that you give due to Allāh—*al-Ḥaqq*—the Truth. Behind self, states and conditions, desires, and wants, is the inexpressible One. Once you are able to do that instinctively without even dwelling on it, you will have passed the test for the Door of *Ri'āya*. You then pass through it, and you move to the next door which is the Door of *Murāqaba*, Watchfulness.

Anṣārī: Protection is only possible if it is done with care and may have three degrees:

1. Protection of your works: to preserve and continue in your works you have to belittle them. You have to undertake them without noticing that you are doing them, as part of your nature and not for show.
2. Protection of your states: to deny that you are having these states so that your exertions and efforts are a reflection of yourself and not for appearances in front of others.
3. Protection of your moment: to stop at the moment and then to efface that Moment and then to efface the effacement.

Protection of others is necessarily to acknowledge that they share with you the immutable qualities of the human soul. It is the state of seeing the Act of the Creator through the being and actions of creation. Protection of yourself is to bend the self towards its highest potential through continuous, conscious striving. The dial on the spectrum of the self will have developed an irresistible tendency towards the higher settings. Protection of Reality is to know that behind all existent realities, states and conditions, desires and wants, acts and actions, stands the inexplicable, inexpressible One. It is this conscious recognition of the Face of Allāh in all people which enables us to value, respect and treat ourselves and each other more beautifully and to believe in our potential and abilities, while encouraging those around us, to build on our heritage and make use of our gifts and talents without risk of arrogance, by crediting their True Source, the Gift Giver, *Al-Wahhāb,* Who Watches over us, enabling our watchfulness.

3.22. The Door of Watchfulness (*Bāb al-Murāqaba*) باب المراقبة

فَارْتَقِبْ إِنَّهُم مُّرْتَقِبُونَ

Fa'rtaqib innahum murtaqibūn

'And be watchful for they are surely watched.' (*Qur'ān*, 44:59)

What is Watchfulness? According to Anṣārī Watchfulness of the heart (*murāqabat al-Qalb*), when you watch your inner being, must lead to a sense of tranquillity and serenity, whereby you are in the Presence of the Eternal. By constantly watching for the signs of Eternity in yourself, you become secure in the knowledge that Eternity is there. When you see these flashes of the Eternal within yourself, it makes you extremely tranquil, sure and certain. *Murāqaba* is not spying on yourself or simply beating yourself with a metaphorical ruler. It is not watching for transgressions as much as watching for the flashes and signs of the Eternal. You may have had these flashes: sometimes an extraordinary set of events takes place and suddenly you know that this is one of the clear signals. Just before a dark and stormy night you take out your binoculars, watching for the lightning and when you see it you become even more certain and it is confirmed.

Anṣārī: Watchfulness is of three degrees:

1. The First Degree: Watchfulness of the Truth is to persevere in the march towards the Truth, poised between incredible awe, the promise of nearness, and the pleasure of the discoverer.

2. The Second Degree is being watchful of the Truth's Gaze upon you and rejecting any resistance [to its implications]; and then rejecting that rejection.
3. The Third Degree: contemplating Eternity by observing the flow of the past in preparation for understanding unicity, and observing the signs of Eternity within the temporal flow.

Watchfulness of the heart of the signs of Eternity must soon give way to the serenity of the heart in the Presence of Eternity. In this manner, the self is secure in the knowledge that the Truth is always present and is observing the self. Tracking and registering the constant flashes of the Eternal in the flow of time is the highest condition of Watchfulness. These three levels of awareness of the Divine Presence could be described as a mystical practice of *taqwa* which is translated as God Consciousness and is, in mainstream practice, the conscious awareness of God's Presence and that He is not only Watching over us all, but also Aware of all our thoughts, feelings and deeds, and therefore no aspect of our existence escapes His Attention and Perfect, Constant, Absolute Wakefulness and Watchfulness. *Bab al-Murāqaba* is our opportunity to learn to watch ourselves at all levels of essence and action and all Stages in the thought process, in our words and our deeds. When we can turn our Watchfulness towards Allāh, we place ourselves in His Sanctuary.

Thirteenth Reflection Day:

Dhikr: Yā Khabīr (O All-Aware) ~ *Yā Baṣīr* (O All-Seeing) ~ *Yā Qawī* (O All-Powerful) *Yā Muntaqim* (O Rectifier)

يا خَبير~ يا بَصير~ يا قَويّ ~ يا مُنتَقِم

WEEK FOURTEEN

3.23. The Door of Sanctuary *(Bāb al-Ḥurma)* باب الحرمة

وَمَن يُعَظِّمْ حُرُمَاتِ اللَّهِ فَهُوَ خَيْرٌ لَّهُ عِندَ رَبِّهِ

Wa man yu'athim hurumāt Allāhi fahuwa khayrun lahu 'inda rabbihi

'And the one who safeguards the limits set by Allāh he is the one who is assured of goodness with his Lord.' (*Qur'ān* 22:30)

The Room of watchfulness opens and once you have mapped out its contours you move into the next room, which Anṣārī calls the realm of *ḥurma* or Sanctuary, which requires the safeguarding of limits. This is one of the difficult conditions for modern wayfarers because it requires that you accept such limits curtailing the popular idea of freedom. Paradoxically, part of inner freedom is to understand your outer limits and boundaries, because we tend to think of freedom as an absence of restrictions or any constraints. When asked to constrain and bound yourself, it seems to be counterintuitive. It could be compared to skiing: you intuitively lean backwards in order to stop yourself going forward. It is against your natural instinct, where outer freedom means removal of chains and so on, in that you need to apply them in order to be free inwardly. The self needs to be contained, there is no question about that; the self is not the soul. The self mirrors the Soul and wants to mimic it, to quote *Shaykh* Fadhlalla Haeri.

In this instance, the act of containment, trying to accept that there are limits to your conduct and that these limits allow you to channel your energies, is essential because they channel your energies ultimately towards the One. By setting boundaries, this flow and at this Stage is not wasted or dissipated. You do not want to be *majdhūb*—people who are attracted as if by magnetic force. You want to channel it so that it can have maximum effect rather than dissipate. That is why for many people at this point the self rebels and does not necessarily commit. Discipline is essential, as is the selection of a path. The path of any *dīn al-ḥanīf*, or primordial religion, says the same thing: the containment of the outer limits are absolutely necessary. With the containment of the outer limits, you end up with a kind of interweaving with your inner reality.

The forms of, for example, the ritual prayers which Islam and other primordial religions prescribe are to do with willingly, and then joyfully, accepting limits. If prayers are seen in terms of a dialogue with the One and as a process of yielding to the Reality of that One, then the nature of that limit becomes limitless as you begin to approximate the Divine Presence. Another example is the Hajj. You can go on Pilgrimage every year but if you do not have a sense of the sacred space that you are going into—and that there is what is known as the Axis Mundi, that this is the central point of physical creation where the outer world meets with the inner—then it becomes a kind of religious tourism. For the wayfarer that knowledge is lost if that outer ritual is not connected with its inner reality. One of the most powerful of the outer constraints is *Zakāt*, because you are giving something that is dear to you, which is unnatural. Fasting is an inversion of the outer senses towards a heightening of the inner senses.

This Stage of Sanctuary is a very large room, and one in which the self rebels against the acceptance of its constraints and limits, or at least attempts to limit to its outer form.

1. Glorifying the commands and limits, not because of fear of retribution, or hope for reward (in the same way of a wage earner), or because of being seen as diligent. These are all manners of self-worship.
2. Accepting the outer dimensions of the commands, without recourse to interpretation or justifications.
3. Sustaining a state of expansiveness and joy at all the commands and proscriptions and establishing a permanent condition of witnessing.

The soul is naturally limitless and boundless, but the self needs to be contained so that it can channel its energies towards the One. Outer limits are at first onerous and appear as breaks on the self's journey. In truth they are essential for the training of the self. In this manner the outer rules and commands are a pathway towards utter freedom. However, this freedom can only be realised if the outer limits and commands become seamlessly interwoven with the limitless freedoms of the soul. All great spiritual traditions have limits and commands as part of their outer practice. In Islam outer rules and commands are all designed to perfect knowledge of the One (*tawḥīd*). Thus, ritual and supplicatory prayer, *salāh* and *du'ā* are periodic spiritual exercises whereby the self enters into dialogue with the One and yields to Its Reality. The *Ḥajj* is to orient the self to the Reality of the Axis Mundi, the central point of the spiritual geography of *tawḥīd*, thereby establishing and confirming the truth of the unseen and subtler universes. The outer limits thus help open up the truth and existence of other dimensions that are essential for the genuine wayfarer.

3.24. The Door of Sincerity *(Bāb al-Ikhlāṣ)* باب الأخلاص

اللَّهَ مُخْلِصًا لَّهُ الدِّينَ

Allāha mukhliṣal lahud-dīna

'To Allāh belongs the sincere [unvarnished] religion.' (*Qur'ān*, 39:2)

Once we have mastered the Door of Sanctuary we go to the next gate which is the Door of *Ikhlāṣ* or Sincerity. *Ikhlāṣ* in Arabic means both Sincerity and unvarnished. Something that is *khālis* is unadulterated. It can be both Sincerity in the sense of being constant in your loyalty or in your exclamations, but it can also mean unadulterated. The second definition is probably more precise here. In the *Qur'ān* it can be either or, both are true. *Ikhlāṣ* removes anything that distorts, pollutes or makes impure, as well as forming faultless consistency. What does Sincerity in deeds and transactions mean? In the outer form it means that you have to be consistent in what you say and do and be prepared to continue and sustain your work. In inner spiritual work, what does it mean? Above all, it means that the effort that you are exerting or the work that you are doing is not something that needs to be recognised, noted or rewarded.

An important element of *ikhlāṣ* or Sincerity is to know that your efforts and exertions are really reflections of something else. You may be acting and doing, but behind it all is the Enabler, the Source of Power, the Grantor of your capacity to work. Everything that drives you in your spiritual work has to be based on the knowledge and recognition that outer work and inner work only leads you to understand that work itself is one of the attributes of the Divine. Therefore, Sincerity is to yield to the patterns and flows that are established by this fact. To the sincere wayfarer, the outcomes of your work are really independent of your exertions. You can exert yourself as much as you want but the outcome is not in your hands. Sincerity, then is the knowledge that is the unvarnished truth.

Anṣārī: Sincerity is to cleanse action from all impurities in three degrees:

1. To stop seeing work whilst working, to be free of asking for recompense for your work, and to be indifferent to contentment in your work.
2. To be embarrassed by the inadequacy of your work in spite of the efforts exerted, and to see work only in light of the degree of recognition by the One.

3. Sincerity is to stop seeing it as work and act only by witnessing the actions of the One, free of all the bondage of seeing work as your own effort.

The degree of Sincerity of your work is a direct function of your shedding the notion of work as effort exerted by you which thus should be either rewarded, recognised or noted. All sincere work can only end in knowing that the origin of effort, the process of work, the power that drives it and the goals to which it moves are all reflections of the manifestations of the Divine Attributes. Sincerity is yielding to the rigour and conformity of patterns and flows established in non-material dimensions. To the sincere wayfarer outcomes are independent of effort, exertion or commitment. وَمَا رَمَيْتَ إِذْ رَمَيْتَ وَلَٰكِنَّ اللَّهَ رَمَىٰ

'...It was not you who hurled when you hurled; but it was Allāh who hurled' (*Qur'ān*, 8:17) *Wamā ramayta idh ramayta walākin Allāha ramā*

Fourteenth Reflection Day:

Fourteen times *Surat al-Ikhlāṣ:*

Bismillāh ir-Raḥmān is-Raḥīm	بِسْمِ اللَّهِ الرَّحْمَٰنِ الرَّحِيمِ
qul hūw Allāhu aḥad, Allāhus-Ṣamad	قُلْ هُوَ اللَّهُ أَحَدٌ اللَّهُ الصَّمَدُ
lam yalid walam yūlad	لَمْ يَلِدْ وَلَمْ يُولَدْ
walam yakullahu kufuwan aḥad.	وَلَمْ يَكُن لَّهُ كُفُوًا أَحَدٌ

'Say, "He, God, Is One, God the Everlastingly Self-Sufficient, Is not born, nor Gives birth, neither does anyone bear likeness to Him"'

WEEK FIFTEEN

3.25. The Door of Refinement (*Bāb at-Tahdhīb*) باب التهذيب

فَلَمَّا جَنَّ عَلَيْهِ اللَّيْلُ رَأَىٰ كَوْكَبًا ۖ قَالَ هَٰذَا رَبِّي ۖ فَلَمَّا أَفَلَ قَالَ لَا أُحِبُّ الْآفِلِينَ

Falammā janna ʿalayiehi al-layeilu ra'ā kawkaban qāla hāadhā Rabbi falammā afal qāla lā uaḥiebb al-āfilīn

'And when night fell he saw a planet and said "That is my Lord!." But when it vanished he said "I do not Love that which vanishes."' (*Qur'ān*, 6:76)

Then we come to the fifth doorway, which is the Door of Refinement, or *tahdhīb*. It is to ensure that your spiritual works, your deeds at the spiritual level, do not become habitual and repetitive. Imam Ali himself said that the bane of all spiritual exercises, and their inability to uplift you, is when they become habitual, and that those for whom every day is the same are lost. You have to be constrained by the bounds and accept that your conduct is contained but this outer containment is a reflection of your inner Refinement. Every act must have within it the courtesy of being consistent, truthful and reflective of Reality that behind it all is the One. That way it will always be fresh, uplifting.

Anṣārī: Refinement is of three degrees:

1. Refinement of service is not to overlook it, due to lapses, neither undertake as a matter of habit nor cease undertaking it because of concern for outcomes.
2. Refinement of state so that one's state is constant, is not subject to preconceptions nor affected by events.
3. Refinement of purpose so that it is not imposed, and it is protected from lassitude.

3.26. The Door of Uprightness *(Bāb al-Istiqāma)* باب الاستقامة

فَاسْتَقِيمُوا إِلَيْهِ

Fa istaqīmū ilayh

'So take a straight course to Him.' (*Qur'ān*, 41:6)

Then we will come to the Door of Uprightness or *istiqāma* which, in the outer forms, means that you become upright, or upstanding, have all the positive virtues and deal with people sincerely and fairly. *Istiqāma* in the inner world literally means to stand up or to move from one condition or level of being to another. It is a movement from lying down to standing up, the spiritual meaning of which is to move from knowledge of what is not real, to what is only real—from what is other than reality to reality itself. This is the process of rising spiritually and is what Uprightness constitutes in the inner dimension. The Uprightness of people in the outer world still abides by the rules and guidelines of the way.

It is the way of moderation, economy and balance, but as the Reality begins to unfold in its Magnificence, and totality, your Vision moves from what is near to the far and farther horizons. A vista opens up to you. It is a metaphorical standing: we are lying down, and suddenly we awaken, stand up and see in front of us a vista, an entire panorama. This is the Uprightness of the spiritual wayfarer. Somebody compared it to a scene of a person who is about to drown and his head pops up; suddenly he sees a magnificent island, and knows he can reach it. It is a scene that is like going up the Swiss Alps and seeing in front of you these magnificent vistas: the reality of the inner world is much more alpine than you will see in Switzerland. The glimpses we have of that are sufficient to know that it is there.

Anṣārī: Uprightness is a force that brings spiritual states to life, while it guides the work of the common people. It is an interspace between separation and gatheredness. Uprightness is of three degrees; strive to understand and implement each:

1. Uprightness in striving towards the end goal without veering from the established creeds and doctrines.
2. Uprightness of one's state is to witness Truth without pretence and to be sustained by its Light.
3. Ceasing to notice one's Uprightness where the desire for Uprightness itself is effaced as the wayfarer sees that it is only the Truth that is Alone Upright.

When the wayfarer moves from what is other-than-reality towards Reality, they are moving from seeing the separateness of the many to the Unicity of the One. The process of rising to full spiritual stature is therefore what constitutes Uprightness. The Uprightness of the people of the outer world is to abide by the rules and guidelines of the way; it is the way of the people of moderation, economy and balance. As the wayfarer begins to see the unfolding of the Ever-Present Reality, their level of vision moves towards the far horizons. Events and things appear to them as only manifestations of Unity. In the final stages, there is no more Uprightness or being upright. The wayfarer's state dissolves into the being of the One. The seer and the seen became one.

Fifteenth Reflection Day:

حسبي الله ونعم الوكيل

Hasbī Allāh wa naʿim Al-Wakīl

Dhikr: at least 99 times: 'God is enough for me and is the Best Disposer of affairs.'

WEEK SIXTEEN

3.27. The Door of Reliance (*Bāb at-Tawakkul*) باب التوكل

We now come to a recurring theme, that of *tawakkul*, or Reliance on Allāh. There are many Qur'ānic *āyāt* referring to it. *Tawakkul* or Reliance in the inner sense is, again, different from the outer. It is very difficult to sustain this state of being. The reason is, when you are truly reliant on Allāh you are refusing to accept, or refuting, the universality of cause and effect. We live in the material, physical world and every single experience that we have in the outer world has to do with cause and effect. Everything has a cause and is seemingly followed by an effect. Our knowledge of the world is determined by the laws of causality. We are trapped and entwined in it and to accept that there is another set of laws, beyond the physical, mental and psychological, that is at least as real, important and significant, is absolutely essential. This is what *tawakkul* is. It is not to go to an exam and write on top of your exam paper *bismillāh ir-Raḥmān ir-Raḥīm* and entrust the outcome by saying '*tawakkaltu* ʿāla Allāh' ('I rely on God').

Reliance is to confirm and verify that the inner world has a different set of laws and that the outer world is only an act of Allāh as The Designer, *al-Musawwir*. He has given the outer world a set of laws and is also *al-Musawwir* of the inner world, its Designer and Fashioner. If you are trapped in time and space, how can you see anything else as being true? That is why it is extremely difficult to be in *tawakkul* and it is a huge escape from the prison of causality if you are. It is like running away from a world that you know is not complete in its own form. But you do not want to fall into another pit—the pit of fatalism—that everything is in the hands of Allāh and therefore your actions are meaningless. That is not true. Your actions are necessary; their outcomes are not up to you. *Tawakkul* or Reliance demands that human beings act in the moment with full vigour and in full knowledge that the outcome is really in the hands of another Power. If you start defining outcomes in terms of either expansion or contraction, favourable or unfavourable, increase or decrease, you are also rendering your statement that you are relying on the Truth invalid or insufficient, by judging the outcomes without seeing the whole picture.

Anṣārī: It is to leave the affair entirely to its Owner, and to depend on His Reliability. This is the most difficult station for most people. It is the easiest station though for the *'urafā* (*inostics*). The Truth Most Exalted has Delegated all matters to Himself. The Knowledgeable person therefore abandons the notion of owning anything. Reliance is of the following three degrees; build them each day, relinquishing control:

1. Reliance, while still requesting (from God) and dealing with causes of things but with the intention of involving the self in higher matters, benefitting creation and abandoning pretence.
2. Reliance, while dropping any request and ignoring causes, expecting to perfect the state of Reliance, quashing the preening self and focusing on maintaining obligations.
3. Reliance, while moving to efface Reliance itself. That is to know that the Truth Possesses all things and no one shares with Him this Possession. This is one of the necessary knowledges for true servitude.

Reliance on God is difficult because human beings are entwined in the realm of cause and effect and are trapped, as part of the ways of the Designer, *al-Musawwir*, in the nexus of time and space. To rely on the Source of Power is to escape from the prison of causality, without falling into the pit of fatalism. Reliance demands that human beings act in the moment with full knowledge and vigour, but know that the outcome is in the Command of the Master of Time. The wayfarer is therefore indifferent to the apparent quantitative increase or decrease of outcomes, whether they are 'favourable' or 'unfavourable'. The most accomplished of wayfarers knows that outcomes are imposters, if they are attributed to other-than-reality. That is the highest level of knowledge in the realm of *tawakkul*. True *tawakkul* in its highest, most refined, pristine sense, is a knowledge and verification that in Truth, there is only one Actor, one Decider, one Fashioner, *al-Muṣawwir*.

3.28. The Door of Delegation *(Bāb at-Tafwīḍ)* باب التفويض

وَأُفَوِّضُ أَمْرِي إِلَى اللَّهِ ۚ إِنَّ اللَّهَ بَصِيرٌ بِالْعِبَادِ

Wa uafawwiūḍu amrī ila Allāhi inna Allāha basSīrun bi'l-''ibād

'And I delegate my affair to Allāh for Allāh knows the intimate affairs of his bondsperson.' ~ (*Qur'ān*, 40:44)

According to *Khwāja* Anṣārī, more important than *tawakkul*, is what he calls the Stage of *tafwīḍ* or Delegation. When you delegate your affairs, to the Great Reality, to the Great Truth, *al-ḥaqq*, you are delegating your powers of action and decision before the event. In *tawakkul* you are doing it after a cause has appeared. In Delegation, when you hand over the entire matter to Reality, to Allāh before anything happens, it is a higher station than *tawakkul*, reliance on Reality, after something has happened. It precedes the cause, rather than following it. You see the hand of the Creator behind the cause, not only behind the effect, which is a much nobler and higher station. Usually, we want to control outcomes, we want to have outcomes that bend to our desires and will, but it requires more subtlety to see that Reality, Truth is also behind the cause. If you are able to see that it is both cause and effect, these two imposters really are only manifestations of the Creator, of the Cause.

To be a person who has attained to this Door of Delegation, *tafwīḍ,* beyond the tongue, this has to be a state that settles on the heart itself, making you indifferent to both cause and effect. This indifference is not a lack of empathy, like seeing a car wreck in front of you and not going to help people. Rather this type of indifference stems from being balanced.

Anṣārī: Delegation is a subtler state than reliance and has a wider meaning. Reliance occurs after the cause; Delegation occurs before and during the cause. Delegation is the tree of yielding (to the Divine Presence); reliance is a branch of it. Delegation is of three degrees; let them take root over the next three days:

1. To know that we have no potential to affect or control the outcomes of our actions, not to feel secure in strategies, neither to depend on good intentions, nor despair from assistance.

2. To see no action that can save us; nor any transgression that can annihilate us; nor hold any cause that can determine outcomes.
3. To see with inner sight that it is only the Truth that possesses the right to action and inaction, expansion and contraction, collection and separation.

Anṣārī's definition that Delegation precedes the cause is in itself the best description of the station of Delegation. By seeing the hand of the Creator behind causes manifested in the realm of space and time,

Sixteenth Reflection Day:

Muḥammad 'Abdul-Jabbār an-Niffari:
I said: How shall I resign to You?
He answered: Do not oppose me with your opinion, and do not seek any guide for my right over you of yourself; for yourself will never guide you to my right, nor will it embrace my right in obedience.
I said: How shall I not oppose You?
He answered: You will follow, and not invent.
I said: How shall I not seek any guide for Your right of myself?
He answered: When I say to you, 'This is yours,' you will say, 'This is mine'; and when I say to you, 'This is mine,' you will say, 'This is Yours.' Then will My Command be yours addresser, and will have a right over you: it will guide you, and you will seek Guidance of it unto it, and by means of it attain it.
I said: How shall I follow?
He answered: You shall hear My Word and tread My Way.
I said: How shall I not invent?
He answered: You shalt not hear your word nor tread your way.
I said: What is Your Word?
He answered: My Doctrine.*

*Niffarī, M. A. J. (1935) *The Mawāqif and Mukhātabāt of Muhammad Ibn 'Abd L-Jabbār Al-Niffarī: with other fragments.* Ed. Trans. Arthur John Arbery. Cambridge University Press for the Trustees of the 'E. : J. W. Gibb Memorial'; London, Luzac & co. p. 127. Niffari (d. 965) lived in the marshes of southern Iraq around Baṣra and Naṣrīya. He is not well known, nor did he write much but his dialogues with the Divine on the halting points along the soul's journey were collected by his offspring and followers.

where material causality is supposed to prevail, is indeed a very high order of realisation. But to go further and allow this state to govern your actions—while knowing that action itself is not in your hands but is only a measure of the empowerment granted you by the Truth—is extraordinary and extremely rare. To be a person who has attained to this Door of Delegation, *tafwīḍ* beyond the tongue, this must be a state that settles on the heart itself, making one indifferent to both cause and effect. This indifference is not a lack of empathy, but is about being balanced on your view of events being good or bad, seeing them as simply what is created as part of the Divine Plan.

WEEK SEVENTEEN

3.29. The Door of Confidence *(Bāb ath-Thiqa)* باب الثقة

فَإِذَا خِفْتِ عَلَيْهِ فَأَلْقِيهِ فِي الْيَمِّ

Fa idhā khifti ʾalayhi fa alqīhi fil-yammi

'And if you fear for him, then cast him in the void.' (*Qurʾān*, 28:7)

The greatest example in the *Qurʾān* is the serenity of Confidence that comes from acting with an empty heart. It refers to prophet Moses' mother who cast him into the river, as she was instructed, and could do so only when her innermost heart was settled and tranquil. The Confidence of this condition comes from the state of delegation, which gave Mūsa's Moses' mother the serenity to put her child into the basket and entrust it to the river, thus delegating his fate to God. There is a *Ḥadīth Qudsī* (Divine Communication to the Prophet Muhammad) the *Khwāja* talks about, which says: 'Oh man, you might will, and I Will, but nought will be except what I Will.' This Confidence of knowing that your will pales into nothingness when you set it against the Will of the One banishes doubt and uncertainty in all of your spiritual and physical actions. For those who are most realised, it leads to the abandonment of any means as a way to an end.

Anṣārī: Confidence is at the heart of reliance, and the fulcrum of delegation, and the kernel of yielding. Thus it has three degrees:

1. Despair of combating the decrees of the Truth, to stop questioning their Wisdom and to liberate oneself from argumentation about them.

2. To feel secure about the perfect balance and justice in the outcomes, gaining contentment from absolute certainty and the veracity of inner sight.
3. Knowing the Eternity of the Truth and thus being free of goals and expectations, and dependence on means towards ends.

Confidence in the veracity of Reality in all its infinite manifestations allows the wayfarer to march onwards knowing that their reliance on and delegation to Truth can only lead to the good. Many of us claim to trust the Divine Plan, while trying to control causes and remaining attached to outcomes, becoming anxious, angry or upset when things do not go according to our plan. The thinking behind this, whether conscious or, more often, unconscious, is that we somehow know better. This is a common form of spiritual arrogance which is even more serious than that which makes us judge or look down upon our fellow humans, as it is against God Himself. It is therefore only forgivable because He Is All-Forgiving and All-Knowing and therefore understands that it is fear-based and due to our inherent short-sightedness, greed, impatience and lack of gratitude, or even recognition of our countless blessings. Allāh Knows Best what we need. We barely even know what we want and, when we do it is often for reasons of overattachment to past patterns or projected outcomes of our own design.

3.30. The Door of Surrender *(Bāb at-Taslīm)* باب التسليم

فَلَا وَرَبِّكَ لَا يُؤْمِنُونَ حَتَّىٰ يُحَكِّمُوكَ فِيمَا شَجَرَ بَيْنَهُمْ ثُمَّ لَا يَجِدُوا فِي أَنفُسِهِمْ حَرَجًا مِّمَّا قَضَيْتَ وَيُسَلِّمُوا تَسْلِيمًا

Falā wa rabbika lā yu'minūn hatta yuhakkimūka fīmā shajara baynahum thumma lā yajidū fī anfusihim harajam mimmā qaḍayta wa yusallimū taslimā

'No indeed and by your Lord! They shall not believe until they take you as judge of what they dispute, then find no resentment regarding your judgement and Surrender completely.' (*Qur'ān*, 4:65)

Surrender, *taslīm* or *istislām,* are among the various nominal forms and meanings of the Arabic verb *aslama,* to yield or submit. When you say I am going to yield, submit or Surrender my will, perhaps harbouring a certain pride in so doing, you must also know that the power to Surrender is granted to you as a gift. The highest stage of yielding is to know that yielding itself is an impostor because the Power that gives you the quality of yielding is granting you the very ability to Surrender to Him. This is the last station of this stage and is a very perilous one because it denudes you of all sense that your self is able to do anything without what is given to you, which Ibn ʿArabi refers to as *iktisāb*—something that is granted to you. The power to think, reflect, yield, breathe, the power to memorise—all these powers are granted to you. The highest stage of yielding is to be effaced from yielding. It is paradoxical but you have to submit to it and then submit to the submission.

Anṣārī: Surrender together with reliance and delegation are the highest station for most people. It has three degrees; Surrender in every moment, on every level, each day:

1. Surrendering to what goes against outer reason, rages against your acquired whims and values, to what appears to be contrary to analogy and example.
2. Surrendering outer knowledge to spiritual station, purpose to unveiling, and outer form to its inner reality.
3. Surrendering what is not the truth to the Truth, while knowing that your yielding to Reality is due to your acquiring the power to yield from Reality Itself.

While Surrendering to the decrees and commands of the Truth is commendable, what is more subtle is to know that the capability of Surrender itself is a power granted to us by the Creator. This is the first step in the passage towards dissolution of the self in the Presence of the One. All around you is the Power, Majesty, Beauty of the One and the immensity of this knowledge can easily overpower the human being. The wayfarer must move on to the next stage, the Stage of Ethics, where the immensity of this condition is tempered, qualified and directed. Before doing so it is highly recommended to repeat and reflect upon the following three Divine Names and their meanings. It is highly beneficial to say each of them at least 33 times, followed by *Yā Allāh.*

Seventeenth Reflection Day:

Suggested *Dhikr* for the Stage of Deeds:

Al-Raqīb (The Overseer) *Al-Wakīl* (The Deputy) *Al-Nāfi'* (The Beneficent)

Yā Raqīb ~ Yā Wakīl ~ Yā Nāfi' يا رقيب ~ يا وكيل ~ يا نافع

4. The Stage of Ethics (*Manzal al-Akhlāq*) منزل الأخلاق

Most of the names and titles that you will come across have their manifestations in the outer realm too. In fact, we are more used to them in the outer realm, because they are at the core of all our ethics, but you should not conceive of them as being simply mirror images. When we talk about the virtues of Patience, for example, or Truthfulness, or excelling in the qualities of good Character, we would tend to know by and large what they mean, colloquially. When you say somebody is patient, we have an idea what that means and we can empathise, sympathise and experience some or most of these states. In the inner dimension, the inner meaning of these terms for the states, takes on a different hue. It is really important to understand that it is not always inverted. The outer forms do not necessarily have to be inverted in the inner context, but in many cases that would be the situation.

The Fourth Stage is the one that Khwāja Anṣārī calls the Stage of *akhlāq*, meaning, for the lack of a better word, Ethics—which does not quite summarise the entire manifestation of the term *akhlāq*. It is derived from the word *khalaqa* (خ ل ق), to create, from which are derived many other terms. *Akhlāq* can mean ethics or, these days, simply good manners. Words like *khulūq*, also derived from *khalaqa*, is a word for the quality of a person's character. *Khallāq* is an innovator. It has an inherent element of creativity, of bringing into being, bringing something into existence. It is from that point that you have to view the perspectives of the *Khwāja* on the internal Ethics that determine the various doors and stages of the fourth landing. All these stages deal with perfecting knowledge of the One. The last door of the last stage is the Door of Unity, or Unicity, where you see and are driven by the One and only the One, and that is the goal towards which you are leaning.

All of these doorways are in order to create within oneself those qualities that allow the self to become so luminous and lustrous, that it can fully yield to and merge with the soul, which is the locus of the perfected qualities inside any being. In the case of human beings, it is the locus of conscious awareness of oneness. In the case of inanimate objects and other beings, it is embedded in their existential blueprint.

They are in unity or unicity without the need to articulate or express it—without even the need to have a consciousness of it. The consciousness of human beings is that element which allows for the self to move towards the soul. Inanimate beings do not have that element, but they still have in their totality the knowledge of unity. In all of the stages of *al-Manāzil,* at the beginning of his descriptions of the various stages and their three degrees, Anṣārī phrases everything in a very succinct, pithy way. His summation of the Stage of Ethics is:

'Ethics are conditions of the self from which emanate instinctive actions, and which reinforce the quality of a person's transactions. Persistence in ethical actions only strengthens the fount of these actions in the self, smoothing the emergence of virtues and goodness along the path.'

Ethics are foundational blocks for the self-in-realisation. They are not simply do-gooding, or a conditioned set of moral rules. They are the expressions of the actions of the Divine Names in the realm of existence. Because their root source is in the Divine Attributes—for example Patience is rooted in the All-Patient, or the Timeless—their inner and outer expression is the propellant that drives the self towards the One. Ethics in the outer dimension are to do with perfecting the qualities by which the outer pathway to Allāh becomes manifested and realised. Ethics of the inner dimension are the foundational blocks of the self trying to realise its potential of being luminous. It is not something that is incidental to the path: it is central and fundamental to it.

Akhlāq is an inflection point in the path of the wayfarer; that is, the ethical dimension of inner conduct is the means by which the wayfarer is able to create a firm and broad foundation, which then allows them to move on to the next stages. It is not a set of moral rules that deal with certain responses to societal demands. Neither is it do-gooding in that sense. There may be an element of that—of being faithful to model precepts—but they are more than that and are also other than that. They are expressions of the Actions of the Divine Names in the realm of existence. When the Divine Names—which are at the core of all entities and all reality—are revealed, everything in existence reflects a Divine Name and every action, every thought, every state reflects one or more of the Divine Attributes, those of Essence or those of Action.

Al-Khāliq, The Creator, for example, is an Attribute of Action, while *Aṣ-Ṣabūr,* The Patient or Timeless is an Attribute of Essence or Being.

These Divine Qualities are named in the *Qur'ān.* Only 99 of them are mentioned, but they are really infinite because they are the Names by which things are called and the Names by which the essences are realised. Human beings, and every being, have two aspects. There is an inner being, which is the realm of meaning, the realm of reality, and there is the outer form, the realm of substance, in which that is expressed. The Names also have these two functions. They are expressing the outer form, in the form of action, conditions and states but they are expressed in the inner form as pointers to the One. When we talk about the Divine Names as being the core of ethics, Ethics in the inner realm are rooted in the Divine Attributes. We talk about the Attributes of Patience, which is the First Door of the Stage of Ethics—and is really an expression of the Essence and the Reality of the All-Patient—this is one of the Names that Allāh gives to Himself, *Aṣ-Ṣabūr.* It is in their inner and outer expressions that the Names propel the self towards the One Reality.

The first door of the Stage of inner Ethics is the Door of Patience, *Bab aṣ-Ṣabr.*

WEEK EIGHTEEN

4.31. The Door of Patience *(Bāb as-Ṣabr)* باب الصبر

'Patience is holding the self back from expressing its resentments and complaints. It is one of the most difficult and solitary states on the path of Love, and the most unrequited towards Unicity.' It is of three degrees, the first of which is the experience of those whose capacities reach a certain level and that level is shared by a large number of people. The subsequent degrees are intended to stretch that capacity to eventually give rise to a deeper and more subtle experience. These are hinted at and mapped out here but are not guaranteed and cannot be hurried, so if you do not always relate to or understand them on first reading, they will clarify with time and occur to you in the appropriate context according to Divine Grace and Will. The First Degree of Patience in the inner way is to generally cease engaging in transactions and transgressions, due to hope for reward and fear of adverse consequences.

Many people tolerate or accept a burdensome condition or situation, because of the belief that there is a reward or spiritual gain to be earned. Anṣārī says that modesty and shamefacedness is better than that type of Patience. Rather than being patient in abstaining from committing an act that you know will lead to a block or an obstacle on the path of realisation, or not committing it because you may lose rewards; you do not commit it because of your shamefacedness. The Second Degree is Patience in obedience, in full Awareness of the norms thereof and the Third Stage is Patience with afflictions, through constant remembrance of God's Superlative Qualities and Gifts. The weakest form is Patience with God's Commands, is that you are patient because this is His Command. Above it is a State of Patience that is bestowed on you by God's Grace. Patience then becomes a condition from which you respond instinctively.

وَاصْبِرْ وَمَا صَبْرُكَ إِلَّا بِاللَّهِ

Wa uṣbir wamā ṣabruka illā billah

'Be patient for none gives you patience but Allāh....' (*Qur'ān*, 16:127)

Anṣārī: Patience is holding the self from expressing its resentments and complaints. It is one of the most difficult Stages for most people, the most solitary in the path of Love, and the most unrequited towards unicity. It is of three degrees:

1. Patience in the inner way is to cease from engaging in transgressions because of the certainty of the rewards that one receives in consequence. However, better than this type of Patience is the one that is driven by modesty and shamefacedness from committing transgressions.
2. Patience in obedience while respecting the norms of obedience.
3. Patience with afflictions while awaiting release from them and accepting their burdens by constant remembrance of the Graces that had been Bestowed on you.

Above all this Patience with God's Command is Patience as a result of your immersion or dissolution in Allāh—this is the Patience of the wayfarer. *Khwāja* Anṣārī was speaking a thousand years ago, not that his understanding of Patience is in any way deficient or incomplete, but there is a different dimension, the reality of which is in its inner dimension, and has to do with the suspension of time. To be patient with someone or something is to allow the passage of time to shrink between the conditions that give rise to the exercise of Patience, leading to its elimination or disappearance. The element of time is essential for you to exercise the virtue of Patience. If time shrinks to zero, Patience becomes infinite. Infinite Patience—God's Patience—is therefore the abandonment of time while wayfaring.

The wayfarer cannot measure states by time. Once you use the yardstick of time and space, you cease to be a spiritual warrior; your referential point becomes the outer meaning of Patience. As Patience is usually related to the response to adversity, which is only an illusion from the perspective of *tawḥid*, human *taqwa* is often overwhelmed by adversity and we may lose sight of the fact that all is from Allāh. That understanding of Patience removes the element of burdensomeness, or the element of suffering, that we all link somehow to Patience. When you are patient with something, there is always a sense that there is a cost attached to it. That cost can be suffering, or it can be loss of something that is being missed, which could be happening while one is waiting patiently for something else to happen or stop happening.

If time is removed from that scale, both the scale of the action and the responses to it, Patience therefore becomes a vitally essential quality for the inner life; not in the sense of suffering or quietly accepting the burden, but in the sense of allowing time to whittle away your assessment of actions and responses to them. The ability to suspend and shrink time is critical if you want to stay on the pathways of realisation. Without it, you keep on falling prey to the idea of Patience as being a burden to be requited or relieved at a point in time, and have basically missed its true meaning. In Anṣārī's understanding and interpretation there is a sense of effort and burdensomeness too. But Allāh is the All Patient and the passage of time goes to zero. Therefore, the expansiveness becomes infinite.

4.32. The Door of Contentment *(Bāb ar-Riḍā)* باب الرضى

ارْجِعِي إِلَىٰ رَبِّكِ رَاضِيَةً مَّرْضِيَّةً

Arji'ī ilā rabbiki rādiyatam marḍīya

'And return to your Lord, content and being contented with….'

(*Qur'ān*, 89:28)

Anṣārī: 'Contentment is the halting point of the sincere ones. It neither increases nor decreases, does not speed up or slow down. It is not displaced or moved. It is the beginning of the progress of the advanced amongst the wayfarers and the most difficult for those who are beginners.'

This is a state of equanimity that, according to Anṣārī, does not go up or down. It is a state of perfect equilibrium or balance that has no shifts in the scale. It is the recognition that where you are at this moment in time, in this condition or state, is a sign of pure perfection and you can be nothing but be contented with perfection. How can you question it? The Third Degree of Contentment is the most difficult to internalise because it deals with abandonment of Contentment. You are no longer content, but you are content with God's Contentment with you, in whatever condition. Therefore, you can transcend Contentment because all is God's decree. Who are you to have a desire for Contentment? At that point, the wayfarer ceases to judge people or events completely, due to their perfection and the recognition of perfection in the Divine Order of things.

1. Contentment is acceptance of Allāh as the only focus of worship. It is a cornerstone of the outer forms of Islam that Allāh is the Most Beloved to the worshipper; and the most worthy of exaltation and obedience.
2. Contentment with what effulges from Allāh and it is with this Contentment that the wayfarer observes the Signs of Manifestation. It is the acceptance and acknowledgement of all that has transpired.
3. Contentment with Allāh's Contentment with one's self. The wayfarer sees no difference then between Contentment and its absence, between reward and punishment. The wayfarer ceases to exercise judgements on people and events.

Contentment in its outer form is a positive quality but is also seen as lacking outer ambition, if a person is contented with doing nothing. But, as previously stated, in many cases you have to invert the meaning of the condition to see what it really means in the inner dimension. Contentment in its highest degree is the condition of observing and marvelling at the perfection of all that has transpired. As *Shaykh* Fadhlalla Haeri has written in his book called *Witnessing Perfection*, it is to do with seeing past events as being not exactly ordained, but falling into an intricately layered matrix with infinite sides and aspects, but

Eighteenth Reflection Day:

Muḥammad ʻAbdul-Jabbār an-Niffari:
I said: Where is Your way?
He answered: My ordinances.
I said: What is my word?
He answered: Your bewilderment.
I said: What is my way?
He answered: Following your own judgement.
I said: What is my own judgement?
He answered: Your analogy.
I said: What is my analogy?
He answered: Your incapacity in your gnosis.
I said: How should I lack capacity in my gnosis?
He answered: I have made a trial of you in everything that proceeds from Me to you, by means of something that proceeds from you to Me. I have tried you in my Knowing by means of your gnosis, that I might see if you follow your knowledge or Mine: and I have tried you in my ordinance by means of your ordinance, that I might see if you judge by My ordinance of yours.
I said: How should I follow my knowledge, and how should I act according to my ordinance?
He answered: You depart from the ordinance concerning my Knowledge, to the ordinance concerning your incomplete knowledge.*

*Niffarī, M. A. J. (1935) *The Mawāqif and Mukhātabāt of Muhammad Ibn ʻAbd L-Jabbār Al- Niffarī: with other fragments.* Ed. Trans. Arthur John Arbery. Cambridge University Press for the Trustees of the 'E.: J. W. Gibb Memorial'; London, Luzac & co. p. 128.

everything is in its place. Contentment is the act of constantly witnessing perfection which can only lead to an astonishment in Contentment.

You are in no position to question why things have happened, because they have happened. In the outer form, you have to question things inside the form. To set things right, you have to try and move towards what is correct in the greater interest of human beings. However, in the Inner world, what is, is because of God's Decrees. Marvelling at the perfection of what has transpired is rooted in the knowledge of God's Realities, Commands, Decrees, and Omnipotence. It is the act of constantly witnessing the perfected conditions and can only reach a state of marvel and astonishment. Now this quality of marvelling is a feature of Contentment because you are in absolute equilibrium in the inner world and you marvel at how this infinite, complex, multi-layered universe of actions, states, of supposed actors or movers, of spirits, of things, entities, meanings, how all of that fits together in a perfected, cosmic uniqueness. When that happens you have to go into gratitude, which is the Third Door, that of *shukr.*

WEEK NINETEEN

4.33. The Door of Gratitude *(Bāb ash-Shukr)* باب الشكر

وَقَلِيلٌ مِّنْ عِبَادِيَ الشَّكُورُ

Wa qalīlummin ʿibādi ash-shākirūn

'And few who worship Me are in Gratitude.' (*Qurʾān*, 34:13)

Anṣārī: Gratitude is the name given to Knowledge of the bounties and that is why Allāh has called faith in Islam a form of Gratitude. Islam here is not just the religion of 'Islam', it is the primordial religion, the religion that encompasses all legitimate pathways, all established paths to Reality. It is the pathway of submission, surrender and trust that Allāh, the All-Bountiful will replace anything that is lost, missing or seemingly taken away with an abundance of graces and bounties. The process of knowing, recognising, and acknowledging this is, in fact, what Gratitude is. The meaning of Gratitude is to see, recognise and know the graces, accept them, and then to acknowledge these graces in Gratitude. He says: Gratitude is to the Beloved and all that people who share a pathway to the Singularity and Unicity of the One have this Gratitude.

He says: Muslims are distinguished by Gratitude in adversity. When things ‘go wrong’, both in the inner and the outer world, you are still in Gratitude because you are contented, and that Gratitude obliges you to hide hardship, cover up complaints and maintain courteous conduct throughout. Gratitude of the highest order, however, is where the bondsperson, for the lack of a better word—slave is also not the right word, perhaps servant—is to be in a state of willing bondage. The bondsperson only sees the Bestower of bounties; they only see that bounties are all from the One so there is no question of adversity, or of elation, and your Gratitude becomes marvellous, as you compare your absolute impoverishment to God’s Absolute Bounty. Even the most constricted condition becomes, in effect, effulgence or emanation of Reality’s Love and Mercy.

Gratitude has three degrees:

1. Gratitude to the Beloved. All true monotheists share this aspect.
2. Gratitude in adversity—this is the condition of a person in contentment and one who hides their hardship, covers up their complaints and maintains courteous conduct throughout.
3. Gratitude of the highest order is where the bondsperson only sees the Bestower of bounties. When witnessing one’s Poverty to Allāh all bounties become marvels; when witnessing Reality as Love, all constrictiveness becomes an emanation of Love; and if Reality is seen as One, then all bounties and afflictions dissolve into that Reality.

You go into a state of Gratitude because all emanations are, by their nature, the source of Gratitude. Gratitude is the self’s acknowledgement of bounties, and where do Reality’s bounties ever end? ‘...And if you try to count the bounties of Allāh you will surely fail.’

تَعُدُّوا نِعْمَةَ اللَّهِ لَا تُحْصُوهَا ۗ وَإِن

Wa in ta’udū ni’mat Allāh lā tuhsūha (*Qur’ān*, 16:18).

For the wayfarer Gratitude is a Stage that has to be attained and then quickly superseded. It is simply an acknowledgement of the obvious. ‘...Whoever is thankful, it is for that person’s benefit; whoever covers up this Reality, God is the All-Sufficient, the All-Praiseworthy’

وَمَن يَشْكُرْ فَإِنَّمَا يَشْكُرُ لِنَفْسِهِ ۖ وَمَن كَفَرَ فَإِنَّ اللَّهَ غَنِيٌّ حَمِيدٌ

Wa man yashkur fa innamā yashkur linafsihi, wa man kafara fa inna Allāha ghanīyun Ḥamīd (*Qur’ān*, 31:12)

4.34. The Door of Modesty *(Bāb al-Ḥayā)* باب الحياء

أَلَمْ يَعْلَم بِأَنَّ اللَّهَ يَرَىٰ

Alam y'ālem bi'enna Allāha yarā

'And does he not know that Allāh is watching.' Qur'ān, 96:4)

The fourth door or the fourth Stage is the Door of Modesty. The word *ḥayā'* in Arabic also has a liveliness about it— *ḥayā'* meaning Life, so it is not about being a shrinking violet type. It is an active Modesty, not a passive Modesty. Your Modesty and your effacement is derived from your knowledge that *as-Samī' al-Baṣīr*, the All-Listening the All-Seeing is watching. Not watching over as Big Brother, but the Reality of the All-Seeing must become part of your equipment in the inner journey. Effacement or Modesty is of three degrees. The first one is modest self-effacement deriving from the knowledge that the Truth is Watching. It allows the wayfarer to bear their responsibilities and burdens, and not to countenance complaining.

The Second Degree of Modesty derives from the knowledge that the Truth is Ever Proximate. He is not just watching but He is nearer to you than your jugular vein, driving the wayfarer towards Love and towards the soul inside. Modesty of the Third Degree derives from witnessing the Divine Presence and marvelling in awe at Truth's Majesty, that is indivisible. Modesty in the wayfarer is knowledge of the certainty of Truth's Presence and Proximity, *al-Ḥaqq,* the Reality of God's All-Encompassing Presence and Being. That knowledge and the acknowledgement of that knowledge pushes a person to recognise the materiality of one's intellect or one's consciousness in light of this Immense Presence and it imposes on one a sense of Modesty. You have to efface the idea that your knowledge, actions, thoughts, even your being, and your independence are anything but conditional. This knowledge humbles a person and obliges one to retreat in the face of the overwhelming Presence, leaving the self-aware of its essential limitations and conditionality.

The Modesty that emerges is not only good, and salutary for the wayfarer on their path, but you recognise that Modesty, which these days seems to be more of a vice than a virtue in the public arena, is in fact a fit and proper condition in the private inner world because it helps to dissolve your will. Your sense of individuality then dissolves into the Divine Presence. In another way it is the retreat of the self, *nafs,* to make way for the soul, *rūḥ*. The self searches for the soul throughout your life. Sometimes it tries to dominate it and sometimes ignores it. Sometimes the self succumbs to it, faces it, opposes it, and then surrenders to it. The soul is ever perfect, the self is ever changing. Modesty of the self is a way in which the self begins to shed its defences in front of the soul.

Anṣārī: Modesty is of three degrees, to be considered one each day:

1. Modesty deriving from the knowledge that the Truth is Watching. It allows the wayfarer to bear their responsibilities and burdens, and not to countenance complaining.
2. Modesty deriving from knowledge that the Truth is Ever Proximate, driving the wayfarer towards Love and to invite the soul inside.
3. Modesty deriving from witnessing the Divine Presence and marvelling in awe at Truth's Majesty that is Indivisible.

> Nineteenth Reflection Day:
>
> Write a list of what you are most grateful for in the order they occur to you and identify a Divine Quality you could attribute them to. Make a *dhikr* out of them or simply repeat *ya Razzaq, ya Wahhāb*—Oh Provider, Oh Gift Giver—and ask The Beloved for their increase.

WEEK TWENTY

4.35. The Door of Truthfulness *(Bāb as-Ṣidq)* باب الصدق

فَإِذَا عَزَمَ الْأَمْرُ فَلَوْ صَدَقُوا اللَّهَ لَكَانَ خَيْرًا لَّهُمْ

Fa idha 'azamal-amru falaw sadaqū Allāha lakāna khayran lahum

'And when matters are grave it would be best for them to have faith in Allāh.' (*Qur'ān*, 47:21)

Anṣārī: Truthfulness is the name given to the reality of things as they originate and exist. It is a confirmation that the existence and being of entities in their inner core, their *jawhar*, in their inner essence, that acknowledgement is Truthfulness. Truthfulness in the world is not just not telling lies. That of course is necessary, but in the inner world you lie to yourself, so it is far more dangerous than lying in the outer world. Because the juxtaposition of truth against lies does not exist in reality. There is only Truth in reality. Lies are the absence or withdrawal of acknowledgement of the truth. There is no condition called lying in the inner world, as there is no condition of evil; it is only the absence of good. The absence of knowledge of things, unwillingness to say things as they are, gives rise to what we call lies or a form of cover, of rejection of the Truth or a non-acknowledgement of it. Truthfulness for Anṣārī is again of three degrees.

The first one is to confirm why you are on this journey: you have to be truthful that the purpose of this journey is something to which your entire self is oriented. This allows the wayfarer to deflect distractions and build on the ruins. By ruins here Anṣārī means the commanding self. If you look at the spectrum of the self, you start from the lowest form: the animal self or the commanding self *an-Nafs al-Ammara*. Then the self that is perplexed becomes aware and self-reproachful, longing for self-improvement. The self can then become luminous, serene and contented. It is like the visible spectrum, from red through orange, yellow, green, blue, violet. The first step of Truthfulness is to abandon the commanding itself so that it is no longer part of your pattern. It may pop up from time to time, like a headache, but it is not your permanent state. The second form of Truthfulness is confirming and acknowledging that the Source of Life is the Truth and the wayfarer only witnesses what is lacking. There is nothing except perfection; wherever there is a lack, it is in the person.

That is a form of *ṣidq,* Truthfulness, the last condition of which is again a paradoxical one, because you go beyond Truthfulness by acknowledging that the Knowledge of Truthfulness is like recognising the complex of consistent geometric patterns that make up the structure of the universe and all it contains. You are conscious of these underlying patterns and universal truths and, knowing that once and for all, you move through life and the world in such a way that your actions and conditions are in concordance with Reality, with the commands and decrees of Allāh. Not only do you reconcile the inner with the outer, but they are in harmonious concord, as opposed to discord. Once you are in that state, whatever you do has within it the core of Truthfulness. There is a big risk here because people think that because they are on this path and have made a decisive commitment to it, they can don the mantle of Truthfulness. If you put that mantle on falsely, that is, if you have not experienced these confirmations of Truthfulness, your praiseworthy works and actions become blameworthy and your sincerity becomes falsehood.

The three degrees of Truthfulness are:

1. Confirmation of the purpose of the journey. This permits the wayfarer to deflect distractions and to build on the ruins (of the commanding self). The wayfarer then refuses the company of those who deny the Primordial Covenant, or who call for its rejection.
2. Confirmation that the source of life is the Truth and that the wayfarer only witnesses what is lacking in themselves.
3. Truthfulness in the knowledge of Truthfulness. Truthfulness in the select is to know that one's actions and conditions are in concordance with Reality, Its Decrees and Commands. If the wayfarer falsely puts on the Mantle of Truthfulness, then all their works become blameworthy, their sincerity turns to falsehood and the limits of their quest is to lie down.

In modern parlance, a more contemporary way of approaching the Door of Truthfulness is to think of it as a form of reconciliation, bringing into accordance intention, action, purpose and meaning, creating a balanced harmony between these four aspects. When these are in unison then all reinforce each other, and the condition and state of the wayfarer can be said to be truthful. Knowledge and direct experience of the Divine Reality in and of itself leads to truthful action. The wheel returns full circle. To know Reality by Its Signs, Symbols and Presence, truthful action is necessary. Obversely, truthful action is the necessary concomitant with knowledge and certainty of the Divine Reality.

4.36. The Door of Altruism *(Bāb al-Īthār)* باب الإيثار

وَيُؤْثِرُونَ عَلَىٰ أَنفُسِهِمْ وَلَوْ كَانَ بِهِمْ خَصَاصَةٌ

Wa yu'thirūna 'ala anfusihim wa law kāna bihim khaṣāṣa

'Who even when needy, prefer them to themselves.' (*Qur'ān*, 59:9)

Here Altruism, *ithār*, means giving preference. Anṣārī is very equivocal about it: he insists that it is something that can only be done voluntarily, as an exercise of free will and free choice. It is not a praiseworthy condition if it is forced upon a person—e.g. if your parents tell you that you have to share your toys with your brother or sister. In the inner world this is a form of compunction, whereas if it is done voluntarily, then it moves to the level of *ithār.* The First Degree of giving preference to others is to generally prefer existent beings in creation to yourself in matters that do not imply contravening the Demands and Decrees of Reality. Here it means essentially the *Sharīʿa* that you must not defer to others when it comes to matters of acting out God's commands and decrees. Any person who tries to block your journey and wastes your time is not to be given preference in the inner realm. The Second Degree of Altruism is to prefer God's Contentment with you to the contentment of all others even if one's burdens are amplified, or one's needs are increased, and afflictions augmented.

The Third Degree of Altruism is to prefer what Allāh Prefers. Your preference for others ceases to be others, who do not feature in your spectrum of preferences, because you have surrendered your right to preference to whatever Allāh Prefers. The reason, he says, is that the notion of preference implies in it an element of dominion over what is being preferred. You are offering something or giving something away. The presumption is that you own that thing or that state. The reality is that you do not own it, so it is best to abandon the notion of having the right to prefer something, when the right is not yours; it only comes by bestowal. It is then the abandonment of that abandonment: you abandoned preference and then abandoned the abandonment of preference. This is the path of the realised wayfarer.

This is exemplified by the actions and the conditions of the outer realm of the Prophet's *ansār* (helpers) in Medina when they were faced with the mass of migrants coming in from Mecca, the *muhājirūn*. It is also quite relevant in today's times too. There are many *áyāt* regarding the virtuousness of taking in others, making them feel at home, giving them comfort and succour. In the inner realm, who are the *ansār*, the helpers, and who are the migrants? The migrant, of course, is the self as it migrates from one state to the next, moving from one landscape to the next. Giving preference is something that requires the element of choice and the element of will, which begs the question: where is the will from? What is the source of your willpower?

Anṣārī: To prefer others to oneself is a matter of selection and choice. Altruism is praiseworthy when done voluntarily but the opposite when done by compunction. It has three degrees:

1. To prefer creation to yourself in matters that do not imply contravening the Commands and Decrees of Reality, do not block your journey's progress and that do not waste your time.
2. To prefer God's Contentment with you over all others, even if one's burdens are amplified, needs increased and afflictions are augmented.
3. To prefer what Allāh Prefers, because preference in itself implies dominion over what is being preferred. Abandoning Altruism and then abandoning its abandonment is the path of the realised wayfarer.

Giving preference to others is what the Prophet's helpers (*Ansār*) in Medina were called to do when faced with the arrival of the migrants (*muhājirūn*) from Mecca. The element of Altruism is essential because it becomes an element in the ethical cultivation of the inner way, if it is directed by the knowledge and experience of unicity. In the outer world, being Altruistic towards those who do not deserve it is in fact an encouragement to their less than good intentions, states and actions, although it could also lead to their improvement by example. The balance of correct Altruism must be related to the march of the self towards its apotheosis in the soul.

Twentieth Reflection Day:

Supplementary to the five obligatory Pillars of Islamic ritual practice which accompany the six Pillars of Faith, are voluntary Pillars of inner spiritual practice, belonging to various denominations and paths (*ṭuruq*). These could be understood as bridging the outer (*ẓāhiri*) rituals of witnessing, *shahāda,* prayer, *ṣalāh,* charity, *zakāt*, fasting, *ṣawm* and pilgrimage, *ḥajj* and the inner prerequisite articles of faith, īmān, in God, *Allāh,* Angels, *malā'ika,* the Holy Books, *Kutub,* the Prophets and Messengers, *al-anbiyā wa'r-Rusul,* the Day of Judgement, *yawm al-qiyāma,* Destiny or Divine Decree, *qadr Allāh* amplifying them by combination of inner and outer, above and below—heavens and earth, *as-samāwāt wal-arḍ.*

Ibn al-'Arabi's four Pillars of spiritual Knowledge (*arkan al-ma'rifa*) أركان المعرفة (first four) included in the nine Principles of Goodness* are one example of these methodologies of augmented Islamic spiritual practice:

Pillar/Principle *arkān*	Spiritual States for the *murīd* and the *muḥaqiq*	spiritual Stations *maqamatāt*	Secrets *asrār*	Knowledge *ma'rifa*
1 Silence *ṣamt* tongue and heart	Safety and intimate conversation	Inspiration *wāḥi*	Truth *Al-Ḥaqq*	Knowledge of God *Allāh*
2 Seclusion *'zla / khalwa*	Transcendance of all attributes	Divine Unity *waḥdānīya*	Uniqueness *aḥadīya*	This world *ad-dunya*
3 Hunger *jū'*	Humility, submission Serenity	Delicacy of feeling transcendence	Eternal self-subsistence *ṣamadīyya*	Satan *shayṭān*
4 Vigilance *sahar*	Cultivation of the moment	Assuming the lordly attributes	Everlasting self-Existence	The (ego/self) self *an-nafs*
5 Veracity *ṣidq*	Lack of self-importance	Truth over self-image	*Qayāmīya* protection	The shadow *aẓ-ẓil*
6 Reliance *i'timād/ tawakkul*	Servility *'ubudīya*	Trust *Ṣidq*	Surrender *istislām*	The beyond *al-ākhira*
7 Patience *ṣabr*	Calm, indigence	Intimacy	Spiritual poverty *faqr*	The Grave *al-qabr*
8 Resolution *'azm*	Absence of base thoughts	Altruistic actions response to needs	Conscious actions/duties	Requirements of the Moment
9 Certainty *yaqīn*	Transcendence of ordinary humanness	non-worldliness non-materialism	Spiritual cause and effect	The Universe All realities

---

*Ibn 'Arabi, M. (2014). *The Four Pillars of Spiritual Transformation.* Trans. Stephen Hirtenstein. Oxford: Anqa Publishing.

WEEK TWENTY-ONE

4.37. The Door of Character *(Bāb al-Khuluq)* باب الخلق

وَإِنَّكَ لَعَلَى خُلُقٍ عَظِيمٍ

Wa innaka lal'alā khuluqin 'aẓīm

'And you are of a character most noble.' (*Qur'ān*, 68:4)

Anṣārī says Character or Ethical Conduct is what reflects of the Attributes onto the wayfarer. This is an extremely subtle point. Whatever the soul is able to impart of its essential Character to the self, that flow in itself is a source of good Character and Ethical Conduct. The more you are able to reflect the qualities of the Divine Names and Attributes and their essential form, the more the quality of your Character begins to rise. And he says it has been agreed, amongst the spiritual leadership of the time, that practical gnosis is the basis of good Character. As much as the soul is rooted in perfecting the qualities of good Character, its practical or outer manifestations, is the basis of the Characters of nobility. It revolves around the axes of the humility of the gnostic and, forgoing any harm, three qualities affirm that: Knowledge, Generosity, and Patience.

High Character implies that you know that created beings are constrained by their capabilities, limited by their powers, and curtailed in their will and action by their destinies. This is when you are dealing with the soul, when it looks at the self, or the luminous self looking at the residual elements of its commanding self. You have to be charitable, accept that conditions and people have flaws, faults and limitations. Once you accept, acknowledge, and imbibe that, the quality of your Character becomes softer, more open to the finer subtleties. The Second Degree by which the quality of Character is enhanced, is when you face the heart and the truth. You are aware that whatever emerges from you is tentative, it is hesitant and whatever comes from the Truth, from Reality, from Allāh demands gratitude and loyalty. That relationship leads necessarily to the enhancement of good Character.

The Third Degree, he says, is to acquire higher qualities through the purification of Character and that happens through spiritual exercises, by which the elements that stop or hinder the progress of the wayfarer are dropped. Gnosis is a practical manifestation of the acquisition of inner knowledge, then dealing with created beings becomes the leitmotif and touchstone of the wayfarer for the highest potential form of Ethical Conduct. Qualities of Character become therefore the outer realisation of the Divine Names and Attributes. ‘Take on the Characteristics of Allāh’ said the Prophet of Islam. In its simplest form it means greeting people by God’s Name, Peace, *As-Salām—Assalāmu Alaykumd.* You praise by invoking that praise belongs to the Praise-worthy *Al-Ḥamīd—Alḥamdulillah.* You thank by invoking the Thankful *Ash-Shakūr—Shukru lillāh.* In essence you are mindful that all created beings have in them qualities that reflect the Divine Names and it is these that you are acknowledging.

For those wayfarers who are rooted and committed to the journey, use of the word *as-Salām* has a very high degree of cognition. You are bestowing the peace of the All-Peaceful onto others, through you as agent.

Anṣārī: Character is what reflects the Divine Attributes onto the wayfarer. It has been agreed that practical gnosis is the basis of good Character. It revolves around the axes of the humility of the gnostic and the foregoing of any harm. It has three degrees:

1. Knowing that created beings are constrained by their capabilities, limited by their powers and curtailed in their will and action by their destinies.
2. Improving the qualities of your Character when facing Truth, by knowing that whatever emerges from you is tentative, and whatever comes from the Truth demands gratitude and loyalty.
3. Acquiring higher qualities of Character through the purification of Character, and then ascending beyond that, towards the perfection of Character.

Whenever you reflect or manifest a condition, a state, in its inner form and in its outer form, when you address people and are in company, you recognise that the driving force behind your actions and states, is one of God’s Names. You reflect, express, and acknowledge that and you are also aware that every created entity has the qualities of the Divine Names so when you approach them, you are acknowledging that. It does not mean that you shirk your duties and responsibilities, but it is always with the knowledge that your actions are rooted in the appropriate Divine Name and Attribute that is within a proper order in the hierarchy. The whole panoply of Divine Names is ordered hierarchically in a particular order and becomes the basis by which the wayfarer conducts themselves and interacts with creation in the broadest sense, including human beings, the natural world and the cosmos.

4.38. The Door of Diffidence *(Bāb at-Tawādhu')* باب التواضع

وَعِبَادُ الرَّحْمَٰنِ الَّذِينَ يَمْشُونَ عَلَى الْأَرْضِ هَوْنًا وَإِذَا خَاطَبَهُمُ الْجَاهِلُونَ قَالُوا سَلَامًا

Wa 'ibād ur-raḥmān alladhīna yamshūna 'alā al-arḍi hawnan wa idhā khāṭabahūm ul-jahilūna qālū salāma

'The true servants of the All Merciful are those who walk the earth in humility and when the ignorant address them insolently, they say "Peace."' (*Qur'ān*, 25:63)

In the inner realm it is to do with bowing in front of the power and force of the Truth. It is again of three degrees: the First Degree is Diffidence in the face of the *dīn,* which is the combined practice described in the previous section. Rather than using the word 'religion', which itself raises a lot of issues, the word *dīn* is far more encompassing of the deep spiritual aspects than religion. Diffidence removes argumentativeness towards the Sacred Texts, adoption of stances that are defamatory or accusatory, and any oppositional stance towards the *dīn* or *adyān* (pl.), or Divinely Inspired Books in general. The Second Degree of Diffidence is to accept the companionship of brothers and sisters on the path of wayfaring, to be just and righteous with your enemies and to accept the excuses of the one seeking forgiveness. The Third Degree is to defer always to the Truth, perhaps retreat from your own justifications and relinquish whatever reward you might expect for your work or service.

Diffidence is a form of spiritual hesitancy; it reflects that there are inner boundaries for one's conduct and that one's knowledge is incomplete by its very essence. Courtesy is imposed upon you when you know that you have boundaries to your behaviour and limitations to your knowledge. Courtesy towards conditions and states that you have not yet achieved. You cannot claim to be where you are not. This sense of hesitancy at one sstage of spiritual advancement on your path, means that you cannot claim the reality of being at a different stage. You are aware of their existence, reality and truth, but you have not experientially reached them yet. There is a certain element of hesitancy in even speaking about what is outside your direct experience. You are pushing the boundary all the time but you have to be aware of the bounds.

The other side of the coin to Diffidence or spiritual hesitancy is spiritual arrogance, in the sense of believing that there is a completeness to your condition and attempt to convince others that you are more spiritually advanced than you are. This of course negates the whole purpose of the journey as you cannot jump to a high *maqam* (station) by bypassing the intermediary stages. Diffidence is the internal condition of the wayfarer as they acknowledge and accept the existence of spiritual hierarchies. There is a hierarchy in existence and to be truthful (*sadiq*) to yourself is one of the conditions of understanding and acknowledgement of that reality and, while it may have an external manifestation, where appropriate, one must never simply go through the motions of Diffidence in an act of false modesty.

Anṣārī: Diffidence is an inner bowing to the power and superior forces of Truth. Diffidence is of three degrees:

1. Diffidence in the face of the *dīn* so that one is not argumentative towards the Sacred Texts, neither adopting an accusatory stance towards them, nor choosing an oppositional path to its tenets.
2. To accept in companionship brothers and sisters on the path of wayfaring; to be just and righteous with your enemies and to accept the excuses of the one seeking forgiveness.
3. To defer always to the Truth, retreat from your own justifications and to relinquish whatever reward you might expect for your work or service.

Anṣārī does not give a complete explanation of the inner ethics of Diffidence or reticence. Reticence is a form of spiritual hesitancy that reflects the presence of inner boundaries as well as the incomplete knowledge of the wayfarer. It is a form of courteous conduct towards conditions and states that one has not yet achieved, but that one is aware of in terms of their existence, reality and truth. It is the condition of the wayfarer as they acknowledge and accept the existence of spiritual hierarchies.

Twenty-First Reflection Day:

Muḥammad 'Abdul-Jabbār an-Niffari (d. 965):

I said: How do I depart from the ordinance concerning my knowledge to the Ordinance concerning Yours? He answered: You make lawful by your doctrine what I have made unlawful by Mine, and you make unlawful by your doctrine what I have made lawful by Mine: and you claim that it is by My Leave, and that it proceeds from My Command.

I said: How do I make claims of You? He answered: You come with an act which I have never Commanded and make judgements for it by My Ordinance concerning an act which I did Command; and you come with a word by which I have never commanded you, and make judgement for it by My Ordinance concerning a Word by which I did Command you. I said: I will not come with an act which You have not Commanded me, and I will not come with a word which You have not commanded me. He said: If you come with it as I have Commanded you, it is My Word and My Act: and by My Word and My Act falls My Ordinance. But if you come with it as I did not command you, then it is your word and your act: and by your word and your act falls not My ordinance, nor do My religion and commandment thereby live.

If you equate My Word and your word, and if you equate My Ordinance and your ordinance then you have made yourself equal to Me.

I said: There is no ordinance, except that belonging to Your Word and Your Act. He said: You have understood.*

WEEK TWENTY-TWO

4.39. The Door of Nobility *(al-Futūwwa)* باب الفتوة

إِنَّهُمْ فِتْيَةٌ آمَنُوا بِرَبِّهِمْ وَزِدْنَاهُمْ هُدًى

Innahum fityatun āmanū birabbihim wa zidnāhum huda

'They were noble youths who believed in their Lord and whom we increased in Guidance.' (*Qur'ān*, 18:13)

Spiritual Nobility is leaving enmity, ignoring insults and forgetting harm done to you. In many ways this reflects the teachings and leadership by

*Niffarī , M. A. J. (1935) *The Mawāqif and Mukhātabāt of Muhammad Ibn 'Abd L-Jabbār Al- Niffarī: with other fragments.* Ed. Trans. Arthur John Arbery. Cambridge University Press for the Trustees of the 'E. J. W. Gibb Memorial', London, Luzac & co. p. 128.

example of all the great prophets. Turning the other cheek is part of that. The Second Degree is drawing near to the person who is trying to undo you, to honour the one who is trying to hurt you and to apologise to one who is causing you harm. The Third Degree is to avoid giving justifications for your actions, thereby tarnishing your responses by preaching. *Futūwwa*, Nobility of action and intentions are the hallmarks of the spiritual warrior and in the realm of the world of Islamic civilization, the peak of spiritual chivalry, and Nobility is Imām ʾAlī. Out of all the 12 largest Ṣūfi Orders, 11 of them place the Imām at the top of their hierarchy. There is a well-known attribution to him, that he was the original *fatā*. * The word *futūwwa* derives from the singular word *fatā*, which means youth, and *futūwwa* is the selfless noble actions of enlivened youth.

In the *Qurʾān* it is applied to the Prophet Ibrahim and to the people in the cave—*Ahl al-Kahf*. In outer practice, it requires the evolution of the self towards the highest spiritual qualities represented by the soul. It is a form of melding intention, effort and action. The Nobility of intention, effort and action is a function of the degree in which you mirror the particular related Divine Quality. In its outer reality *futūwwa* was the guild system. The entire economic order of the world of Islam was girded together by these guilds, which combined within them both Devotion and work towards enlivening, improving and elevating the self in its spiritual journey. Work has a very profound spiritual, sacred side to it. The organisation of the workplace, the whole system of masters and apprentices girded the Islamic world order until around 100 years ago. It was then undermined and replaced by trade unions and the sense of rupture between work and the spiritual meaning of work became defined.

Anṣārī: The essence of Nobility is not to see in your self any preference nor that your self has any rights. It has three degrees:

1. Leaving enmity, ignoring insults and forgetting harm done to you.
2. Drawing near to the one who is trying to undo you, honouring the one who is trying to hurt you and apologising to one who is causing you harm.

---

* *Lā Fatā illā Alī* لا فتى إلا علي literally means: there is no hero but Ali, said at the Battle of Uḥud by the Archangel Gabriel, according to a *ḥadith* attributed to the fifth Imam Muḥammad al-Bāqir. Shah-Kazemi, H.R. (2019). *Imam ʿAli: From Concise History to Timeless Mystery.* London: The Matheson Trust for the Study of Comparative Religion.

3. Not to give justifications for your actions, or to tarnish your responses by preaching.

4.40. The Door of Exuberance *(Bāb al-Inbisāṭ)* باب الانبساط

أَتُهْلِكُنَا بِمَا فَعَلَ السُّفَهَاءُ مِنَّا ۖ إِنْ هِيَ إِلَّا فِتْنَتُكَ تُضِلُّ بِهَا

Atuhlikunā bimā fa'āla asfahā'u minnā in hīa illā fatnatuka tuḍillu bihā

'Will you destroy us now for what the reprobates amongst us have done? This is nothing but a trial from You.' (*Qur'ān*, 7:155)

The last door that *Khwāja* talks about in the Stage of Ethics (*akhlāq*) is the Door of Joyfulness, Exuberance or *inbisāṭ*. Your sense of elation dissolves into greater advancement towards the Most Expansive, as Allāh calls Himself *Al-Bāsiṭ* in the *Qur'ān,* although it only reaches its fullness in Stage Nine. Exuberance is a condition of limitless joy that expresses itself by an ease and serenity and dealing with created beings, secure in the knowledge of the One. This is best articulated by *surah 94 al-Inshirāḥ*; it is a very short *surah*—'Have We not Soothed your heart? Have We not Relieved you of the burden that weighed upon your back? Have We not Exalted your Remembrance? For with hardship comes ease, with hardship comes ease. And when your work is done, turn to devotion, and make your Lord your sole quest.'

Bismillāh ir-Raḥmān ir-Raḥīm *Alam nashraḥ laka ṣadrak wa waḍā'na 'anka wizrak alladhi anqaḍa ẓahraka wa rafa'nā laka dhikraka fa inna ma' al-'usri yusrān inna ma' al-'usri yusrā fa idha fara-ghta fanṣab wa ilā rabbika farghab*	بِسْمِ اللَّهِ الرَّحْمَٰنِ الرَّحِيمِ أَلَمْ نَشْرَحْ لَكَ صَدْرَكَ وَوَضَعْنَا عَنكَ وِزْرَكَ الَّذِي أَنقَضَ ظَهْرَكَ وَرَفَعْنَا لَكَ ذِكْرَكَ فَإِنَّ مَعَ الْعُسْرِ يُسْرًا إِنَّ مَعَ الْعُسْرِ يُسْرًا فَإِذَا فَرَغْتَ فَانصَبْ وَإِلَىٰ رَبِّكَ فَارْغَب

The risk of being in that stage is that you neglect the boundaries. The nature of Exuberance is to spill over, to overflow. You always have to contain—and be contained—to the maximum of containment, contained within the limits of expensiveness. Otherwise, you may have a false sense of freedom and empowerment. The summation of the Stage of Ethics are the essence of goodly conduct in the outer form. *Akhlāq* or Ethics become the basis by which you discriminate or differentiate between the accepted, the prohibited, the good, and the not so good. The ethical understanding of the outer ordinances, *Shari'a* is an essential element in its practice, and Ethics ultimately come down to the condition of the self. There are societal ethics that have a different dynamic, but the Ethics of the self express themselves inwardly, through the perfection of these qualities—Patience, Contentment, Gratitude, Effacement etc.

In their other form, they become a mechanism by which you gauge the appropriateness and the timeliness of Decrees, of Commands, that are subject to variation and change in their essential character. It becomes a way of understanding and orienting yourself in the world, while rooted in the knowledge of One. In the inner world, the human kingdom, *al-Mamlaka al-Insaniyya*, as Ibn 'Arabi called it, that we all have, has its own king, its own viceroy, and enforces its own laws, its own judges—there is a world inside. This inner kingdom must also have a fulcrum and the precision of that fulcrum is the ethical basis. The more one is attuned to the ethical foundations of inner conduct, the more balanced the discriminating quality becomes and the more it is honed and able to differentiate and discriminate, as well as to move on.

Anṣārī: Exuberance is to despatch grief, to avoid the solitude of humility; it is to march with the upright. It is of three degrees:

1. Exuberance of created beings, that is not to isolate yourself from them but to engage them with your virtues and to tolerate them with your qualities of character.
2. Exuberance of the Truth, that is neither to be stopped by fear nor lulled by excessive hope, nor allow any human being to enter between you and your Lord.
3. Exuberance by rolling up Expansiveness. The wayfarer enfolds his joy in the Expansiveness of the Truth Most High.

Twenty-Second Reflection Day:

Suggested *Dhikr* for the Stage of Ethics:

Aṣ-Ṣabūr (The All-Patient) *Ash-Shakūr* (The All-Grateful) *Al-Ḥalīm* (The All-Clement)

Yā Ṣabūr ~ Yā Shakūr ~ Yā Ḥalīm

5. The Stage of Origins (*Manzal al-ʾUṣūl*) مَنزِل الأُصول

Overarching Names:

The Resurrector *Al-Bāʾith* الباعث

The Mighty *Al–ʿAẓīm* العظيم

Anṣārī on the Stage of Origins: 'The Origins are the structures for appropriate conduct and the bases for progressing along the path. They are the halting points for the heart from which the intellect proceeds.'

Before we continue on the Fifth Stage of Origins (*ʾuṣūl*), it is worthwhile summarising and taking stock of where we are, where we came from and whether the exercises so far have been of use to those of us who wish to be on the path of wayfaring, and whether there have been obstacles or issues that we may need to look at, so that this does not become just an academic exercise or scholarly study. If you look back at the Preliminary Stage, these thirteen doors are part of the preparatory work of the modern wayfarer. Each of them has a quality to it, a certain aspect and they are all intended as platforms from which to ascend to a higher degree of spiritual awareness and consciousness. That is the whole purpose of this book. It is not to explain the finer intricacies of the thoughts of great masters, although they are quite interesting in their own right, but rather as tools and guides for those who want to use them as part of the package for progressing along this path.

If they have not yet achieved that, would its repetition or revisiting provide an advantage, or would we become disconnected? They may become such a thicket of stations, doors and degrees that we get lost in them. You could try to situate yourself at one or other of the stages or doors or at a different level or another height or condition that governs your reality. Ask yourself or those who are spiritually intimate with you. Most of those who skirt along the path and feed from it, when and if they feel the need, will probably get stuck in the Pre-Stages. Some may move on to a form of awakening or alertness and begin to experience the vitality and reality of these doors. The vast majority of people dabble on the way. This is not a condemnation; it is a non-judgemental description. Most people dabble because they are driven by this agitation and the need to make some sense of the various spiritual conditions that they find themselves in and address this sense of anxiety or perplexity that prevails.

These are ephemeral conditions; you can dwell in them without leaving and spend your entire life in a state of perplexity or agitation. This is not what this path is about; it is about moving, advancing, ascending, not constantly wallowing or dithering at the lower levels. The lower levels themselves are intrinsically worthwhile on their own terms but you have the capacity to move up, to ascend and you should not stop simply because you are comfortable in that state. The *Qur'ān* says that you are enjoined to exercise to your limit. Most people think 'it is the limit, I'll do my best', but you have to do your best up to the very limit. If your limit includes your capability for moving on to the next stage, then you should do so. The whole point of this, or any spiritual exercise, is to invert the sense of perception. You have to develop or recognise a different way of looking at things and if you constantly refer to them as what is comfortable, what is familiar, then you have not yet fulfilled your potential as a person who can act as an interface between the two realities, the seen and the unseen.

Human beings, by their very nature, have the capacity of being *barzakhi* creatures, creatures of the interspace—creatures who are able to unite what appear to be irreconcilable worlds into their own reality. This is what *maraj al-baḥrayn* is all about. The *Qur'ān* talks about the two oceans of the seen and the unseen approaching each other, but with an isthmus between them, like the Panama Canal. So you are the Panama Canal, between the Atlantic and the Pacific, as an isthmus, a *barzakh*, an interspace, or a bridge. Your potential is not only to see the realities of both, but to act as the vehicle or vessel for yourself to traverse that isthmus or that bridge. It is worthwhile, now or later, for you to go back to each of these stages. Maybe the jumble in which they come in is not cast in stone, and that you start with the Door of Awakening and finish with Endings.

These are very malleable ideas and conditions and you have to stretch them, bend them and mould them to fit your own reality. By and large they serve as guideposts, indicators and signs. The world of the unseen is really a world of signs, symbols and examples—*amthāl*, as the *Qur'ān* says. Without the capacity to understand symbols (*amthāl*) you would not have the necessary language to converse with this other reality. All this is designed to awaken in a person a language of spiritual consciousness. There is a language of spiritual awareness which has to do with the outer reality—that is the language of the rituals—but they are not necessarily the same. The inner reality has its own form, rules and guidelines. Since we cannot experience them in the substantive sense, but only by inference, by example, by symbols, we sometimes even encounter them in myths, in the sense of Mythos—the encoding of ancient history in archetypal stories, rich with symbolism— not as in fiction but as an archetype.

All of these stations and archetypes are ideals that are stripped of the denseness and veils of darkness and polarities, to become luminous doorways. When you see words that appear to make sense to you in the mundane world, they do not necessarily have the same significance or meaning when you relate them to spiritual reality. This is a very important lesson that one should obtain through this experience and while reviewing them, reflecting on and thinking about them, it is essential that you see them in the context of this inner language that you need to evolve. This inner language has been spoken about by many of the masters before. It is not worth simply regurgitating what they said as it was for a different time, a different age. There is a certain universality to it but that universality has to be conditioned by our own circumstances, which have to remould these works so that they become as real to us as they were to our predecessors, even in our outer world which has lost its capacity to engage with the unseen or even with the sacred.

With that in mind, you can go to the Fifth Stage of the *Manāzil*, which is the Stage of Origins (*'uṣūl*). Looking at this, at this Stage, you might think we are moving backwards as the previous Stages seem to be dealing with sets of virtues, that in some ways have been discussed in different contexts before. The fine definitions are not scientific. It is a science in the sense that it is an access to realities that are natural, but not a science in the sense of an empirical science, which you can observe and measure. It follows different kinds of programmes and methodologies and looks at them with the eye of inversion. By placing Allāh at the centre of understanding, rather than yourself, you will then see these words and concepts assume a different kind of reality.

Summary: Origins is the Stage where the intellect of a person comes to the fore, acting on the earlier Stages where the self was the focus of the wayfarer's endeavours. By intellect is meant the reasoning faculty that can discern the luminous and subtle. It is not so much the mind—although the mind is part of the intellect; but rather the bedrock of action which is based on will and desire. This Stage is where the intellect is refined towards the higher goal of purposeful action, where the intellect is aware of its powers but is also aware of their limitations and their source in the One. When consciously connected with its Source, The All-Knowing, *Al-ʿAlīm,* the intellect, *al-ʿaql,* perpetually expands and becomes infinite.

WEEK TWENTY-THREE

5.41. The Door of Purposefulness *(Bāb al-Qaṣd)* باب القصد

وَمَن يَخْرُجْ مِن بَيْتِهِ مُهَاجِرًا إِلَى اللَّهِ وَرَسُولِهِ ثُمَّ يُدْرِكْهُ الْمَوْتُ فَقَدْ وَقَعَ أَجْرُهُ عَلَى اللَّهِ ۗ وَكَانَ اللَّهُ غَفُورًا رَّحِيمًا

Waman yakhruj min baytihi muhājiran ilā Allāhi warasūlihi thumma yudrikul-mawtu faqad waqaʿa ajruhu ʿāla Allāhi wakāna Allāhu ghafūrar Raḥīmā

'Whosoever leaves his home as an emigrant to God and His Messenger and is overtaken by death, his reward falls upon God for God is All-Forgiving, All-Merciful.' (*Qurʾān*, 4:100)

The first Door of the Stage, *bāb al-qaṣd*, which is translated here as Purposefulness, can also mean the end, intention, objective, the target, or justice in the sense of putting things in their proper places. Generally, for the Stage of Origins, Anṣārī says: 'The Origins are the structures for appropriate conduct and the bases for progressing along the path. They are the halting points for the heart from which the intellect proceeds.' What he means here is that the heart can comprehend the unseen; it is a vessel that relates to the subtler realities. The intellect has that purpose too, in the outer form, but the intellect in the inner world is a different kind of faculty. It is not the calculating mind of logic or reason, that weighs and measures, that is the central point of understanding cause and effect. The intellect of the inner world is the faculty that points to the limitations of that mode of thinking and is in fact its opposite.

Reason, or *al-ʿaql,* in the inner reality is not only something that is ever expanding; it is a faculty that includes human reasoning but also understands the limitations of the empirical base of human knowledge. Therefore, it is a kind of metaphysical entity, which relates to the unseen. It is that faculty that has a will and a direction. The direction of that is to understand the way to Allāh, not merely to understand causality. We always have to make that conversion when you are dealing with the inner realities. The Purposefulness of focus in the inner Life of the human being, is to understand the pathways and mechanisms that can relate, combining all the inner faculties towards that objective. At Stage Five, Anṣārī builds the doors around that specific function of the *al-ʿaql,* the intellect. His commentary is that throughout this entire stage, where the intellect of a person comes to the fore, it is acting and building on the earlier stages, where the self was the focus of the wayfarer's endeavours.

Previous stages had more to do with improving the quality of the self, the virtues. Now we come to the point where the assumption is that your qualities have emerged and you can see how they relate to heightened spiritual consciousness. You can see, for example, how in many of the stages beforehand, the perfection of these specific virtues are, in their own ways, an indicator towards Allāh. Here the ball is passed on from the virtues to the intellect, but not the intellect of logic or reason. It is a unifying element that combines mind and the heart. By intellect is meant the perceptual faculties that can discern the luminous and subtle, it is not so much the personal mind, at least not the mind of psychiatrists. It is not the ego, superego, the Id of psychoanalysis, nor even the psyche in the sense of soul; it is close but much more than that. The mind is part of the intellect, but the mind by itself cannot discern the luminous.

The heart is the driving motor of the intellect in the spiritual realm, through will and desire. These are the two elements, like the hydrogen and oxygen molecules of water. Some of these ideas have also been appropriated into modern philosophy. Will and desire are at the heart of, for example, Schopenhauer's philosophy but it is a different kind of will. It is the will to action on the mundane level. It is not the will that seeks realisation and *tawḥīd.* The focus and purposes are different.

Anṣārī talks about desire in the same vein as the nineteenth-century idealists, but the goal is not to create a superman, as in Nietzsche's *Übermensch.* The goal is to create the complete self that understands their origin and can see the One behind multiplicities. It is the bedrock of action which is based on will and desire. This is a stage where the intellect is refined towards the higher goal of purposeful action, where the intellect is aware of its powers, but also its limitations.

This is *qaṣd*, the target, the end result, fortified by the above Qur'anic *āya* (*Qur'ān*: 4:100). We are immigrants, *muhājirīn,* on this path. The wayfarer is a traveller, an immigrant from one condition, one realm, one familiar abode to another zone that is unknown or different. Think of yourself as a nineteenth-century immigrant leaving the wilds of Russia and emigrating to the States. But this is an inner journey, a different kind of journey. It has the same kind of fears, anxieties and expectations which can overwhelm the wayfarer but as you have your eye focused on the outer world wherever you are going, whichever country you are emigrating to, here your eyes focus on proximity to the Station of Oneness. Anṣārī says: 'Purposefulness is determination to abjure all but obedience.' Again, it is a kind of inverting of the idea. If you are utterly obedient you basically give up your will, so how is that related to having a goal?

That is the meaning of the highest station of any realised being, the Station of Servitude, where absolute freedom originates. Here to be purposeful is to abandon all other objectives except the one that is pointed out to you. It is a form of absolute obedience, although in the outer world purposefulness might be the opposite of obedience. You cannot be purposeful and obedient at the same time, if somebody else's will prevails over yours or your will prevails over them. He defines these stages or conditions in the usual three degrees, dependent on the level of accomplishment. The First Degree focuses on maintaining one's commitment to the spiritual exercises, overcoming all obstacles and banishing hesitancy. The Second Degree is where you do not allow any negative, obstructive impediments to arise in your quest. You brush them aside, ignore them, or deflect them.

The Third Degree is the Purposefulness of surrender to the rules of outer knowledge, responding to their demands and determined to dissolve in the Ocean of Oblivion, which is one of the States called *fanā'*, Annihilation. The objective of Purposefulness is to ensure that the wayfarer does not waiver from their objective, and that the intellect—as well as the self—are now trained to be single-minded in moving towards their goal. No obstacle, be it social, religious, political, cultural or intellectual is allowed to block or force a deviation in the path of the wayfarer. Observance of outer law becomes immediate and not debatable; while the wayfarer is always on the lookout for the appearance of the Ocean of Unity, into which they are preparing to dive. You constantly keep your target in mind and when you see glimpses of it you know that it is within your grasp. To be purposefully focused on the objective, you also have to have Resolve, which is the following Door. When you are resolved on the matter, you put your trust in Allāh.

Anṣārī: Purposefulness is the determination to abjure all but obedience. It is of three degrees:

1. Purposefulness that leads towards the spiritual exercises, banishes hesitancy, and calls for overcoming obstacles.
2. Purposefulness that cuts through all objections, does not allow any negative states to arise, and carries burdens lightly.
3. Purposefulness of Surrender to the rules of outer knowledge; responding to the demands of God's Commands and determination to dissolve in the Ocean of Oblivion, *fanā.'*

5.42. The Door of Resolve *(Bāb al-'Azm)* باب العزم

فَإِذَا عَزَمْتَ فَتَوَكَّلْ عَلَى اللهِ

Fa idhā 'azamta fatawakkal 'al Allāh

'And when resolved on a matter, put your trust in *Allāh.*' (*Qur'ān*, 3:159)

This is a very well-known *āya*, and is usually said in conjunction with people embarking on some expedition, dangerous task, or action that they are hesitant about. Where we are going, there is another twist to it. Anṣārī: 'Resolution is to realise a purpose, whether voluntarily or by compunction.' It is a very unusual explanation or explication of what resolution means. It has three degrees. Firstly, by not allowing the state of the wayfarer, now experiencing flashes of unveiling, Intimacy and intimations of oblivion, *fanā'*, to cause the wayfarer to retreat. What Anṣāri means here is that sometimes the shock of recognition is so great that you step back, become afraid, unsure, you think it might be some kind of delusion. Or it is such an overwhelming flash that you are not sure whether you want to experience it again. For those who have seen these flashes, it is easy to understand the sense of fear that overwhelms, rather than awe.

That is the initial response: you want to turn away and run. It is like walking along and suddenly an elephant emerges, it shocks you. Resolution has to do with that. Whenever you are graced and these intimations occur, they are not to be ignored. If you want to stay on this path, you must not retreat from them. You cannot claim that you are on the path of the wayfarer and reaching your personal purpose if you are not able to face these realisations. The Stage of Resolve or Resolution is a bridge between righteousness, goodly action and the Station of Proximity. It is not enough to stay at the lower rungs of the ladder. You have started something and you want to finish the job. You do not want to give it up at any stage, but the self seeks preservation—it is natural. The degree of self-preservation becomes more acute if the projected future has within it the idea of oblivion or obliteration. Why would you Resolve to an end that involves the possibility of oblivion?

Anṣārī: Resolution is to realise the purpose, whether voluntarily or by compunction. It has three degrees:

1. By not allowing the state of the wayfarer—now experiencing flashes of unveiling and intimacy, and intimations of oblivion—to cause the wayfarer to retreat.
2. To immerse oneself in the glories of witnessing, illuminated by the lights of the path, and gathering the forces of uprightness.
3. To know the cause of one's Resolve, then resolving to abandon resolution and its obligations. Resolution does not bequeath the person more satisfaction than knowing the Source of resolution itself.

The Stage of Resolve is a bridge between right action and the Station of Proximity. At this point the wayfarer experiences a fundamental shift in perceptions and experiences. Verities fall by the wayside and a new world of luminosity and subtleties beckons. The temptation is always to fall back. After all, the state from which one had emerged is in itself a noteworthy state. You are not emerging from ignorance and darkness. You are coming from Stage Four, the Stage of *akhlāq* and you are supposed to have gone through doors of Patience, Gratitude, and then Expansiveness. It is not that you are retreating to a kind of darkness, you are simply retreating to a different degree of light, but your Resolve still pushes you forward. Ahead lies a condition about which one has had no previous knowledge or experience, which engenders a certain fear of the unknown. One's survival instinct might be activated, along with one's sense of self-preservation while the future threatens oblivion; one's Resolve is here tested to the limit. The wayfarer must plough ahead, and in order to do so you need, not only Resolve, but also will and desire, *irāda*.

Twenty-Third Reflection Day:

Dhikr: 99 times *Yā Qawī ~ Yā Muntaqim*

يا قوي يا منتقم

WEEK TWENTY-FOUR

5.43. The Door of Will *(Bāb al-Irāda)* باب الإرادة

قُلْ كُلٌّ يَعْمَلُ عَلَىٰ شَاكِلَتِهِ

Qul kulli ya'malu 'alā shākilatihi

'And say: Each person acts according to what befits the person....'

(*Qur'ān*, 17:84)

This is a very powerful *āya*. It is used in the outer sense to explain how each person, group or community thinks that it is doing its best by acting according to its own rules. This is the nature of things. It is not condemnation, but it is also not commendable in the outer world for each one to act according to what they think is in their own interests, as it is not necessarily in the interests of others or the community as a whole. In the inner world, the community, or the kingdom is within you—the elements within you have to be aligned. Anṣārī makes this point of inversion time and time again'. Whatever *Allāh* Presents or what Reality impinges upon, falls on you, that is your Will. It is not for you to resist; it is for you to yield completely, as a matter of voluntary action, to the demands of the *ḥaqq*, the Truth.

Anṣārī: Will is to respond voluntarily to the demands of the Truth. It is of three degrees:

1. Leaving habits behind while fortified by the *Sharī'a*; holding fast to the path of wayfaring with truthfulness in one's purpose; and staying away from those who distract and disturb from one's path and condition.
2. Breaking away while keeping true to one's state, freshened by the breath of intimacy, and moving between expansiveness and constrictiveness.
3. Astonishment while maintaining uprightness and ensuring courteous conduct.

Will in the wayfarer is the response to the irresistible pull of Reality. In essence it expresses itself as the degree to which the wayfarer opens up to the forces of attraction. In the inner reality, what passes for human Will is actually the loss of Will to the All-Wilful. This is the heart of the *Ḥadīth Qudsi* whereby Allāh says that for every step toward Him by human beings, Allāh Will Take ten steps towards them. The surrender to the Will of Allāh—expressed as human Will—is a geometric relationship and is compounded as one draws to the Station of Proximity, which is always there in any case. The effort to climb the hill is rewarded by the effortlessness in descending, but one has to always maintain the balance on the slope towards proximity. It means that every time you yield, the degree of success is geometrically enhanced. As you get higher and higher, your outer will becomes apparently incredible but your inner Will, which is expressed in a way that loses its outer realisation, merges into this sort of magnetic field.

5.44. The Door of Courtesy *(Bāb al-Adab)* باب الأدب

وَالْحَافِظُونَ لِحُدُودِ اللهِ

Wal-ḥāfiẓūna li-ḥudūdillah

'And the respecters of the bounds of God.' (*Qur'ān*, 9:112)

The Fourth Door is Courtesy or *adab*. Here, the Qur'anic *āya*, those who respect the boundaries, limits, conditions, and the courtesies, understand, acknowledge and respect the boundaries. Anṣārī says that Courtesy is preserving the line between excess and bareness, while knowing the dangers of slipping into either extreme. You abandoned Courtesy of the final degree because the whole act of being courteous creates a sense of false power to be courteous. The power to be courteous, the relationships of Courtesy and the person or the object of it becomes, at the highest level, incidental because you do not have the power. You acknowledge that, like being thankful or being in gratitude implies that you have the power to be grateful, but you do not have the power of gratitude, it is one of the Divine Attributes that you have borrowed from. At the highest level, you recognise the relationship as being a borrowed one and, therefore, you return it to its Possessor.

Anṣārī: Courtesy is preserving the line between excess and bareness, while knowing the dangers of slipping into either. It is of three degrees:

1. Courtesy is stopping fear from moving into despair, hope from moving into false security, and controlling joy from turning into disappointment.
2. Courtesy is moving from fear into the Field of Constrictiveness, and climbing from hope into the Field of Expansiveness, and from joy towards the Field of Witnessing.
3. Courtesy is knowing its essence and then abandoning it by relying on Truth and then altogether being free of witnessing the boundaries of Courtesy.

Courtesy is knowing the duties that are incumbent on one without addition or subtraction. On the path of wayfaring it is often that one encounters states and conditions that are entirely new and can lead to inappropriate responses unless the balance is kept. There is an element of equilibrium in the idea of Courtesy and when you come across new states and conditions, the temptation is to be absorbed into them. Therefore, they may have their own dynamic and create their own demands on you, which may lead to inappropriate action. You have to know the boundaries and be limited by what is courteously acceptable in the condition that you are in. A state of utter helplessness, for example, can lead to despair. If you feel absolutely helpless, in front of Allāh, one of the potential outcomes is to despair of your condition. What am I good for? If everything emanates from the One, what role do I have? What potential do I have in realising my own spiritual reality? A sense of being in complete impoverishment to Allāh must be counterbalanced by another condition, if you are not to fall into despair.

Twenty-Fourth Reflection Day:

Reflect on instances in which the imposition of your will might have encroached on the bounds of Courtesy. You may have said or done something in the spirit of upholding the good and preventing evil and, even though you were convinced you were right and your will was to the good of all concerned, your insistence tarnished your *adab* and may not have been appropriate, as it could have infringed upon the free will of others or even the Divine Will.*

WEEK TWENTY-FIVE

5.45. The Door of Certainty *(Bāb al-Yaqīn)* باب اليقين

وَفِي الْأَرْضِ آيَاتٌ لِّلْمُوقِنِينَ

Wafil-arḍi Āyātul lil-muʾminīn

'And on earth are signs for people of certain faith.' *(Qurʾān*, 51:20)

Glimpses of realities can lead to joy and then to unexpected shock; this can happen very frequently. You may want to recreate a high which does not materialise and then you fall into 'have I been abandoned?' The Prophet (Pbuh) was in that condition when the Chapter of the

* Freedom is a complex subject on which philosophical treatises are written. E.G. Regin, D. & Schiller, F. (1965) *Freedom and dignity. The historical and philosophical thought of Schiller.* The Hague: Martinus Nijhoff. Steiner, R. (2011) *The Philosophy of Freedom (the Philosophy of spiritual Activity): the Basis for a Modern world Conception.* Special ed. Forest Row: Rudolf Steiner Press.

Dawn Light *sūrat aḍ-ḍuḥa* descended. It is a necessary station to be at so the wayfarer does not transgress and begin to attribute to themself Attributes and Qualities that belong to the Truth. Another word for knowledge of Absolute Proximity is Certainty, *yaqīn.* We know of the three Stages of Knowledge of Certainty, *'ilm al-yaqīn*, the Eye of Certainty, *'ayn al-yaqīn* and the Truth of Certainty, *ḥaqq al-yaqīn.* Knowledge of the fire is not the same as seeing a fire, which is not the same as being inside the fire.

Anṣārī says that Certainty is the vessel for those who are on this path. It is the last stage of the common folk but the first step of the adept. What he means is that the knowledge and witnessing of Certainty that most people aspire to, brings the comfort and confidence they want to anchor. But for those who are starting on a much more intense experience of spiritual realities this is not the endpoint but the starting point. The Knowledge of Certainty or *'ilm al-yaqīn*, he says, is to accept what Truth has revealed itself and has sought to conceal of Itself and to be satisfied with what is established by Truth. The Eye of Certainty or *'ayn al-yaqīn* is to be strengthened by intuition and not by rational proof and by insight, rather than information. *Ḥaqq al-yaqīn* or the Truth of Certainty is to know beyond mental or sensory experience and then to abandon Certainty that comes from oneself, returning all to Allāh and then to be obliterated in the Truth of Certainty.

Anṣārī: Certainty is the vessel for those who are on this path. It is the last stage of the common seeker but the first step of the adept. It is of three degrees:

1. The Knowledge of Certainty is to accept what Truth has revealed of Itself, and what Truth has sought to conceal of Itself, and to be satisfied with what is established by Truth.
2. The Eye of Certainty is to be strengthened by intuiting and not by rational proof, and by insight, not by information.
3. The Truth of Certainty is to know beyond mental or sensory experience, then to abandon Certainty that comes from oneself, returning all to Allāh and then to be obliterated in the Truth of Certainty.

The degrees of Certainty of the wayfarer are best expressed in the example of the fire. Knowledge of the fire is to be told of the properties of fire, its heat, its light and its colour. The eye of the fire is to actually be hurled into the fire, experiencing its heat and its rage. The truth of the fire is to be the fire, its fuel and its flames. The wayfarer in the First Degree of Certainty knows of the existence of the Truth; in the Second Degree the wayfarer knows the Attributes of the Truth; in the Third Degree the wayfarer has to efface their own personal existence in the All-Encompassing Truth, *al-ḥaqq al-wāsi`*.

5.46. The Door of Intimacy *(al-'Uns)* باب الأنس

سَأَلَكَ عِبَادِي عَنِّي فَإِنِّي قَرِيبٌ

Sa'alaka 'ibadi 'annī fa'innī qarība

'If My worshippers ask you about Me, I Am Near.' (*Qur'ān*, 2:186)

Intimacy, Anṣārī says, is the soul of the heart—being the vessel of perception of subtle realities. The Heart of the heart, which is known as *al-fu'ād*, the kernel of the heart. The Kernel of the kernel is called the *lubb*. There are three degrees to the experience of spiritual reality. The heart in its outer form that can engage with the unseen, has within it an inner Heart, which does not deviate. It is always oriented towards the Truth. There are many *āyāt* in the *Qur'ān* which talk about the heart that has emptied. For example, when the Prophet Mūsa's mother was asked to cast her infant son into the river, she was asked to do that after her heart had emptied. It is the emptying of a heart, even though it is a vehicle of perception, that leads to the spiritual core. The Core of the core is called *al-lubb*.

Al-albab in the *Qur'ān* deals with those who have reached the highest state of spiritual realisation, those who are governed by the Kernel of the Core of the Heart. *'Uns* is also the root word for *insān*, which means human being in Arabic. One of the definitions of a human being, if you use the linguistic root of *'uns*, is the entity that maintains Intimacy. It can also mean the entity that forgets from *nisyān*, but it is more often related to *'uns*, as an intimate, a creature that seeks outer Intimacy. Also a creature that necessarily seeks inner Intimacy, not only between the self and the soul, but between the self, the soul and the Origin of both. The more intimate the self becomes with the soul, which is the ambassador or the messenger to the unseen within the person, the more it becomes gradually absorbed into it and takes on its colour.

Anṣārī: Intimacy is the soul of the Heart and has three degrees:

1. It is to taste remembrance *(dhikr)*, be nourished by listening *(Sama')*, and to ponder the signs *āyāt.*
2. Intimacy by the light of unveiling. This emerges from the First Degree of Intimacy. It is struck by the Onrushes and the waves of obliteration. This is what drives some into mindlessness, others to impatience, and others to shed the bounds of knowledge.
3. Intimacy that is inseparable from being proximate, and which cannot be expressed by sight, nor by pointing out, and which is indefinable and ineffable.

Intimacy is to be gradually absorbed into the One. It comes first as flashes and brief rapture, but then becomes established as absorption into the One. The State of Intimacy gives total confidence, security and power to the wayfarer; but with it comes also risks. It can lead to taking on the colouring, but then confusing the colourings with the Essence; confusion as to who is subject and object can lead to heedlessness and immanence. Courtesy then comes into play, which is why it precedes Intimacy; putting these states into their proper condition keeps the outer bounds clear, while dissolving them in the inner reality that all returns to Allāh.

Twenty-Fifth Reflection Day:
Reflect on the three levels of certainty: The Eye of Certainty *'ayn al-yaqīn* عين اليقين Knowledge of Certainty *'ilm al-yaqīn* علم اليقين and Truth of Certainty *ḥaqq al-yaqīn* حق اليقين*

WEEK TWENTY SIX

5.47. The Door of Remembrance *(Bāb adh-Dhikr)* باب الذكر

وَاذْكُر رَّبَّكَ إِذَا نَسِيتَ

Wa adhkur Rabbaka idhā nasīt

'And remember your Lord if you had forgotten.' (*Qur'ān*, 18:24)

The Door of *dhikr* or Remembrance. Anṣārī talks about *dhikr* elsewhere, but again it is one of those Arabic words that can have different inflections.

*Ṭāhā, M. M. (1987) *The Second Message of Islam.* 1st ed. Trans. A. A. An-Na'im. Syracuse, New York: Syracuse University Press.

In an earlier context in Stage One, what he calls the Door of *tadhakkur* means memorising, recollection, Reflection or remembering. At the very earliest Stage your intonations and recollections and Reflections are acts of volition that are generated by your striving to remember—this is *tadhakkur.* This stage is the one wherein you are within the notion of Remembrance, rather than going through the process of remembering. There is no exertion involved, you are simply in that state. He defines Remembrance or *dhikr*, rather than *tadhakkur*, as to be free from the heedlessness of forgetting. Another condition which is seen more by subtraction than by addition is the *lā ilāha* part of the statement of *tawhīd—lā ilāha illa Allāh* (there is no deity but God). That is why we start with a negative, the state of forgetting.

The less you forget the more you remember. Like an equation. The decrease of heedlessness automatically leads to an increase of its opposite. Heedlessness is, in fact, non-existent in the inner realities, as darkness is non-existent in the inner reality, there is only light. The less Light you have, the less inner reality. Heedlessness in human beings has no existential reality. The Reality is Allāh and your Remembrance of Him. If you forget, it does not give any substance to your forgetfulness. It is a state of negation rather than a positive attitude. That is why the *shahāda* (testimony) starts with *lā ilāha.* It starts by negation because there is only Allāh and the less that you attribute existence to anything else, the more your knowledge becomes secure, the more proximate you become and the greater the intensity of your existence. The First Degree of outer Remembrance is to glorify and to supplicate. Hidden Remembrance is to be absorbed in witnessing and determined to persevere.

Anṣārī: Remembrance is to be freed from the heedlessness of forgetting by degrees:

1. Outer Remembrance is to glorify and to supplicate.
2. Hidden Remembrance is to be absorbed in witnessing and determined to persevere.
3. True Remembrance is to witness the Remembrance of Truth within you, to be liberated from seeing your own Remembrance, and knowing the conditionality of the one remembering while confirming their permanence in the Remembered.

The act of remembering itself, the condition of being in Remembrance of Allāh is, in the final stages, Remembrance of that which embraces existence in its entirety. The soul cannot forget its Creator but the self can displace its Remembrance. An illumined self can forget what is other-than-Truth, and thereby confirm its Remembrance. This type of forgetfulness is commendable for the wayfarer, as it always puts the Truth before all else. The more the Truth emerges the less other-than-Truth can have any consequence or significance. The Stages of *dhikr* are steps towards reaching the unveiling of seeing only the Truth within oneself. The realised self cannot accommodate two realities: there is only One Reality and Infinite conditional realities. One can acknowledge their conditionality and then use them as pointers to the One Reality but never give them their own independent reality. This sense of being impoverished, the realised self knows that it owns nothing and is in a state of absolute *faqr,* impoverishment, which is the next door.

5.48. The Door of Poverty *(Bāb al-Faqr)* باب الفقر

يَا أَيُّهَا النَّاسُ أَنتُمُ الْفُقَرَاءُ إِلَى اللَّهِ

Yā ayyuhan-nās antum ul-fuqarā'u ila Allāh

'O mankind, it is you who stand impoverished to Allāh.' (*Qur'ān*, 35:15)

Poverty is the denial of ownership, it is not to own anything, to deny the notion of ownership, which is the false notion in the spiritual realm. If you cannot own something, or if the idea of ownership does not arise, like living in a country where everything is leasehold, there is no freehold, so it does not occur to you that you can actually own something, some other landlord owns it, this is probably, irrespective of the lease terms or duration, which can be a billion years. Still, in the year 999 million, when the last second comes, you still do not own anything. Recognising that as an existential reality, as a truth, is very important for wayfarers, not for other people. Poverty of the ascetics (*az-zuhhād*) has three degrees: it is to abandon the world by not desiring or wanting to remain in it, keeping the tongue quiet, by neither praising or blaming the world and seeking safety by staying away from it.

This type of Poverty, of which much has been spoken, the Poverty of the ascetics, is the realisation that, no matter how much we apparently own, we do not own anything; it is all entrusted to us by the One Creator of all things. This Poverty is owning nothing, neither wanting anything, nor caring much for the worldly, while still caring about the world which has been entrusted to us as guardians (*khulafa'*). Imam Ali says, this is the Poverty of the *zuhhād*, it is not necessarily to own anything, but rather not to have anything own you. To see the signs of eternity in all the favours that one has received, leads you to not seeing your own hand behind your works and stops you from attributing to yourself your highest achievements, conditions and states. Thirdly, to see only the perfection in what has transpired, yielding into the Hand of the One and remaining within the circle of proximity. Anṣārī: Poverty is the denial of ownership or being the owner.

Poverty is of three degrees, to be considered one by one daily:

1. Poverty of the ascetics, which is to abandon the world by not desiring it or wanting to remain in it; keeping the tongue quiet by neither praising nor blaming the world; and seeking safety by staying away from it.
2. To see the signs of eternity in all the favours that one has received. This leads you to seeing not only your hand behind your works, but primarily that of God.
3. To see only the perfection in what has transpired, yielding to the Hand of the One, and revelling in remaining within the circle of proximity. This is the Poverty of the Sūfis.

The essence of the Poverty of the Sūfis is not to attribute any signs of ownership and acknowledging that the Owner and the Inheritor are One. Allāh is *Al-Wārith*. The rights of ownership are not ours and the condition of possessing anything or anyone simply does not arise. The elaborate rituals that we use to establish ownership are in reality struggles over illusory rights. They have only a conditional reality, an inferior and insubstantial one. In the realm of dealings and transactions, other rules apply, but the quality of one's dealings is immeasurably enhanced, ethically and in terms of personal enlightenment, if it is qualified by this knowledge—Allāh is the Owner and He is the Inheritor. Those on the highest rung of illumination simply dwell in a realm where the notion of possessing and owning is simply accepted as being the sole property of the One. Personal existence itself is a gift of the Owner so where does the right of ownership originate? Allāh is the One Who is the All-Wealthy, *Al-Ghanī Al-Mughni.*

Twenty-Sixth Reflection Day:
Invoke *Dhikr* on all the Names of Allāh you can remember; try to remember all of them by heart.

WEEK TWENTY-SEVEN

5.49. The Door of Wealth (*Bāb al-Ghinā*) باب الغِنَى

وَوَجَدَكَ عَائِلًا فَأَغْنَىٰ

Wa wajadaka 'ā'ilan fa aghnā

'And you were dependent and then He enriched you.' (*Qur'ān*, 93:8)

The Wealth of the heart is the lowest degree of realisation of Allāh as *Al-Ghanī.* It is liberation from seeing only causality, understanding only in terms of cause and effect. Acceptance of His Commands and its resulting freedom from seeing other than Him. That is the Heart. The Wealth of the self is to stand upright in front of what it truly desires and being spared from its own vanities. The Second Degree of Wealth has to do with one of the inner faculties that human beings have lost, the faculty of *wahm*, which is the faculty that gives true value to things.* The Wealthy self is the self that has true *wahm*, i.e. the ability to ascribe value to what is really important to that self. Lastly, Wealth by the Grace of the Truth has three aspects: His Remembrance of you, your enthralment by His Oneness and your victory by His Being.

Anṣārī: Wealth is the Name given to the Absolute Owner. It is of three degrees:

1. The Wealth of the heart, which is its unchaining from seeing only causality; acceptance of His Commands; and freedom from seeing other than Him.
2. The Wealth of the self, which is to stand upright in front of what it truly desires; and being spared from its own vanities.

*This term has been inverted in modern Arabic to mean its opposite, that is 'illusion'.

3. Wealth by Grace of the Truth. This has three aspects: His Remembrance of you; your enthralment by His Oneness; your victory by His Being.

The Wealth of the wayfarer is, in simple terms, their recognition and acknowledgement that the Owner, Fashioner and Inheritor is One. The state of plenitude and fullness can only therefore be associated with its Originator and not to some subsidiary reality. The greater the recognition the greater is one's spiritual Wealth.

5.50. The Door of Desired End *(Bāb al-Maqām al-Murād)*

باب المقام المراد

وَمَا كُنتَ تَرْجُو أَن يُلْقَىٰ إِلَيْكَ الْكِتَابُ إِلَّا رَحْمَةً مِّن رَّبِّكَ

Wa mā kunta tarjū an yulqā ilayka al-kitābu illā raḥmatam mir Rabbika

'You had not expected the Book to be delivered to you, were it not from a mercy from your Lord....' (*Qur'ān*, 28:86)

The last door is the Door or Desired End, *maqām al-murād.* We started this Stage with *qaṣd*, purposefulness. What ends are we seeking?

Anṣārī: They indicated the desired ones by pointing to the Desired End. It has three degrees:

1. To make the worshipper immune to wrongful acts and dispositions by banishing desires and blocking transgressions.
2. To turn the worshipper aside from seeing deficiencies in their actions and absolve them from blaming themselves, as was the case with the Prophet Moses when he threw down the tablets and admonished his brother Aaron. God did not chastise him.
3. To shield the worshipper by the Truth and to pass on more of Truth's Attributes, as in the case of the Prophet Moses when he carried fire to his people, which he had made for himself but kept its borrowed form for others.

The station of the Desired End is when the wayfarer begins to assume more of the Attributes of the Truth as is their higher purpose, in seeking proximity to the Truth and to be Its true reflection. The actions of the wayfarer might seem angry or even fierce, but they are protected by the state which they had reached. Anger becomes righteous anger for which there is only recognition and ferocity becomes passionate single-mindedness in redressing wrongful acts or transgressions. Alternatively, the Desired End might lead to utter peacefulness and serenity. Both are conditions that emanate from the same Source. The condition of the Prophet Moses is one of ferocity and righteous anger—driven by the Name of Majesty, *Jalāl*. The condition of the Prophet ʿIsa (Jesus) is of Love, tranquillity and repose—driven by the Name of Beauty, *Jamāl*.

The Desired End of the Stage of Origins is one that, Anṣārī says, is related to your own predilection, the way that the Names which are most emmanent in an individual are expressed in different grades with different quantities. If you have a Mosaic (Moses-like) temperament, then the Desired End would be one where you are seized by it, you become desirous and driven to campaign, write petitions, apply for grants or redress injustice and right the wrongs. If your constitution is more Isaic, Jesus-like, it will become more oriented towards service in a serene engagement with the Station of Proximity to the Absolute.

Abraham was in a different kind of state; he could see into people's hearts and conditions and was extremely agitated. He could see them in evil, in the absence of good. These kinds of insights that come to you, if they come to you, must be weighed against your own state and composition, so as not to stray too far from your natural predisposition. All the great beings have a certain flavour to their message. Solomon was able to manage the powers that exist in different realms, through the Solomonic powers bestowed upon him. There are certain individuals who have been given some degree of these assigned powers, which allow you to engage with beings that are of a different composition, comprehend and relate to them. These doors can open and have to be related to your own composition, condition and constitution.

Twenty-Seventh Reflection Day:

Suggested *Dhikr* for the Stage of Origins:

Al-Muqtadir (The Source of All Power) *Al-Mu'min* (The Bestower of Faith) *Al-Mughnī* (The Bestower of Wealth)

Yā Muqtadir ~ Yā Mu'min ~ Yā Mughnī يا مقتدر ~ يا مومن ~ يا مغني

6. The Stage of the Valleys (*Manzal al-Awdiya*)

منزل الأودية

The All Aware *Al-Khabīr* الخبير

The All Seeing *Al-Baṣīr* البصير

This Sixth Stage of the *Manāzil as-Sā'irīn* is entitled the Stage of the Valleys or *Manzal al-Awdiya*. Valleys are a recurrent theme in most of the literature of the inner way of *taṣawwuf.* They feature quite prominently in the Conference of the Birds, *Manṭaq at-Ṭayr*,* where the birds as they have assembled, move on to find the legendary King of Birds, the Simurgh. As they reach towards the end of their journey, the 30,000 who set out are reduced to only 30 as they enter into the final Stage of the spiritual adventure. *Si murgh* turns out to mean 30 birds. The journey is a constant theme of gradual, but relentless ascent, spiralling through the Valley of Annihilation, the Valley of Perplexity, the Valley of Love, Fear and Hope. The reason why they are called valleys is that they offer both an easy route, in the sense of being valleys within a range of mountains offering a relatively straightforward way through, but at the same time, roads along which one can be ambushed by those on top of the commanding heights.

The Stage of the Valleys has ten doors:

Anṣārī, on the Stage of the Valleys:

> This Stage is termed that of the Valleys since most of the aspects of journeying and appropriate conduct are undertaken within it. Exertions are recognised, as are the efforts of the intellect; but Satan also finds in it a playground…There are dangers and risks in this Stage…because of the prevalence of ambiguities for the mind. The plotting of Satan finds its foothold in it. And were it not for the divine support, the guidance of the law and the sacred proofs, most sojourners would have stayed in it without ever leaving...But Allāh guides with His Light whomever He wishes...*yehdi Allāha linūrihi mayyashā.*

The Stage of the Valleys is deceptive. The qualities of goodness, knowledge and so on are self-evidently commendable but many

---

*'Aṭṭār, F. al-D. (1974) *The conference of the birds: Mantiq ut-Tair: a philosophical religious poem in prose*. London: Routledge and Kegan Paul.

seekers become ensconced inside them, especially if they are expressed effortlessly and spontaneously. The self becomes satisfied with its achievements and assumes that it has reached its desired Stage of Awareness. In reality, these are all virtues with the possibility of opening the gateways to the Divine Presence, but if they are not seen as doorways to higher levels, then their true significance can be lost. As in everything else in the *Manāzil*, these are Halting Points, enough for the wayfarer to establish their features and qualities within themselves and then move on to other levels on the path of Oneness or *tawḥīd*. The first doorway is the Door of *Iḥsān*, Goodness, and he starts with the *āya*: '...Can the reward of goodness be other than good?' *Iḥsān* is a central element in *taṣawwuf.*

WEEK TWENTY-EIGHT

6.51. The Door of Goodness (*Bāb al-Iḥsān*) باب الإحسان

هَلْ جَزَاءُ الْإِحْسَانِ إِلَّا الْإِحْسَانُ

Hal jazā'ul-iḥsāni illal-iḥsān

'Can the reward of goodness be other than good?' (*Qur'ān*: 55:60).

Anṣārī: Goodness has been interpreted in the Ḥadīth '...To worship Allāh as if you were to see him', which is the act of witnessing. It has three degrees:

1. Goodness of purpose, by divining one's purpose with knowledge, by seeking it with firmness, and by purifying it.
2. Goodness in one's condition, which is to jealously safeguard it, cover its essence with integrity. And to correct it with verification.
3. Goodness in time, which is never to allow your witnessing to diminish, nor to dwell on your concerns, and to make a beacon of your journey to the Truth.

Goodness is a multifaceted word that encompasses all virtues. Allāh perceives people's acts. Therefore, it stands to reason that all one's acts must be driven by this knowledge which is the Good. Thus, purposefulness of Goodness becomes infused with the knowledge of the Truth, constrained by the courtesy that what comes from the Good is the property of the Good and not the person who is its carrier.

self-aggrandisement is banished with this knowledge, and acts of Goodness are not only meritorious in and of themselves, but also because they are reflective of the Good Itself. When one does good, or has the intention of doing good, then its importance on the road to unity is directly proportional to the certainty that the Source of the act and the intention rests in the Good—in God.

Valleys or *Awdiyā,* in the way of *Tasawwuf,* have both of these polar opposite aspects: the aspects of ease and the aspects of being ambushed. What does being ambushed mean in the context of these stations and stages? It is the ambush of the self that has not yet disconnected from its spatio-temporal, material moorings. The self is also reflected in the work of Satan, (*Shayṭān*). *Shayṭān* is both an external actor and an internal one who pulls you back to what is more comfortable, what is more secure and away from your goal. This stage is to do with being in a state of ease. Most of the states are doorways that some of us think we are already in, or in one way or another are no different from the normal ethical behaviour or conduct of individuals who are aspiring to the good. For example, Goodness, knowledge, wisdom, inner sight are all states that we believe we have in our daily existence if we are ethically minded people, but in the context of the spiritual journey they have a different dimension, a different meaning. They embody the commonly understood notions of goodness but they are also entrapments, because the self becomes content.

If you are a good person, a person with knowledge, not just outer but also inner, spiritual knowledge, if you behave with courtesy and wisdom and have a bit of insight into how others think and behave, and if from time to time you are inspired, you might think that these are conditions and states that are in fact commendable and should be nurtured and centred. That is true, to a point. You have to be established in them and then move on. These are progressive Stages which are hierarchical, like the rungs of a ladder. When you climb a ladder and use one of the rungs to climb up, you do not want to go back to the lower rungs. Establishing yourself in these states and conditions and then moving beyond them, using them as launch pads for the next phase in your journey is what these stages are all about. These are not static descriptions of individual states, which you may or may not have.

It is a dynamic process, the end goal of which is to be in the presence of oneness and to see oneness before, after, in and above all things.

Anṣārī makes the definition of Goodness part of a prophetic *Ḥadīth* which defines *iḥsān* as to worship Allāh as if you were to see Him, which is the act of witnessing and he says it has three degrees. The degree depends on your own level of accomplishment; the *iḥsān* of *qaṣd,* Goodness of purpose, he says is accomplished by divining one's purpose with knowledge, by seeking it with firmness and by purifying the intentions behind that purpose. *Iḥsān fi al-aḥwal,* the Second Degree, is Goodness in one's condition, jealously safeguarding it, covering its essence with integrity, and correcting it when necessary, with verification. Lastly, Goodness in time. By time he means Goodness in the sequence of states, not just the progression of time, that is never to allow your witnessing to diminish, not to dwell on your outer concerns, and to make your journey to the Truth a beacon to others, leading by example. Goodness or *iḥsān* is actually a multifaceted word which encompasses nearly all the virtues.

If you ask what is Sufism, Islamic Mysticism, or *Taṣawwuf,* it is *iḥsān*. This comes from the *Ḥadīth* of the Prophet, when he was asked by the Archangel Gabriel to define the *dīn* of *Islām*. What are the aspects of it? *Iḥsān* is one of the three:

Islām (Submission/Surrender)
Imān (Faith/belief)
Iḥsān (Goodness/improvement)

Iḥsān is the path of *Taṣawwuf,* the inner way that connects the outer rituals and jurisprudential aspects, with the inner path to Allāh. It is the bridge between the *Sharīʿa* and the *Ḥaqīqa*, and is the work of the *Tarīqa*. By its very nature it encompasses all the milestones on the way, which mark out the way itself. The way Anṣārī does that is as has been defined in the prophetic *Ḥadīth*. It is the state of the *ʿabd* (servant), the state of the person who is Witnessed by Allāh. The Act of Allāh Witnessing itself embodies the totality of Goodness. If you act with that knowledge, then it stands to reason that this kind of knowledge drives you to the good. So the purpose of good actions is to become infused with the knowledge in the heart of the Truth, constrained as they are by a degree of adequate courtesy. And everything that comes from the good is necessarily good. We partake in it as carriers, not as its originators.

On the path of Goodness one reflects some of God's Goodness. With this kind of knowledge that your Goodness is not due to your being somehow a more moral person, or more ethical, that definition of Goodness destroys the self-centredness associated with one thinking that he is a godly person, because the Origin and Source of it is elsewhere. Like all virtuous acts, in order to be tools and aids along the path of reaching a sense of Oneness, Goodness can only be so if they are seen to be emanating from the Origin, and knowledge of that element is essential when it comes to the second doorway. The Door of Goodness leads to the Door of Knowledge. Anṣārī defines it in very modern and scientific terms, although his knowledge is not scientific. He defines it: 'Knowledge rests on evidence and the removal of ignorance.' It sounds very much like Karl Popper in that it implies evidence-based empirical knowledge, testing hypotheses and theories, resulting in their verification or falsification.

6.52. The Door of Knowledge *(Bāb al-ʿIlm)* باب العلم

مِّنْ عِندِنَا وَعَلَّمْنَاهُ مِن لَّدُنَّا عِلْمًا

Min ʿindinā wa ʿallamnāhu milladunnā ʿilmā

'And to whom We from on high had brought Knowledge.' (*Qurʾān,* 18:65)

Khwāja Anṣārī, through his brilliant insight, has identified the nature of Knowledge well before the empiricists—the outer Knowledge which we all think is true, as it is based on evidence and testing, on verification or, more likely, falsification. We think of it as the basis of all the material world. It would be very hard to travel on an aeroplane, for example, which is not designed in accordance with this kind of Knowledge. If the engineers who have designed your aeroplane and built its engines decided that they will not use empirical evidence and theories or hypotheses that have been verified by evidence, you would not board that plane. Similarly, here the outer Knowledge is subject to outer evidence and outer observation and witnessing and that removes the veil of ignorance. There are three degrees of Knowledge, according to Anṣārī:

Firstly, clear knowledge that is obtained by sensory evidence, a correct deduction, or established verifiable procedure and routine, using deduction rather than induction in terms of establishing the coherence and veracity of the process of confirming knowledge. That is, you go from the particular to the general. To him spiritual evidence is based on an accumulation of confirmable experiential encounters, rather than from a grand theory; as there was no grand theory of the soul, it is evidence that is painstakingly accumulated. Of course, in the real world, the painstaking part of it can be instantaneous, especially if you have the second or third degree of Knowledge. The Second Degree of Knowledge is Hidden Knowledge that emanates from spiritual Exercises and righteous actions, as manifested in one's inner Secrets. It is a Knowledge that reveals what is hidden, or absent and gathers in what is scattered.

This type of Knowledge and common experience is a Knowledge associated with ecstatic states, in which the constraints of reason fall away. These can happen in certain instances during Devotions, where a kind of Certainty emerges, through the dissolution of the bounds of containment. The Third Degree of Knowledge is the Highest Knowledge. It is top-down Knowledge from on high and its proof is very Presence itself. That is why you cannot speak about it. Awareness of it is to know its truth, with no veil between it and the witness. This is a type of Knowledge that is given to very few people, mainly to Realised Beings, such as Prophets, *awliya,* Imams and Saints. One cannot really prove it, as they will not speak of it.

That level of Knowledge is without veils or ambiguities. This is one of the key propositions in *Taṣawwuf*, that the entire scheme has within it a sense of hierarchy. You have to understand that there are these Degrees of Knowledge and that there are barriers between them. That is, you cannot use your empirical knowledge, your knowledge of the First Degree, to suddenly understand the nature of Knowledge of the Third Degree. You have to be prepared, conditioned, moulded, to be receptive. The kind of knowledge that we think of as the only one that makes sense of the material world is, according to the hierarchy of Knowledge in *taṣawwuf*, of the lowest degree. It is the knowledge that comes from empirical evidence and sensory experience. It is not knowledge that you have to throw out the window, simply because there are other grades. This is an essential form of knowledge if you want to deal with the world. You cannot deal with the world if you are constantly in an ecstatic state—it does not work. We should not therefore, denounce it or denigrate knowledge. *Taṣawwuf* does not imply the complete denial of the rules of the outer world which are governed by outer knowledge.

Anṣārī: Knowledge rests on evidence and the removal of ignorance in three degrees:

1. Clear Knowledge that is obtained by sensory evidence, or a correct deduction or established verifiable routine.
2. Hidden Knowledge that emanates from spiritual exercises and righteous actions and is manifested in one's inner secret. It is a Knowledge that reveals what is hidden, absents the witness and gathers in what is scattered.
3. Knowledge from on high; its proof is its very presence, being aware of it is to know its truth, with no veil between it and the witnesser.

It has its own truth, but it is circumscribed by higher forms of Knowledge, which empiricism, almost by definition, cannot understand. The second form of Knowledge can be derived not only from these special states but also from action that is driven by ethical purpose. This model introduces the idea of a dynamic framework for Knowledge. Here you cannot divorce knowing from acting. So you cannot be a knowledgeable person if you do not act upon it. You can theoretically be a good person, but if it is not experienced through action, through interaction, then it becomes inert. It is something that has potential kinetic energy, because the highest form of Knowledge is entirely by *luṭf* (subtlety); it is not something that you can work on or strive for. It is the one that comes to us by hurling into a receptive vehicle. This is a Knowledge of Prophets and realised beings, which is why it cannot be subject to proof because its source is the unknown. Knowing that is a form of wisdom itself, which brings us to the third doorway, the Door of Wisdom.

Twenty-Eighth Reflection Day:

Contemplate the different levels of knowledge present in your life: how and whether you know certain things to be true, what is purely conjecture, how you learned to do your work, what do you simply know intuitively? What is received wisdom, where or who does it come from? Are there certain things you have always believed to be true or taken for granted? Is it time to examine certain assumptions for veracity? Are your opinions being challenged by further evidence? Are they allowed to be? What would you like to know more about? What is the knowledge you are seeking and which questions do you need to ask?

WEEK TWENTY-NINE

6.53. The Door of Wisdom (*Bāb al-Ḥikma*) باب الحكمة

يُؤْتِي الْحِكْمَةَ مَن يَشَاءُ ۚ وَمَن يُؤْتَ الْحِكْمَةَ فَقَدْ أُوتِيَ خَيْرًا كَثِيرًا ۗ وَمَا يَذَّكَّرُ إِلَّا أُولُو الْأَلْبَابِ

Yu'tī al-ḥikmata may-yashā waman yu'tal-ḥikma faqad awtīya khayran kathīran wamā yadhakkaru illā ulul-albāb

'He grants wisdom to whomsoever He Wills and he to whom wisdom is granted has been granted abundant good.' (*Qur'ān*, 2:269)

Anṣārī's definition of Wisdom is extremely profound and succinct. Wisdom is the name given to the rules of placing things in their appropriate places. Very simple, true and deep. To know where to place things is not that difficult; to know where to place things appropriately is sometimes more difficult. The wise person does not go beyond their limits, nor do they usurp the rights of others, or try to rush things into being. The element of appropriateness must always be there. As that becomes embedded in your spiritual DNA, you begin to see the Wisdom in all of the actions, in the sense of seeing the perfected outcome of all your actions and the actions of the world around you. You see behind them and ahead of them God's Will, Bounty and Subtlety (*lutf*).

Wisdom has three degrees to be considered one per day for the next three days:

1. To give each thing its due measure, not to exceed its limits or to hasten its being.

2. To see the Truth of Allāh Most High in His Promises, to know His Justice in His Commands, and notice His Righteousness in His Constrictiveness.
3. To reach inner sight whenever you deliberate, to utilise the truth in your advice, and to achieve your purpose whenever you allude to matters.

Wisdom is also to see God's Bounty and Mercy in all Actions and to see the Hidden Hand of Truth behind all states, stations and movements. Allāh says: '...For all you know, you may hate something and it is good for you; For all you know you may love something and it is harmful to you' (2:216). Modesty in knowing the bounds of Wisdom is itself a form of Wisdom. If you recognise the limits of your capacity, and that your wisdom is not overarching, does not embrace everything, and that you are not necessarily wise in each matter, this gives you a sense of proportion and humility. The Third Degree of Wisdom is where the discerning faculty, the capability within a person to exhibit Wisdom, merges with inner sight, the next doorway, which subsumes all other forms of wisdom and has another range of qualities.

6.54. The Door of Inner Sight (*Bāb al-Baṣīra*) باب البصيرة

قُلْ هَٰذِهِ سَبِيلِي أَدْعُو إِلَى اللَّهِ ۚ عَلَىٰ بَصِيرَةٍ أَنَا وَمَنِ اتَّبَعَنِي

Qul hādhihi sabīli ad'ū ila Allāhi 'alā baṣīratin ana waman attab'ani

'This is my way. I call to Allāh, clear-sighted—I and those who follow me.' (*Qur'ān*, 12:108)

Inner Sight contains the elements of wisdom, covers it and goes beyond it. It differs from Insight, which is an onrush that allows you to see things in a flash. Inner Sight is the reverse of outer sight. As you need eyes to see the outer world, you need inner eyes to see the inner world that is hidden from outer sight. Anṣārī says that Inner Sight is what saves you from perplexity, *ḥayra*, which is an earlier station. When you see an entirely new landscape, you can immediately take in its shapes, contours and major features. Outer sight gives you that ability. Inner Sight does the same, but gives a more complete picture by showing you, at least intuitively or theoretically, that there is a spiritual reality behind all matter and revealing something of a story of how things may have come to be the way they are. Rather than being confused by what you see, or falling into uncertainty, you can see with a higher degree of clarity and sharpness, and the perplexity of being in an entirely unknown landscape or strange and incomprehensible universe is removed.

From time to time in his Stations, Anṣārī brings us back to one aspect which we may forget or not give due weight or credence to, which is that you have to be anchored in the law, to come back to the *sharī'a*. Without devotional practices and commitment to the sacred law, the whole process becomes at best theoretical or self-serving, at worst illusory or in danger of drifting into delusion, falling into the elaborate traps of the *nafs*. This path is a complete package and, although you can read Ibn'Arabi without reference to *sharī'a*, it will be an incomplete and insufficient reading and naturally impracticable. Anṣārī throws out these reminders to stop people from believing that they can create their own rules of the game. Inner Sight requires you to know that the manifestations of the *sharī'a* emanate from an unerring Source, and that you relish its Certainty and safeguard it with alacrity.

You might ask, 'What kind of *sharī'a*? Whose interpretation?' To embark on a path of enlightenment requires some outer bounds and constraints, and the constraints and this path are that of the Muḥammadan *sharī'a*. All paths are perfect at Source as they have their Origin in the One and are brought to humanity by realised beings through Divine Inspiration and Guidance. After the demise of their guiding Prophets and Imams, however, the message invariably becomes corrupted and the more their original sources become interpreted by fallible human being. Even though they may be great scholars with the best of intentions to guide and teach people in the best possible way, corruption sets in when elements and groups start using their pure teaching for political ends and with power-driven agendas. In light of this knowledge, derived from many historic and contemporary examples, these questions are relevant and justified.

The development of Inner Sight may help the wayfarer to discern more accurately and effectively which translations of the *Qur'ān* remain truest to the original Arabic, which interpretations uncover more of the meanings and which *Ḥadith* collections are most reliable in contextualising jurisprudential inferences and transfer them with greater understanding to our contemporary contexts with least ideological contaminations. As the eye of the heart opens to Inner Sight you will find the least sectarian, most balanced, forgiving and moderate rulings ring truer than the extremely strict, exclusivist ones. This does not mean opting for the path of least resistance or doing the bare minimum in terms of practice. On the contrary, often the harshest, more literalist interpretations are the most minimalistic in practice, content with the basic five obligatory pillars, while the more flexible, inclusive and perhaps lenient rulings tend to call for more ascetic practices and maximising *sunnah* prayers and *dhikr*.

Anṣārī: Inner Sight is what saves you from perplexity in the following three degrees:

1. To know that the manifestation of the *shariʿa* emanates from an inerrant Source, and that you relish its certainty and safeguard it with alacrity.
2. To witness the justice in the guidance that comes from the Truth, to witness righteousness in its diversity, and to draw close to it as a means of reaching the Divine Presence.
3. Inner Sight that overwhelms knowledge, confirms the signs from the unseen, and from which grows clairvoyance.

Contrary to what some might believe, Inner Sight is not possible without constraining oneself by the Commands of the Sacred Law. The acts of devotion and affirmation of oneness are a necessary requirement in the launching stage of achieving Inner Sight. They are the anchor for the maturation of Inner Sight. In the Second Degree of the evolution of Inner Sight is the ability to see the perfection in all the manifestations of diversity that are a feature of creation. Behind them all are the actions of the One. The full flowering of Inner Sight is when the person affirms continuously the presence of oneness, beyond signs, symbols or evident knowledge. At that point, everything dissolves. To get to that point you have to know where you came from. You do not reach your sanctuary on a leaky craft. The Door of Inner Sight leads to the doorway of spiritual acumen, the Door of Clairvoyance.

Twenty-Ninth Reflection Day:

He was manifested from the water of Maryam
And the breath of Jibrīl in the form of man existing from clay.
The spirit was in essence purified of nature which it called prison
For that reason, the spirit stayed in it
For more than a thousand years in the designation of time.
A spirit from Allāh no other
For that reason, he revived the dead and formed the bird from clay.
Since his relation with his Lord is proven
By it he has effective action in both the higher and the lower worlds.
Allāh purified his body, and made his spirit pure, and He made him a model of taking-form.*

Dhikr: Yā Laṭīf Yā Ḥalīm Yā Ḥakīm يا لطيف يا حليم يا حكيم

WEEK THIRTY

6.55. The Door of Clairvoyance *(Bāb al-Firāsa)* باب الفراسة

إِنَّ فِي ذَٰلِكَ لَآيَاتٍ لِّلْمُتَوَسِّمِينَ

Inna fī dhālika lāyāti lil-mutawassimīn

'In this are signs for those who scrutinise and reflect.' (*Qur'ān*, 15:75)

Anṣārī defines Clairvoyance as having the spiritual acumen to reach a decisive conclusion without sensory confirmation or relying on testing and experimentation. It is an ultra-modern understanding of very subtle realities, far ahead of his time. He thinks that Clairvoyance (*firāsa*) does not happen to the ordinary adept. He says that many times, not only here but elsewhere. The lowest degree of Clairvoyance is sudden and infrequent; it might occur once in a lifetime, asserting itself because of the dire need of the seeker for it and for its benefit. If you are a sincere seeker, sometimes you need the aid of the unseen as a matter of emergency. This is when it can happen to you; without necessarily knowing why, you suddenly experience a clarity of vision that may become Clairvoyance. You may make a decision that turns out to be spot on which has no relationship, he says, to the knowledge

* Ibn al-'Arabī (1980) *The Seals of Wisdom*. Norwich: Diwan.

or insight of that person. You just get it when you need it. You may not have needed it, but when you need it, you will get it.

The Second Degree of Clairvoyance is that which appears from the depths of truth, the vigour of one's state, and shines with the light of unveiling. This happens to many people, even to those who are not that far advanced on the spiritual path. The capabilities of reaching inner Sight are much greater now than they were perhaps a thousand years ago. While some forms of Clairvoyance have retreated and degraded, by and large the insight of people on the path of realisation now can quickly generate and increase this capability. There is some evidence of its prevalence in the seventh century in this prophetic saying: 'Be wary of the Clairvoyance of a true believer for they speak with true insight.'

The Third Degree of *firāsa*, is where you actually see into things, and the spiritual reality behind them, all the time. Independently of your sight, speech or physical hearing, you can see into the hearts of people.

That power, of course, can be abused. Some people have the capacity to see, with mesmerising eyes, into your soul. That power of Clairvoyance can also have a very dark side and this is one of the tricks of these gateways, where the self or Satan can gain or give this power without the responsibilities and constraints that must necessarily accompany them. Many people have abused that power and you can see results of it around the world. For example, Reverend Jim Jones manipulated 800 people into committing mass suicide in Guyana in 1979. He apparently had this very powerful way of psychically drilling into people. He had *firāsa*, but in diabolical form. One blessed with that capacity has to manage it with great care, skill, responsibility and reticence so that it does not hurt or frighten people, which is why we need all the other doors and stages to balance with ethical qualities and safeguards (Steiner said that for every step we take spiritually, we should take ten morally).

According to Anṣārī, Clairvoyance has three degrees:

1. A sudden and infrequent Clairvoyance that might occur once in a lifetime, asserting itself because of the dire need of the seeker in a

particular moment. This has no relation to the knowledge or insight of the person.

2. A Clairvoyance that appears from the depth of faith, invigorates one's state and shines with the light of unveiling.
3. A secret Clairvoyance that is independent of sight, speech, hearing or allusion.

Clairvoyance requires no proof or evidence. It is a quality that enters into the heart and clarifies the spiritual reality behind things to ascertain their purpose and meaning. For many, such a state can descend on one only in times of dire need and is thus most uncommon, unless their need increases. As the spiritual condition of the wayfarer grows, Clairvoyance and Clairaudience develop accordingly, occur more frequently and become almost second nature. The wayfarer sees with an astute vision that ought to make those who are subject to the wayfarer's Clairvoyance cautious of what they hold in their heart. At the highest level of attainment, the Clairvoyance of the wayfarer is established as an essential characteristic of their person. It melds imperceptibly with the other qualities and virtues and the wayfarer no longer needs any prompting—by vision, sound or speech—to understand the purport and direction of phenomena.

6.56. The Door of Exaltation *(Bāb at-Taʿẓīm)* باب التعظيم

مَّا لَكُمْ لَا تَرْجُونَ لِلَّهِ وَقَارًا

Mā lakum lā tarjūna lillāhi waqāran

'Why are you not in awe of Allāh's Majesty?' (*Qur'ān*, 71:13)

The best antidote to any abuse of power is Exaltation, as it acknowledges, affirms and recognises that there is no power independent of or other than the All-Powerful, *al-Qawī*. This awareness may bring you back from the edge to which *firāsa* can take you. It is also very important to know that through *tāʿẓīm*, by exalting Allāh and His Attributes and Qualities you are, by implication, reducing or shrinking the space for the lower self or an outer diabolical force to take over your being. Consciousness of God's Exaltation prompts one's abasement, *tadhallul* in front of a greater force, rather than a sense of your own worthlessness. Once you recognise that your self-worth is linked to a Higher Source, then the nature of abasement changes. By its very nature, *tāʿẓīm* of the

Attributes and Qualities of Allāh pulls you back to the medium path of modesty and moderation.

Anṣārī: Knowledge of Exaltation of Allāh implies one's own abasement in front of it. Exaltation has three degrees; try to experience one each day:

1. Exaltation of the Commands and Prohibitions by not opposing them with barely acceptable justifications, or dishonouring them through excessive zeal or placing on them impossible conditions.
2. Exaltation of the Commands from those who wish to distort or replace them and to defend them with knowledge.
3. Exaltation of the Truth so that you affirm that there is no cause, reality or choice apart from the One.

Exaltation necessarily leads to holding to the median path. The wayfarer seeks no excuse, even when allowed, to distort the intent of the Commands and Prohibitions. It is the path of prudence and caution when it comes to divining the intent of the One. When this principle is applied to the broader realities beyond the self, it is not to confuse apparent benefits or licence with the intent of the law. For example, the prohibition on intoxication does not give one the right to consume intoxicants below the point of drunkenness. Another example is if you say that pork meat was banned because it has been proven scientifically that it has parasites, that is not the point. It is not your job to justify them. Your job is to understand them in a way that is commonly accepted, even if there seems to be justification for limiting or altering Commands.

Yet another example is foregoing prayer because of the difficulties of praying in an office context, then it would not even register with the wayfarer's resolve. The command is not subject to time and place. You cannot say, 'Well, I'm in an office environment, and if I start praying, people will point at me and it will become a sore point of contention.' You can always retreat to a corner or do it in a different form. You may have the licence to do this but exalting the Command for prayer means that you give it priority over the circumstances. You do not have to make a hue and cry about it or do it in an exhibitionistic way, but you have to understand that there is a priority, that there are certain aspects of it that cannot be wished away. Do it in ways that cause minimum disruption and reaction.

Thirtieth Reflection Day:

'The sun with loving light makes bright for me each day, the soul with spirit power gives strength unto my limbs. In sunlight shining clear I revere, Oh God, the strength of humankind, which thou has planted in my soul, that I with all my might, may love to work and learn. From thee stream light and strength to thee rise love and thanks.'

— Verse by Rudolf Steiner

'Whoever seeks higher knowledge must create it for themselves. They must instil it into their soul. It cannot be done by study; it can only be done through life. Whoever, therefore, wishes to become a student of higher knowledge must assiduously cultivate this inner life of devotion. Everywhere in their environment and experiences they must seek motives of admiration and homage. If I meet a man and blame him for his shortcomings, I rob myself of power to attain higher knowledge; but if I try to enter lovingly into his merits, I gather such power. The student must continually be intent upon following this advice. The spiritually experienced know how much they owe to the circumstance that in face of all things they ever again turn to the good, and withhold adverse judgement. But this must not remain an external rule of life; rather it must take possession of our innermost soul.'*

WEEK THIRTY-ONE

6.57. The Door of Inspiration (*Bāb al-Ilhām*) باب الإلهام

قَالَ الَّذِي عِندَهُ عِلْمٌ مِّنَ الْكِتَابِ أَنَا آتِيكَ بِهِ قَبْلَ أَن يَرْتَدَّ إِلَيْكَ طَرْفُكَ

Qāl alladhi ʿindahu ʿilmummin al-kitābi ana ātīka bihi qabla an yartadda ilayka tarfuk

'Said one who had Knowledge of the Book: "I shall bring it to you before you blink your eye".' (*Qurʾān*, 27:4)

Next door is a doorway of *ilhām*, or Inspiration. Anṣārī says that Inspiration is the state of those who are advanced on the path. It is

* Steiner, R. & Collison, H. (1937) *Knowledge of the Higher Worlds and its Attainment: a Revised and Enlarged Edition of 'The way of Initiation' with 'Initiation and its Results'*. 3rd. ed. / Authorised English translation by G. Metaxa / Edited by H. Collison. S.l: Rudolf Steiner Publishing Co.

above the state of clairvoyance, which may occur only rarely, and its expression could trouble the wayfarer. Inspiration, on the other hand, can only occur if one is on a firm foundation. He divides it into three categories. The lowest form of Inspiration is one deriving from a live source confirmed by hearing or not. He has a tendency, perhaps partly due to his Ḥanbali environment, to be very strict and *sharīʿa* minded in many ways and sometimes he gives a physical understanding of what could be subtler realities, but here he has a very strong point when he does that. When he talks about his own Inspiration coming from a live source, he actually means that a source outside the person can provide Inspiration. It can be an individual, a sound, movement or an onrush. You can confirm it or not but it is an external source acting on the individual. It has three degrees:

1. Inspiration deriving from a live source, confirmed by hearing or not.
2. Inspiration from a visual source, as long as it does not cross barriers or bounds.
3. Inspiration that comes from the heart of verification and speaks with the authority of eternity.

Inspiration in the spiritual realm is the onrush that cuts out all uncertainty and establishes the truth of a matter. It is a subtle energy that galvanises the self and overwhelms the intellect. A true Inspirational Onrush such as a *khātir* (flash) or *wārid* (an inflow) are among the most common forms of Inspiration, and preserve the limits and boundaries of the natural world and *sharīʻa.* For example, it could never abrogate the scale of measurement nor push the person into committing what would normally be considered transgressions. At the highest level of realisation, Inspiration becomes established in the person and becomes a state of permanent unveiling—in which the thing and its essence are experienced or seen simultaneously.

The highest form of Inspiration comes from the heart of verification and speaks with the authority of eternity. In the spiritual realm, when you say that you are inspired, what it really means is that it removes uncertainty. It is not necessarily that you are inspired to create high works of literature or composition, but rather that you cut out uncertainty in your actions, thus establishing the truth of the matter. Inspiration may also come from visual sources, as long as it does not cross barriers or bounds. If it does, then that inspiration is false. That is why the Stage of Valleys has in it this element of trickery. True Inspiration can never push you into doing something that is in itself a transgression. It is good to dwell in this valley for some time because it is a very important tool for weighing and measuring the outer world. Events seen with the light of inner sight take on a different dimension, because you remove yourself from the daily hurly-burly.

If you are in the middle of a battle, for example, you are too busy trying to maintain your balance and defend yourself. As you move up, the whole thing takes on a different dimension and its true meaning becomes evident to you. If you are sitting on top of a mountain looking down at people fighting and shouting at each other, you are situating them in a broader context. That state allows you to deal with the outer world in a much more effective way and to weigh and measure things properly, so do not get carried away by events; whether they are the Arab Spring or the war on Palestine or in Sudan, you see in them the cycle of long duration, in which their meaning manifests itself. That gives you serenity, which is the next doorway.

6.58. The Door of Serenity (*Bāb as-Sakīna*) باب السكينة

هُوَ الَّذِي أَنزَلَ السَّكِينَةَ فِي قُلُوبِ الْمُؤْمِنِينَ

Huwallathī anzala as-sakīnata fi qulūb il-mu'minīn

'It is He who sent down the spirit of Serenity into the hearts of the believers.' (*Qur'ān*, 48:4)

Unusually Anṣāri gives no definition. He has from time to time, a tendency to materialise what seems to be a subtler reality, and he does that here with Serenity, *sakīna.* He specifically relates the first level of Serenity to the experience of the Israelites who came from the Ark (*at-tabūt*). It is very unusual to see a definition of how a subtle reality is somehow embodied in what seems to be an outer force, but he does see it and gives room for the physical embodiment of Serenity. He says that the Serenity the Israelites were given in their Ark, was akin to a breeze with a human visage, and he seems to mean that quite literally, not metaphorically. For their prophets it is a miracle; for Josef and Jacob—for their kings—a sign of impending victory. It puts fear into the hearts of their enemies, when a mighty and terrifying sound emanates as the Israelites face them in battle.

For us who have become distant from these times and think that our minds and perspectives have evolved, we cannot conceptualise the reality of a breeze with a human face on it. It becomes more difficult to accept this specific interpretation, but as you reach back to the axial prophetic Age, these events took place with far greater recurrence, and we should not be that dismissive. We think a subtler reality supposedly cannot have external aspects to it.

The Second Degree of Serenity is what emanates from the tongues of those who have their veils removed. It is not something belonging to them, but one of the subtle Graces of the Truth. It imparts wisdom to the tongues of realised ones and is the breeze that transported revelation to the hearts of the prophets. Anṣārī visualises that when the Archangel Gabriel imparted the revelation, the breath that came out of him was the breath of Serenity. It allows the realised ones to speak with the tongues of truth and the eye of certainly, preserving the inner secrets while exposing the false or dubious one.

The Third Degree of Serenity is a breeze that descended on the heart of the Prophet and the hearts of the believers. It combines light, force and spirit. It has a set of components which create the conditions in which the fearful ones are becalmed, the sorrowful or angry ones consoled, and the transgressing repulsive and prideful ones are contained. It is also possible to appear serene, while suffering inner turbulence and conversely to be internally serene while dealing with external turmoil. He then goes on to discuss the other type of Serenity with which we would feel more familiar or comfortable, which is metaphysical Serenity.

Anṣārī: [unusually, Anṣārī has no definition]. The spirit of Serenity is of three degrees:

1. The Serenity of humility when one performs devotional duties with presence and exaltation.

2. The Serenity from correct deeds and transactions when the self is made accountable for its actions in dealing with creation and the Truth.
3. The Serenity out of which grows contentment with what one has been allotted. This Serenity did not descend except on Prophets, Imams and Saints *awliyā'*.

Metaphysical Serenity is an aspect of spiritual dignity that is often the mark of the realised ones and is the shine that derives from this last form of Serenity. Anṣārī understands Serenity as an active agent in the world. It is not an intangible state that is associated with the spiritual condition of the wayfarer, as it may now be obtainable through sincere striving—due to the evolution of consciousness. Rather, it is a specific force from the subtle realities and takes different expressions with different groups. His *sakīna* includes the Hebraic *shakina* and is probably the same force that aided Constantine during his battle to bring Christianity into the Byzantine world. Anṣārī clearly affirms the continuity of this force which came with the prophetic experience. We, however, are unlikely to see the Third Degree of Serenity, as we tend to strive for more or other than our lot, but the metaphysical one—the Serenity of spiritual dignity—may be in reach.

Thirty-First Reflection Day:

Read, recite, and reflect upon this affirmation(*du'ā*) of Abraham from *Qur'ān*, 26:78-81:

Alladhī khalaqanī fahuwa yehdīni — ٱلَّذِي خَلَقَنِي فَهُوَ يَهْدِينِ
He Who Created me will Guide me
Walladhī huwa yut'imunī wa yaskīni — وَٱلَّذِي هُوَ يُطْعِمُنِي وَيَسْقِينِ
And He Who Feeds me Gives me water
Wa idha mariḍtu fahuwa yashfīni — وَإِذَا مَرِضْتُ فَهُوَ يَشْفِينِ
And if I am ill He Heals me
Walladhi yumītunī thumma yuhhyīni — وَٱلَّذِي يُمِيتُنِي ثُمَّ يُحْيِينِ
And He Who Causes me to die Gives me Life.

WEEK THIRTY-TWO

6.59. The Door of Assuredness (*Bāb aṭ-Ṭama'nīna*) باب الطَمأنينة

يَا أَيَّتُهَا النَّفْسُ الْمُطْمَئِنَّةُ

...Yā ayatuhan nafs ul-muṭma'inna

'O self at peace.' (*Qur'ān*, 89:27)

Assuredness is a degree of evolution of the self in the spectrum of the self which you may have come across before in the cosmology of *taṣawwuf* and is briefly described in the introductory chapter. You start with the lowest self, the commanding self, *an-Nafs al-Ammāra;* then you move up to the blaming self, *an-Nafs al-Lawwāma*; to the inspired self, *an-Nafs al-Mulhama;* and then to the self that is at peace, secure, and assured, *an-Nafs al-Muṭma'inna;* then the contented self, *an-Nafs ar-Rāḍiya;* and finally to the self with which Allāh is Contented *an-Nafs al-Marḍīya*. There is a spectrum which you can often find yourself moving along in either direction, and if you reach that point of *Marḍīya*, you are quite high on the dial, with only *kamāl* (completion) beyond. Anṣārī says Assuredness is serenity understood in the sense of spiritual dignity and is strengthened by true security.

Even the Prophet (Pubh) went through periods when there was a lull in the revelatory experience and he became very agitated; that was when the *surat ad-Ḍuḥā* and *al-Inshiraḥ* descended, which reassured him. Assuredness occurs at different levels up to the type of Assuredness and certainty experienced by prophets, saints, *awliya'* and by the ancients. On the other hand, Anṣāri says: 'Assurance of the self by the remembrance of Allāh is the assurance of one who is scared, needy or afflicted, knowing that their condition will only be alleviated by recourse to the One.' You do not ignore your condition, but you know that you have a solution to it.

The Second Degree is Assuredness of the soul and its purpose of unveiling is desire for what is promised and drive to be in-gathered. Thirdly, Assuredness on seeing the subtle presences, knowing that in-gatheredness is the way to eternal being.

Anṣārī: Assuredness is serenity strengthened by true security. There are two main differences between it and serenity:

Firstly, serenity can be sudden and can lead to becalming while Assuredness is a secure presence in which the self can find repose.

Secondly, serenity can be itinerant with the person, while Assuredness is established and irremovable. It has three degrees:

1. Assuredness of the self by the remembrance of Allāh is the Assuredness of one who is scared, needy or afflicted, knowing that their condition will be alleviated by recourse to The One.
2. Assuredness of the soul in its purpose of unveiling, its desire for what is promised and in its drive to be in-gathered.
3. Assuredness when seeing the subtle presences, knowing that in-gatheredness is the way to eternal being.

Assuredness is a higher form of certainty and serenity because it is a permanent condition inside the wayfarer, independent of external conditions, not subject to itinerant inner and outer fluctuations. It is also *sui generis*, in the sense that it is an established inner condition rather than one emerging from an external force. It is therefore more stable than *sakina* for the wayfarer. Assuredness is the necessary condition of the self as it reaches the highest level of realisation as it gives you a sure footing and a firm basis. It is the spiritual nuclear force that connects the opposites: fear and hope, expansion and contraction, beginning and end. It is the force that takes over after the subtler realities are revealed. It is the force that connects the drive of the soul to be with the eternal presence, in balance with modesty or self-effacement. It is the force that reconciles opposites.

6.60. The Door of Resolve *(Bāb al-Himma)* باب الهمّة

مَا زَاغَ الْبَصَرُ وَمَا طَغَىٰ

Ma zāgha al-basaru wa mā taghā

'The eye neither veered nor overreached.' (*Qur'ān*, 53:17)

Lastly, the Door of *himma*, Resolve, Concern or Diligence. Anṣārī says Resolve or *himma* is the force that propels the believer towards the goal without let up. It is a relentless force that pushes you on and on toward resolution. It has three degrees: Resolve or *himma* that fortifies the heart in dwelling in Annihilation and pushes it to desire to remain there eternally. The Second Degree is a Resolve that pushes one away from Immersion in causes, towards work, trust and hope. Thirdly, Resolve that lifts one beyond states and conditions, away from Attributes and towards Essence. Spiritual Solicitude, Diligence, Concern and Resolve—all these words are insufficient to translate *himma*—are the ever present drive of the true wayfarer that keeps you going, pushes you harder and harder and steers you away from what is transient and temporary towards what is permanent and true.

Anṣārī: Resolve is the force that propels the believer toward the goal without let up. Resolve or Solicitude is of three degrees:

1. Resolve that fortifies the heart in dwelling in annihilation and pushes it to desire to stay in The Eternal.
2. Resolve that pushes one away from immersion in causes and towards work and trust in hope.
3. Resolve that lifts one beyond states and conditions and away from Attributes towards Essence.

As you progress that force also changes its nature like a stagecoach moving through different landscapes as you travel from one valley to the next, from one *Manzal* to the next. You have only one goal which is the Truth in front of you and so you ride roughshod over everything else—the tricks of the self, the enjoyment of these states and conditions. These states in themselves can be very pleasant to dwell in. It is an ever striving force that channels your spiritual energies towards the permanent and real. Obstacles and impediments vanish and the drive towards the One is relentless. It is the Newtonian force that pushes you on and on, like a force applied to a body without friction. If there is no friction, the body will continue forever. The stronger the force, the more it can overcome friction. Friction in this context is all the distractions and tricks of the *nafs*. The force of *himma* drives relentlessly onward. Once you remove the *himma* you tend to stop, as there is nothing completely frictionless.

Thirty-Second Reflection Day:

Suggested *Dhikr* for the Stage of Valleys

Al-'Alī (The Most High) *Al-'Alīm* (The All-Knower) *Al-Ḥakīm.* (The All-Wise)

Yā 'Alī ~ Yā 'Alīm ~ Yā Ḥakīm يا علي ~ يا عليم ~ يا حكيم

Wasṭ Al-Manāzil—Beyond the Halfway Point—Golden Section—وسط المنازل

The first part of the book focuses on our selves—our true state and condition—to ascertain whether we are fit to embark on the journey. Like a mountaineer, the scaling does not commence at base camp: it begins with months, if not years of preparation. The prerequisites for embarking on the journey are to shed as much as possible the accoutrements of a sensibility mired in the material and the physical. This, in short, is the sensibility that does not or cannot see or experience the actions of the unseen in the landscape of time and space, or cause and effect. It is the absence of the sacred in our everyday lives, perhaps even in spite of repetitious cycles of devotion and rituals. Even before we try to scale the heights, we have to have the predisposition, or taste, for this type of endeavour. Otherwise, the entire exercise is pointless. The wayfarer is thus a person who has already prepared themselves for this task and is willing to take the plunge.

The Stage of the Preliminaries is a prerequisite that prepares us for Anṣārī's Stages. When seen in the light of their sequencing, the *Manāzil* begin to form a whole picture as to the purpose and direction of this journey. The following is a brief summary of each Stage you have covered so far in the order presented in the book, but they can also be reviewed in reverse:

1. The First Stage (Chapter 1) dealt with what Anṣārī called the Stage of Beginnings. It has to do with the fundamental grounding of the wayfarer. We need to be alert, aware and, above all, willing to let go of the certainties that define a person in the modern context. These certainties are very hard to give up, because it is through that prism that we see or appreciate reality. By the end of the first set we have to be prepared to let go.
2. The Stage of Gateways (Chapter 2) dealt with the beginnings of immersion in the realm of the intangible, the cultivation of the qualities of doing without, self-effacement and quiet confidence in the outcome are established and a need to begin to interact with what is not physical, temporal, or subject to cause and effect in a familiar way.

3. The Stage of Deeds (Chapter 3) is where the early qualities are now manifested in the outer realm, through a person's dealings with others, as well as with the inner realities. sincerity, sanctuary and reliability and consistency lead to the state of yielding to the force of a Higher Reality and you consciously become aware of its actions, and that it is a force that prevails, overpowers and overwhelms. You begin to sense it and sense its contours, boundaries and its power.
4. The Stage of Ethics (Chapter 4) dealt with the grounding of the wayfarer's qualities in spiritual Ethics or chivalry, and the cultivation of the nobler qualities in human beings that then become established in the wayfarer's character, where Ethics begin to colour their actions, dealings, perceptions and interactions of the individual.
5. The Stage of Origins (Chapter 5) dealt with the reassertion of will and purposefulness to propel the wayfarer into new terrains of consciousness, where the will to continue becomes paramount. It is no longer a question of being propelled by a force that is partly due to reason and partly due to intellection. It is a force that drives you forward, creating in you the will and desire to move towards the objectives. Once this wheel is set in motion, the wayfarer begins to experience different perceptions that form the beginnings of a new consciousness.
6. The Stage of Valleys (Chapter 6) dealt with the ease and pitfalls that accompany the wayfarer's journey into the Valleys that combine great promise with hidden threats. The first breezes of being pulled rather than being propelled are felt here. The wayfarer begins to surrender to the force of attraction that emerges towards the end of this stage. With this new attainment you enter into the Sixth Station, where there are risks as well as great rewards because these valleys have within them the conflicting contradictions of ease and hardship. You become aware of the new consciousness, are amazed and dazzled by it and may overlook the need to maintain limits and boundaries. Here, in the Station of Valleys, the nature of what pushes you changes from being one that emerges from your inner realities, advanced awareness—your greater sense of awareness and focus on the subtler realities—to a different kind of magnetic force that has its own reality.

As has been discussed, the *Manāzil* are not a mechanical or deterministic path towards enlightenment, rather they are milestones that the wayfarer may experience if they are primed to receive and imbibe the signs and signals. Their importance is magnified several times if we conjoin what we know from reason, the intellect, and the faculty that is able to connect with the unseen in practice, which is a fundamental aspect of making these Stations not only part of one's inner being, but allowing one to refine and perfect them as one continues. Practice can be at the individual level and also at the group level—or a mixture of the two, according to personal predisposition. For one person collective *dhikr* can open doorways; for another it is invocations; for yet another it is through acts of service to certain communities, the destitute, the elderly. It could take a solitary form or be within a group, in a formal or an informal setting, through a strict organisational framework or through a loose confederation of like-minded people, but above all, there has to be an element of praxis to it.

It is important to draw on the understanding of the *Manāzil* at the level of practice, according to individual taste and what works for you. It is a matter of disposition, desire and will. The mix of these will determine the extent and degree of the wayfarer's passage along this path. Like the thousands of birds that embarked on Attar's epic journey to the Simurgh, only thirty end up in its presence as the appropriate mix only applied to a few. Similarly, many will drop out on the three hundred rungs of Anṣārī's *Manāzil* and this is not a failure in the conventional sense: it is a recognition that the mix noted earlier may not exist or be available in the optimal proportions for each wayfarer. This recognition is in itself a victory, but becomes so only at the limit of our exertions.

You do what you can to the limit of your ability within your constitution, which is the way in which the unseen interacts, the way that spirit acts upon the soul within your self and how these engage with each other. Each one then becomes a unique vehicle or vessel. Do not feel that you have not met a promise of complete unfolding. The important thing is to exert yourself within this mixture. The *Manāzil* are not a substitute for, or a displacement of, the outer forms of devotion.

Neither are they a separate creed. No inner path can exist without an outer form to contain it, and vice versa. The outer form protects it, covers it and the inner form acts as its secret. This leads you to the end result, which is total immersion in *tawḥīd*, Oneness. The end goal is not guaranteed, although the Mercy of the All-Merciful is guaranteed.

7. The Stage of the States (*al-Aḥwāl*) منزل الاحوال

Overarching Names: The Fair or Just *Al-ʿAdl* العدل

The Sustainer *Al-Ḥafīdh* الحفيظ

WEEK THIRTY-THREE

With this introduction, we approach the Seventh Stage of the States. Anṣārī talks about this stage, as all the stages, having ten doors. Each door leads to the next, and if you go through Door One, you are supposed to reach the beginning of Door Two at its end. The ten doors of the Stage of States are the Door of Love, *maḥabba;* the Door of Vigilance, *ghīra,* Longing or *shawq*; Anxiety or *qalaq*; Thirst, which is *ʿatsh*; Ecstasy, *wajd;* Astonishment, *dahshe,* Overwhelm, *hayamān;* Lightning Flashes, *barq;* and finally, Taste, *dhawq.* A certain continuity is apparent from the titles of the doors, which may be more or less the case with the preceding and following stages. They all follow an order which, if not obviously logical, nevertheless has a coherent plan on a spiritual level.

According to his structure, Anṣārī always begins the stages with a succinct summary:

> When the wayfarer is still in the Stage of Valleys, Stage Six, the element of yearning and striving still prevails. The wayfarer then gradually moves into the Stage where the forces of propulsion and inspiration are evenly balanced. When inspiration overcomes the efforts exerted by striving, which tends to happen in the doors of the Stage of Valleys, and resolve, solicitude, concern and tranquillity are firmly established, then they will enter the Stage of States. It starts with Love, which originates with the Love that the Truth has for creation. Love obviates the strains of effort and struggle and the path becomes strewn with expressions for joy and ecstasy.

The Stage of the States coincides with a change in the nature of the journey. It is to do with the nature of the force which propels and moves you. Before it was a force that was generated within. You were moving because of your desire, will and resolve. You have now entered a condition where the doors are beginning to open and what pulls you is more important, more significant than what propels you. You do not need to exert the same degree of inner effort. You are drawn. The engine that moves is no longer your own exertions and has more to do with inspirations, flashes and is more or less continuous. These can come in the strangest places and at the most unexpected times. They are real and act as constant signs or affirmations. The cornerstone of that is Love, the force that brings two together.

The Stage of States has ten doors.

7.61. The Door of Love (*Bāb al-Maḥabba*) باب المَحَبَّة

يأتي اللّٰه بِقَوْمٍ يُحِبُّهُمْ وَيُحِبُّونَه

Ye'ti Allāh biqawmi yuḥibbuhum wa yuḥibbūna

'Allāh Will bring forth a people whom He Loves and who love Him.'

(*Qur'ān*, 5:54)

The first doorway is the Door of Love, *maḥabba.* Anṣārī describes Love as 'when the heart is suspended between concern and intimacy on the one hand and self-effacement and modesty on the other'.

Here is meant Love as it applies to the passage of the journey by the wayfarer.

> Love is the First Station along the path of annihilation and the first step towards the Station of Dissolution. It is the point where the most accomplished of the beginners meet the strides of those who are already advanced on the path and it has three degrees. At the First Degree it is Love that cuts away some whisperings, revels in service and brushes away afflictions. It is a Love that grows from concentrating on the bounties of Allāh and is reinforced by following the prescribed patterns of action and devotion, growing with the need for the Beloved.
>
> At the Second Degree it is Love that gives preference to the Truth over all else, occupies the tongue with constant remembrance and causes the heart to cling to witnessing the Truth. It is Love that emanates from contemplating the Attributes, witnessing the signs and being content with one's station of knowing. At the Third Degree, the most realised form, it is a gripping Love that cuts all circumstance, overpowers the signs and continues without let up. This type of Love is the peak of this

gateway. Otherwise, it would only be the love of the tongue and what all creation claims it has.

The word from which *maḥabba* derives is *ḥobb*, which is love in noun form, and *maḥabba* is Love, a noun derived from *aḥabba*, the fourth form of the verb, and is the act of extending it. Its special significance has been eroded by its association with the kinds of love that we find easier to understand, for example emotional, filial, romantic and Platonic.

These patterns have seeped into the vernacular, even sacred, language. They have in them an element that is incomplete. A far better, more appropriate and comprehensive word, which is used in the *Qur᾽ān*, is *widd*, which is unconditional Love, and it has the right aspect in its descriptive power. Allāh refers to Himself at *Al-Wadūd*, not *Al-Maḥbūb*—that is in absolute form, which is more of a field, an Energy, rather than a specific bond. It goes beyond duality. *Mawadda* is possibly what Anṣārī was talking about. *Maḥabba* was probably the right word two or three hundred years ago but its erosion through overuse, misuse and abuse in modern times creates a different connotation. So the true significance of this gateway is the creation of this unencumbered, unconditional field, where in the final analysis there is no duality, and if you can remove the subject and object of Love from your understanding of it, then we have *Mawadda.*

Love, according to Anṣārī has three degrees:

1. Love that cuts away any doubts and whisperings, revels in service and brushes away afflictions.
2. Love that gives preference to the Truth over all else, occupies the tongue in constant remembrance, and causes the heart to cling to witnessing the Truth.
3. A gripping Love that cuts all circumstances, overpowers the signs and continues without letup.

The term *ḥobb* (love) or *maḥabba*—the act of extending Love that Anṣārī uses—is not much evident in the *Qur᾽ān*. In many ways its full import in the lexicon of spirituality has been eroded by its association with the more ordinary familial types of love, which have been denuded of their power to express the state that Anṣārī is depicting. As stated, a far better word is *widd* (unconditional Love) which is used in its many forms in the *Qur'ān*, Allāh Manifesting His Truth as *Al-Wadūd*—the unconditional expression of Love, by elevating it far above the notion of physical, emotional and romantic aspects of Love. It becomes an energy field or a state that is neither other person-focused nor inwardly focused. It is subsumed within the meaning of the Truth. This is the true significance of the gateway of Love: *mawadda* rather than *maḥabba*.

7.62. The Door of Vigilance *(Bāb al-Ghīra)* باب الغيرة

رُدُّوهَا عَلَيَّ فَطَفِقَ مَسْحًا بِالسُّوقِ وَالْأَعْنَاقِ

Rudūhā 'ālayya faṭafiqa masḥan bis-sūq wal-a'nāq

'Bring them back to me. And he proceeded to stroke their shanks and necks.' (*Qur'ān*, 38:33)

Vigilance at the First Degree is the Vigilance for retrieving what one has lost, conscious of what has been missed and keen not to see it disappear. At the Second Degree it is to ensure that time is not wasted any longer. This Vigilance can be overpowering because it can lead to regret. If you are at an advanced age and you have not been through this path, another path or engaged in any progressive spiritual activity, it can very well lead to a sense of regret that you have wasted your time, so the earlier you start, the better, so that this sense of regret does not emerge. On the other hand, every activity has a spiritual dimension and, when reviewed with the insights accumulated along the path, will reveal a unique tapestry of all your Life experiences that have made you who you are, lead you to this point and prepare you to embark on this path, so nothing is lost. Knowing that, you have started, are well on your way, and you will want to preserve what you have achieved.

Anṣārī says that time is quick to anger, unforgiving and slow to return. The Third Degree is the Vigilance of the gnostic, for the keenness of their inner sight, for protecting their inner secrets from tarnishing and for the prevention of the self from slipping back. It is the quality of the guard or the sentinel. In this case, who is the sentinel? It is the self trying to realise its potential. This inner sentinel is there to safeguard jealously what one has acquired through effort or through inspiration and guidance, to understand the meaning of time as a feature which can be best put to use in understanding and experiencing the passage of the wayfarer. Time in this context is at the level of spiritual evolution, and its main purpose is to understand where we are.

Anṣārī: Vigilance is not to allow one's expectations or loss of patience to distract you from single-mindedness. It has three degrees:

1. Vigilance of the faithful for retrieving what they have lost, consciousness of what has been missed, and keenness not to see it disappear.
2. Vigilance of the adept to ensure that time is not wasted any longer. This Vigilance can be overpowering. Time is quick to anger, unforgiving, and slow to return.
3. Vigilance of the gnostic for the keenness of their inner sight, for protecting their inner secrets from tarnishing, and for preventing the self from slipping back into mere hope and expectancy.

Vigilance is the quality of the sentinel—in this case the self-in-realisation. It is to safeguard jealously what one has acquired through effort, and yearning—or through Inspiration and Guidance from the Most High. It is to mark the meaning of time as a feature which is best put to use in understanding and experiencing the passage of the wayfarer from and to the One.

Thirty-Third Reflection Day:

(1) Love's perfection is blame (*malāmat*) which has three faces:
One toward the world of creation, one towards the lover, and one towards the beloved.
The face towards the world of creation is the beloved's jealousy (*ghayra*); it consists in keeping the lover from paying attention to things other than the beloved.
The face towards the lover is the sword of Time's jealousy, and it consists in keeping him from paying attention to himself.
Finally, the face towards the beloved is the sword of love's jealousy; it consists in making him take nourishment from nothing but love, as well as keeping him from being caught in covetousness, and in compelling him to seek nothing from outside (love's essence).*

*Ghazzālī, A. (1986) *Sawāniḥ: Inspirations from the world of Pure spirits: The Oldest Persian Sufi Treatise on Love.* London: KPI. pp. 23. Quote continues in the thirty-fourth reflection.

WEEK THIRTY-FOUR

7.63. The Door of Longing *(Bāb ash-Shawq)* باب الشوق

مَن كَانَ يَرْجُو لِقَاءَ اللَّهِ فَإِنَّ أَجَلَ اللَّهِ لَآتٍ ۚ وَهُوَ السَّمِيعُ الْعَلِيمُ

Man kāna yarjū liqā'Allāhi fa'inna ajal Allāhi la'ātin wahū as-samī' ul-'alīm

'Whosoever desires the encounter with Allāh, his final destiny shall arrive, He is All-Hearing, All-Knowing.' (*Qur'ān*, 29:5)

Anṣārī defines Longing as the upsurge of the heart towards what is absent. It is a very profound definition. It is something that you desire, and its absence overwhelms and overpowers you and that response is yearning and Longing. For the believer, it is a desire, a yearning for Paradise, a place of security from fear, and joy in receiving what has been promised you. In the Second Degree it is Longing or yearning for the Divine Presence of Allāh and this ardour, which has been planted by the force of Love (*mawadda*), has grown from His Graces and Attributes, and the heart has become attached. It is a yearning to be within the Divine Proximity. In the Third Degree it is a fire that is fuelled by the purity of Love, ignoring the imperatives among daily existence and whose flames will not be extinguished until the appointed hour.

Here we are getting to the point where it is very hard to express the wayfarer's condition in normal terms. This is the vision of the essence of certainty, *'ayn al-yaqīn, 'ilm al-yaqīn, ḥaqq al-yaqīn.* It is where the entire affair becomes subsumed within your being and you merge in an exchange of spiritual DNA and are consumed by the force which propels you towards what you know is Ever Present. It has degrees of intensity, like all fires, all Longings and all yearnings. At the first level, it is the ardour of the true believers who conduct themselves with expectations of the promise being fulfilled. At the next level you are seized by an unconditional Love that comes from yielding to the One. Lastly, it is the essence of *ḥaqq*, a pure intense Longing that is fulfilled in every instant, ever growing aspect.

Anṣārī: Longing is the upsurge of the heart towards what is absent. It has three degrees:

1. Longing of the believer for Paradise, seeking refuge from fear, and joy in receiving what has been promised.

2. Longing for Allāh Most High, which has been planted by Love that has grown from His Graces and to Whose Attributes the heart has become attached. It is a yearning for His Subtle Generosity and the signs of His Favours.
3. Longing is a fire that is fuelled by the purity of Love, ignoring the imperatives of mundane existence and whose flames will not be extinguished until the appointed hour.

We are now entering the realm where the wayfarer's conditions become inexpressible in normal terms. This is the eye of the fire where the wayfarer is consumed by a force that drives them to what they know is ever present (*mawjūd*) but is only visible to the one from whom the veils are removed. Longing, *shawq,* is an intensity of many degrees. At the first level is the Longing of the explicit believers, rightly awaiting their just rewards. At another level it is the Longing which has become ignited by the unconditional Love that only comes from surrender to the One. Lastly is the Longing that is the essence of ardour, a pure, intense, Longing that is fulfilled in each and every instant.

7.64. The Door of Anxiety *(Bāb al-Qalaq)* باب القلق

وَعَجِلْتُ إِلَيْكَ رَبِّ لِتَرْضَىٰ

Wa ʿajiltu ilayka Rabbi litarḍā

'And I hurried on to you, my Lord, that You may be content with me.'
(*Qurʾān*, 20:84)

The Fourth Door is the Door of Anxiety. If you recall, at an earlier stage, Patience was a very important gateway. It is now superseded by Anxiety or *qalaq*. The earlier rungs, where patience was an important key to unlock that particular gate, are now subsumed or give way to Anxiety and apprehensiveness. That is, if longing does not overcome patience in order to attain the result, then you become apprehensive. You want to escape and be in the company of realised beings; and if they are not available, not around or cannot be found you want to distance yourself from creation and the problems thereof. Whenever you do interact, you are apprehensive that this contact may change your perceptions or alter your state. Anṣārī says here that it is a state where you welcome your physical end, to escape from the prison of existence.

Anṣārī: Anxiety is to push forward with Ardour at the expense of Patience. It has three degrees:

1. Anxiety about staying in the realm of creation, which annoys created beings. It is one that welcomes death to escape the prison of existence.
2. Anxiety that struggles with the intellect, enjoys listening, 'audition' or *sama*ʿ and overcomes patience.
3. Anxiety that has no mercy, accepts no delay and exalts no one person.

The Apprehensiveness that Anṣārī alludes to is all about Anxiety of losing what you have gained and impatience to achieve the desired end. You are now on this path, you know it is the correct path for you, everything is fully equipped, your vehicle is moving, and you want to get there. Patience—one of the virtues in the early stages—is now a positive hindrance before the longing to achieve the Divine Presence. At the first level, it is to seek the realisation of what one has been promised. Manifest existence becomes an irrelevance and people are seen as either obstacles or agents of forgetfulness for the wayfarer. They are best avoided unless they contribute to the passage of the wayfarer. Listening (*sama*ʿ) becomes a tool for agitating the power of that longing in the heart by which you can enter into this Love, while the mind is seen as a critical instrument that might dampen or extinguish it.

Anxiety thus grows in regard to the tricks of the mind—that the force of logic and reason might pull you back again. It is not that you abandon mind, logic and reason; it is that you are always aware that if you allow these faculties to transgress, to move into the realm where they do not have a part to play, then they will deflect, detract from or distract your thinking. In the final stages, Anxiety becomes driven by the desire for laser focus so as not to be distracted or deflected from the annihilation that the wayfarer seeks. This is not a literal annihilation but a complete paradigm shift, in which what seemed important previously is now no more than a distraction from what is of the essence. You may often feel at this stage that the end is nigh, although there are still several stages and many doorways through which you must yet pass.

Thirty-Fourth Reflection Day:

(2) Since I seek nothing in this world from you except love
Union with you and separation are the same to me.
Without your love my being is in disorder.
Choose, as you may: union or separation.

These three are the swords of jealousy for cutting the attention (of the lover) from things 'other' (than love, even if it be the Beloved); because this process may reach the point where not only the lover but even the Beloved function as something 'other' (*ghayr*). This is the power of love's splendour, because love's nutriment in its state of perfection comes from unison, (*ittiḥād*) and there is no room in unison for the separation of the lover and the beloved.*

WEEK THIRTY-FIVE

7.65. The Door of Thirst (*Bāb al-ʿAtash*) باب العطش

Allāh says with reference to His friend (Abraham):

فَلَمَّا جَنَّ عَلَيْهِ اللَّيْلُ رَأَىٰ كَوْكَبًا ۖ قَالَ هَٰذَا رَبِّي

Falammā janna ʾalayhil-laylu raʾā kawkaban qāla hādhā Rabbī

'When night enveloped him, he saw a star: He said "This is my Lord".' (*Qurʾān*, 6:76)

The Fifth doorway is the Door of Thirst. The above *āya* is in reference to Abraham (Ibrahīm). He wanted signs. He was Thirsty for confirmation of the Divine Presence and he wanted to see physically, in his own inner being, the reality of this Presence, and that is why he was seeking Lordship. He was Thirsty for Lordship and he saw it in various forms and jettisoned them all. Anṣārī says Thirst (*ʿatash*) is a term for an obsessive search for the promise. The Thirst of those in the early stages of this journey is for a witness, a sign or reflection that can confirm. It is something that Ibrahīm wanted and sought. At the Second Stage you want your quest to end, and the day when all the scales will fall away.

---

*Ghazzālī, A. (1986) *Sawāniḥ: Inspirations from the world of Pure spirits: The Oldest Persian Sufi Treatise on Love.* London: KPI. pp. 23.

You want a halting point where you can stop, finally, for repose. Thirst changes its intensity and form. The thirst that comes from a salty drink is different from the thirst that comes if you are denied water. Each one of these levels has its own degree of thirstiness.

Anṣārī: Thirst is a term for an obsessive search for the promise. It has three degrees:

1. Thirst of the adept for a witness, a sign or an inflection that can quench them.
2. Thirst of the wayfarer for an end to their quest, for a day in which they will see what they have been seeking, and a halting point wherein they can find repose.
3. Thirst of the lover for a clear manifestation that has no shadow nor a veil of separation, a confirmation that there are no further stations to seek.

In the early parts of this station, the adept seeks confirmations for his state and condition and eagerly accepts a signal from the unseen or an assurance by a realised being. In the intermediate phase, the wayfarer seeks an end to their efforts and exertions and is thirsty for experience of oneness. In the last Stage, the wayfarer ardently seeks the manifestations of the One without any layers of veils or shadows, knowing that beyond this station there is only nullification of individual being. This is not a complete reversal of the individuation process but rather the acquisition of nearness and ultimate union with the Beloved which is the longed for culmination of that process, the just reward for that struggle and the requiting of that Love and longing, and the final quenching of this Thirst and of this initial agitation that began the search for this path.

7.66. The Door of Ecstasy (*Bāb al-Wajd*) باب الوَجد

وَرَبَطْنَا عَلَىٰ قُلُوبِهِمْ إِذْ قَامُوا

Wa rabaṭṭnā ʿalā qulūbihim idh qāmū

Allāh says: 'And We strengthened their hearts when they rose up.' (*Qurʾān*, 18:14)

Anṣārī says Ecstasy is a flame that increases in power when it faces that which disturbs it. What disturbs it could be like oxygen to fire.

Sometimes you see the flame becoming that much more intense when exposed to higher levels of oxygen, like in oxyacetylene welding. Ecstasy that is ignited by a passing event which awakens spiritual listening (*sama*ʿ), seeing or reflecting. It may or may not have a lasting effect on the person. The Second Degree is Ecstasy that awakens the soul with the eternal light or a primordial sound or a true force of attraction. It can impart a cloak of awareness, or its light might persist. At the Third Degree it is Ecstasy that splits the person from the world of the earth and the cosmos, the seen and the unseen, liberating the wayfarer from all that is material, which he calls water and clay. If the person is so seized, their own name is lost to them, and one could impart onto them another name, one derived from the 99 or more Divine Names.

It has three degrees:

1. Ecstasy that is ignited by a passing event that awakens spiritual listening, seeing or reflecting. It may or may not have a lasting effect on the person.
2. Ecstasy that awakens the soul with an eternal light or a primordial sound or a true force of attraction. It could impart a cloak of awareness or its light might persist.
3. Ecstasy that whisks the person away from the two worlds, liberating the wayfarer from all that is material (water and clay). If the person is so seized, their own name is lost to them; alternatively it could impart onto the person its own Name.

True Ecstasy can arise from a powerful experience of listening (*sama*ʿ), focused prayer or act of devotion, or by seeing things in their true nature. Openings from the unseen are a way in which true meanings are established. In the early stages, such openings deriving from ecstatic states can be fleeting or intermittent; they can disappear as soon as they arise. In the intermediate stages, Ecstasy becomes associated with the condition of the realised self without any external promptings of witnessing, hearing or reflecting. It is an opening that descends on the heart and thereby creates the ecstatic circumstance. In the last phase, the Ecstasy becomes overwhelming, effacing the person's identity and individuality. It is here that the wayfarer must be armed with caution and courtesy. Seeing only the One does not make you the One.

Hence, Hallāj's utterance 'I am the Truth' (*Anā al-ḥaqq*), though true in its own way because he had lost his sense of individual being, emptied himself of his personal self or ego and was filled with the Divine Presence, was no longer able to distinguish self from soul, and had become completely transparent to the spirit. However, it is also un-utterable, as it is too easily misunderstood, taken externally or taken out of context. Hallāj later realised and demanded that he be executed for transgressing the bounds, saying during one of his trials, 'Kill me, my trusted ones, for there is Life in my death' (*Uqtulūni yā Thiqātī, fa fī mamātī ḥayātī*— اقتلوني يا ثقاتي وفي مماتي حياتي). He had seen the Truth but he assumed the Name of the Truth without Permission, even though what he said was true. Once one gets to this level of spiritual realisation, you are in a state of muted astonishment, or *dahshe*.

Thirty-Fifth Reflection Day:

It* drew me, substituting Itself to me in me;
It replaced me, certainly, but where then am I now?
I became It, and It is myself;
There exists for It no singular being which desires It.
I subsist through It in It; there exists no 'thou' between us.
My state with It was in the past as it will be in the future,
However, I have elevated my soul, and it has removed the partition;
I have awoken from my sleep, and arisen from my bed.
It has shown me to myself through the eye of my Essential Reality;
It is on the forehead of the Beauty that I read these characters.
I will polish my interior beauty, before the mirror
Where the traits of Plenitude are printed.
Its qualities are mine, my essence is His,
And in Its virtues the sun of Beauty rises for me.
My Name is really Its Name; and the Name of its Essence is my name,
And all these attributes come to me through nature.
[Quṭb al-Jīlī (d. 1424)]

*The Divine Reality (*al-ḥaqīqa*). Quṭb al-Jīlī, ʿAbd al-Karīm ibn Ibrāhīm & Burckhardt, T. (1983) *Universal man.* Sherborne: Beshara. A second poem from this book is in the thirty-sixth Reflection Day.

WEEK THIRTY-SIX

7.67. The Door of Astonishment (*Bāb ad-Dahshe*) باب الدَهشة

فَلَمَّا رَأَيْنَهُ أَكْبَرْنَهُ

Falammā ra'aynahu akbarnahu

'When they saw him, they greatly admired him.' (*Qur'ān*, 12:31)

Astonishment is when you start seeing the interconnectedness of things falling in front of you as a matter of routine. Like the wings of a butterfly in Beijing creating tornadoes in Mexico. Seeing instantaneously the interconnectedness gives you this sense of muted Astonishment.

Anṣārī: Astonishment of the wayfarer is when one's intellect, patience or knowledge is overpowered. It has three degrees:

1. Astonishment of the adept, when their state engulfs their knowledge; when ecstasy overpowers their potential and when unveiling covers solicitude.
2. Astonishment of the wayfarer, when gatheredness collects separate forms; when the outcome precedes the event; and when the witness sees only one's soul.
3. Astonishment of the lover, when the intimation of union surrounds the bounties of graces; when the light of proximity overshadows the light of mercy and the longing and yearning of witnessing overcomes that of the expectation of the actual event.

Astonishment is the dazzle associated with spiritual attainment. The light of recognition increases with intensity as one proceeds along the Stations of the Wayfarer. At the beginning, one is amazed by the intensity of the inner eye, drilling into the outer realities and the inner concerns to achieve a panorama of insights into the true nature of things. The interconnectedness of things and events become evidently manifest so that the wayfarer need not make a conscious association between them. They emerge almost spontaneously. In the last Stages, it is the Astonishment of seeing the light of proximity displace all else, including its own shadow of separateness. When that happens, you become overwhelmed and enter the eighth gate, the Door of *hayamān*.

7.68. The Door of Overwhelm (*Bāb al-Hayamān*) باب الهَيَمَان

مُوسَىٰ صَعِقًا

Mūsā sa'iqā

'Moses collapsed senseless.' (*Qur'ān*, 7:143)

Anṣārī: Being Overwhelmed is to abandon wonder or perplexity. It is a firmer and more durable station than astonishment. It has three degrees:

1. The first flickers of being Overwhelmed, when the adept embarks on their quest and recognises their inadequacies, lowly position and trivial reality.
2. Overwhelmed by the pounding waves of verification when its proofs become evident, its wonders become continuous and its lights burst through.
3. Overwhelmed by the first footsteps in the reality of non-time, seeing the master of eternity and drowning in the sea of unveiling.

The sense of being Overwhelmed is akin to drowning. It confirms the inadequacy of the will or desire to master the condition that one is in. Thrashing about to regain one's footing is useless as the adept has abandoned their reliance on the outer faculties. The drowning thus becomes a doorway into the engagement with another set of realities, more true and long lasting. As these realities are confirmed and verified, the wayfarer now scales the heights of vertical drowning—the inverse of the physical one. You do not go down into the Mariana Trench; you do the opposite, but the opposite has no limit. Rising to the heights rather than sinking to the depths. You may start by free falling without the anticipated fatal impact. You may say your *shahada* ahead of your perceived imminent end but just keep falling indefinitely. As the spiritual realm is non-spatial, there are no heights to ascend nor depths to plummet, no up or down. Here a different force applies—the force of lightning.

Thirty-Sixth Reflection Day:

The creature only has being by contingent attribution
In reality it is nothing.
When the Divine Lights appear,
They efface this attribution,
So that the creatures were not, now ceases to be.
God has extinguished them, but in their essences, they have never existed,
And in their extinction they subsist…
When they are annihilated, the Being returns to God;
He Is then such as He was before they became;
The servant becomes as if he had never existed, And God Is as if nothing had ever ceased.
However, when the Divine fulgurations appear,
The creature is invested from the Light of God and becomes one with Him.
He extinguishes him, then He substitutes Himself for him;
He lives in the place of the creatures, and yet they have never occupied anything.
Like waves, for which the principle is the unity of the sea,
And which, in their multitude, are united by it;
When it is in movement, it is the waves which are it in their totality,
And when it is calm, there are neither waves nor multiplicity.
[Quṭb al-Jīlī*]

WEEK THIRTY-SEVEN

7.69. The Door of Lightning Flashes (*Bāb al-Barq*) باب البَرق

إِذْ رَأَىٰ نَارًا

Idh ra'ā nāran

'When he saw a fire….' (*Qur'ān*, 20:10)

Lightning Flashes are like riding a chariot of light. The pathway is either towards the Divine Presence undertaken in full awareness or by the Divine Presence with a guiding chariot. This is a common theme in

*Ibid.

Taṣawwuf and the journey has four aspects to it, as described by Mulla Ṣadra:* the journey from creation to the One; the journey from the one to the One; the journey from the One to creation; and then the journey from creation to the individual. From the first we are now entering the second: you are now journeying towards the Divine Presence within the Divine Presence with Its limitless perimeters. So the beginning of this phase of the journey is the pull towards Allāh according to Anṣārī: the Flash of Lightning beckons the adept and invites them to enter the path. The difference between it and ecstasy is that ecstasy occurs after one has entered the path. Ecstasy is a reward while Lightning Flashes are a permission to enter.

It has three degrees:

1. The Flash of Lightning that shines from the side of the promised end in response to sincere pleading. The adept happily accepts whatever is offered, ignoring all the side-effects and accepting the bitterness of living the decrees.
2. The Flash of Lightning that shines from the side of the promised end in response to the urgings of caution. The adept sees only the shortness of the road, becomes indifferent to creation and is urged to purify his inner awareness.
3. The Flash of Lightning that shines from the side of the subtle graces illuminating the poverty of the wayfarer, giving rise to the clouds of joy, and the raindrops of ecstasy onto the rivers of bliss.

The pathway is either towards the Divine Presence, undertaken in full awareness, or by the Divine Presence Whose Guiding Chariot is the Lightning Flash. The former starts with creation while the latter state starts with Allāh. It is a passage inside God's Names and Attributes. If the entire world and what is in it are mere manifestations of the Names and Attributes of the One, then His Names and Attributes are only manifestations of His Essence. The journey from the world of existences to the One is different from the journey inside the Names

*Ṣadr al-Dīn Shīrāzī & Peerwani, 2008; *Falsafa-ʾi ʿaālī yā Ḥikmat-i Ṣadr al-Mutaʾal-lihīn : talkhīṣ va tarjuma-ʾi qismat-i umūr-i ʿāmma va ilākhiyyāt-i Kitāb-i Asfār.* Mullā Ṣadrā (Ṣadr ad-Dīn Muḥammad ibn Ibrāhm̄) Shīrāzī.; Muṣliḥ, Javād. 2nd ed.; 1353 1974.

and Attributes. The steed which the wayfarer mounts in the latter case is the Flash of Lightning. At the First Degree, the Flash is a confirmation of the promised end. In the Second Degree, the Flash has a different purpose. It cautions the wayfarer about the hubris of their ways and urges them to be prepared for all outcomes. In the last Degree the knowledge and certainty of the wayfarer's absolute impoverishment becomes the doorway into the end state of harmony and delight, which is the last doorway of the stage, the Door of Taste or *dhawq*.

7.70. The Door of Taste (*Bāb adh-Dhawq*) باب الذَوق

هَٰذَا ذِكْرٌ

Hādhā dhikrun

'This is a reminder....' (*Qur'ān*, 21:24)

Taste is more durable than ecstasy and clearer than lightning. It is of three degrees, the tasting by verification of the fruits of efforts without any doubts, unburdened by expectations of hope, tasting by the will of the fruits of intimacy, without interruptions or impediments and with no possibility of separating from it, and lastly, the tasting by separateness of the fruits of union and tasting by solicitudes. *Dhawq* is a key word in the science of the inner way. It is both a state as well as a predisposition, and it is manifested in different guises throughout the journey; the entire period of preparation is predicated on a person having the Taste for the Supreme. You cannot consume a meal if you are allergic to one or more of the ingredients or if you cannot abide the dish. You can acquire a Taste, but it is not the same as having an instinctive Taste for something. This is one of the necessary qualities that must be present in the early stages of the journey. The nature of that case changes as you progress.

Again, using the analogy of taking a meal: a Taste for simple dishes may not be sustained as the meal becomes complex and vice versa. You may like to have very simple meals, but if the meal becomes more complex and elaborate, you may not like it. Or you may like very complex French foods with all kinds of sauces, and you may not, therefore, enjoy a piece of bread. When you fully realise, however, that all of our provision comes from The Beloved, even the most meagre morsel will taste like a gourmet meal. Even bitterness becomes sweet. This science is not for everyone and you have to be clear and open with yourself; it is only for those whose spiritual Taste buds have metamorphosed. As it becomes easier, as the nature of the forces acting on you changes, as you move from going towards the One to acting by the One, each of these stages requires the states for them as your predisposition does not push it forward. In this case, it explains why Taste is a higher quality to have than either Inspiration, Ecstasy or bedazzled astonishment.

Anṣārī: Taste is more durable than ecstasy and clearer than lightning. It has three degrees:

1. Tasting by verification of the fruits of efforts, without any doubts, and unburdened by expectations or hope.
2. Tasting by the will of the fruits of intimacy, without interruptions or impediments, and with no possibility of separating from it.
3. Tasting by separateness of the fruits of union and the tasting by solicitude of the fruits of gatheredness.

Taste (*dhawq*) is a key word in the science of the inner way or *taṣawwuf*. It is a state as well as a predisposition and is manifested in different guises throughout the journey. The entire period of preparation before the person commits to the path must be predicated on having the Taste for this endeavour. This is a matter of one's essential blueprint—whether one has the qualities that would prevail especially in the early stages of the journey. The nature of one's Taste also changes as one progresses along the path. A Taste for simple dishes may not be sustained as the meal becomes more complex; and vice versa, as the journey progresses, so that Taste is always there no matter what the station. Hence the higher station that Taste is given.

Thirty-Seventh Reflection Day:

Suggested *Dhikr* for the Stage of the States:

Al-Wadūd (The All-Loving) *Al-Matīn* (The Steadfast) *Al-Muhaymin* (The Protector)
Yā Wadūd ~ Yā Matīn ~ Yā Muhaymin يا ودود ~ يا مَتين ~ يا مُهَيمِن

8. The Stage of Guardianship (*Manzal al-Walāyāt*) منزل الولايات

Overarching Names: The Guardian *al-Wāli* الوالي
The Close Friend *Al-Walī* الوليّ

WEEK THIRTY-EIGHT

This is the first opening in which the wayfarer has moved from being pushed by their own desire, will and volition to being pulled by another force, where the motor changes from one's own will (*irada*) or desire, or longing (*shawq*) to one where the circle of attraction's remote pull becomes greater. The force attracting overcomes the will of the wayfarer and they are no longer self-propelled. It is important to understand this inflection point, because here we are now, in realms where very few people have entered, and few who have entered ever return. *Shaykh* al-Anṣārī has clearly crossed this bridge and is reporting to us veraciously what he experienced. It is not something that came as a result of discursive intelligence or logic and reasoning. It is not something that moves smoothly from one stage to the next; thus here we have a break.

Stage Seven is where the force of attraction pulls the wayfarer into the Circle of Divine Presence. The natural character of the matter changes and the various categories we use to try and understand the significance of this Journey become more difficult to experience spiritually, because it is a very heightened state. It is easy to explain intellectually in terms of the logical flow of the Stages, but it is difficult to express experientially because of the inflection from the first seven stages. Because the adept—who then becomes the wayfarer—is pushed by their own desire and will, there is an element of comparability to our own experience. Once you tip over to this other realm, that of attraction, it becomes difficult to rationalise, express or describe, unless you have reached that state of realisation.

From his writings and the way that *Khwāja* Anṣārī expresses these states, it is clear that he crossed that threshold and was moved into a stage where attraction is greater than in other realms. We now come to realms that are ambiguous in terms of the way that we relate to them. We may see glimpses of them experientially. It is a reality that is basically imposed upon them by proximity to the Divine Presence and this will continue until we end the journey that we are now on in a different order. The title of this Stage is Guardianship. This is the *Manzal* of the friends of Allāh—those who are proximate, those whom Allāh has selected for Himself— as the *Shaykh* says, it is one of the waystations of annihilation. By annihilation he means the effacement of all the qualities that give a person the illusion of having desire, will, or control.

A person who is in the Station of *walāyāt* knows that whatever actions, drives or forms existence and reality take, it has no depth to it. In fact, it vanishes in the Face, in the Hands of what *Shaykh* Anṣārī calls the Irresistible Annihilator, *Al-Qahhār*—one of God's Names. It is the annihilation of the illusion of separation, as well as that of any essential character that is seen to be independent of the One. There is a prophetic saying that you leave yourself in the Hands of Allāh as a corpse in the hands of the person who washes it, because you have no more will, no desire, you become an instrument of a Higher Authority. There are ten states in this Stage of Guardianship.

Anṣārī on the Stage of the Guardianship:

> *Manāzil* are waystations of annihilation (*fanā'*), when the Truth directly takes charge over the wayfarer, they no longer have any control over their affairs. One has no existence, no essence, no description and no action. They are Landings in annihilation in the hands of The Irresistible Annihilator, Who does with the wayfarer what He Wills, even by effacing their name and presence, removing them from sight and leaving no traces. The wayfarer is brought to life by God's Life; and achieves permanence by His Permanence.

The Stage of Intimacy is the first entry into the realms of the self's annihilation. The wayfarer no longer has any will, action, thought or presence that is not connected, inspired by and driven by the One. The wayfarer becomes a feather, floating on the breeze of the Breath of the All-Merciful. There is no more inner sight, vision, desire or striving. This is when the person becomes as a corpse in the hands of the One who prepares it for its destiny.

8.71. The Door of Instant Recognition (*Bāb al-Laḥḍ*) باب اللحض

انظُرْ إِلَى الْجَبَلِ فَإِنِ اسْتَقَرَّ مَكَانَهُ فَسَوْفَ تَرَانِي

Anẓur ila al-jebeli fa'in istaqarra makānahu fasawfa tarāni

'Look instead upon that mountain. If it remains firmly in place you shall see Me.' (*Qur'ān*, 7:143)

The common word in Arabic is *laḥḍa*, which means an instant or a Moment. But *al-Laḥḍ* is even more sharply defined, it is Instant Recognition and goes beyond the moment. It is a kind of instantaneous awakening that has in it a recognition. It is not just seeing a flash, it is knowing the meaning and spiritual substance behind it. Anṣārī defines *al-laḥḍ* as the vision of the bondsperson. When a person in the Stage of Guardianship sees events, phenomena, the flow of time, anything that is ordinary or extraordinary, they see instantaneously the meaning behind it. For those in this exalted state, it comes in three degrees of intensity. The first one is the Instantaneous Recognition that whatever happens to you is a gift, a form of blessing or bounty, and the last stage is when you see events and phenomena, people, the march of time and all the accompanying changes, and understand that these are all manifestations of the One. They all gather back into the One and you see things with the eyes of unity.

1. Recognising the past bounties. It stops one questioning their origin except to affirm with humility one's dependence on The Sustainer. It generates Joy except when caution is warranted from the actions of The Planner. Gratitude is poured out except when one recognises from Whence comes the Source of giving gratitude.
2. Recognising the lights of unveiling. It covers the wayfarer with the garment of dependence, causes the wayfarer to taste the fruits of manifestation and protects from any harm that could arise from the exuberance of these bounties.
3. Recognising the eye of gatheredness, which is to make easy the path of struggle, to be rid of any resistance to it and to benefit from seeing its origins in the beginnings.

The Qur'anic *āyāt* is most apt in that it showed Moses the utter futility of trying to see other than the One. Moses did look at the mountain but as he looked it had disintegrated. There is no reality, solidity, materiality or even spirituality outside of the One. Your own essence disintegrates. Where the One Is, duality necessarily vanishes; so with the wayfarer in the first station of the Stage of Guardianship otherness disappears. There is only He and not-He. If we look at creation we are in fact seeing what is not-Allāh. If we look to Allāh we see only the One. We may think that we have the tools to be able to engage in Reality but when the spirit emerges, your own essence disintegrates, leaving only that One Reality. Where there is The One, all twos, all dualities and all multiplicities vanish. Any sense of otherness disappears. There Is only He.

Instant Recognition thus becomes a state where otherness is banished. Whatever you see, experience and even contemplate becomes instantaneously referred to as its Source. For those who have not yet earned this station, but are aware of it, as some of us might be, but have not yet earned it through absorption of earlier stages, we have to be extremely cautious because this condition can be overwhelming. Seeing the Actions of the One behind the multiplicity without having the filter of the various Stages of Guardianship and are not protected by the force of attraction, it can overwhelm, as you are not able to relate to this constant, Infinite shift between the One and the many. The true wayfarer, in the Station of Guardianship, would have surrendered their essential being to the One, erasing all terms such as will, desire, destiny, individuality and outcome, so there is an element of containment.

All dangers become immaterial, literally and metaphorically. The wayfarer's identity is now effaced and there is only One Reality that prevails: yielding to the One Reality.

8.72. The Door of Moment (*Bāb al-Waqt*) باب الوقت

ثُمَّ جِئْتَ عَلَىٰ قَدَرٍ يَا مُوسَىٰ

Thumma ji'ta ʿalā qadarin yā Mūsā

'And then you came back at a time appointed, O Moses.' (*Qur'ān*, 20:40)

This instant, this *laḥḍ*, is a Moment. *Waqt* in Arabic is a very important word commonly understood as time. Those in *taṣawwuf* are sometimes known as *ibn al-waqt*, Child of the Moment, which means that they have no sense of the past and no expectations of the future, but live in and of the Moment. Time has absolutely no meaning, because the flow of time to that Moment—and the flow of time after it—has no relationship to being within that Moment, that occasion of the manifestation of an entity. This is also significant because the way that God's Manifestation takes place is entirely due to His Power and His Will. Manifestation is constantly reaffirmed on an instantaneous basis infinitely. It is true that we tend to see things in sequence and in a certain continuum. For example, this table is here. It was here a few seconds ago, and it is very likely to be here a few seconds from now. But this is not necessarily a determined condition or limitation on God's Actions.

Anṣārī: The Moment is the occasion of the manifestation of an entity. It has three meanings:

1. The Moment of true ecstasy, seeing the Lights of The Bountiful, accompanied by true hope, or inspired by a shock, or by a burning Love.
2. Being poised between the possibilities of realising and realisation itself. At times, the wayfarer seeks knowledge; at other times their states overpower, and their affliction is between these two. Sometimes tasting the fruits, at other times continuing their struggles, and in yet other times, veiled by separation.
3. It has been said that there is 'The Moment is Truth'. By this is meant the Moment is effaced by the realisation of the Existence of the One Reality.

With true inner sight whatever manifested entities exist are brought into creation at every Moment, in every second. The Eye of *ḥaqq*, Truth, sees that all possibilities of existence are brought into existence at that particular Moment, due to the Divine Will and Command. There is no deterministic pattern. What we believe is determinism is, in reality, the realisation of infinite potential at a certain time. Moment, for us on this path, is the constant re-manifestation of entities being continuously brought into existence. When you see things and events in this light, you have to wonder and be in amazement as to how these things appear to have a certain solidity to them, but we know that in every instant, they exist only due to the Actions of Allāh. The Moment is when potentialities are realised and brought into existence. Time thus becomes a series of infinite manifestations being brought into existence at each Moment. When we see time in this light, we see the wonders of creation and the bringing into existence of one of many possible outcomes. This is the essence of the famous paradox of Schrödinger's cat.

Quantum mechanics can confirm some of these major insights, although it may be the other way around, that the insights of *taṣawwuf* find their confirmation in life, as well as in the actions of the most advanced forms of quantum physics. It is to do with the Qur'anic *aya*: 'At each instant, Allāh is undertaking His Creative Act.' The Act of Creation does not start at a certain point and then end, then continue in time, pointing to predetermined laws. The Act of Creation, including created beings' acts and laws, are constantly brought into being as a result of decisive Action of the Observer—Allāh—on manifest creation where there is no entity that has been brought into existence. The act of bringing things into being is God's Choice out of infinite choices. The fact that we are here is because of Determination, at that particular instant that this is the created entity who will be manifested. If you see reality in the form of infinite manifestations, infinitely recurring, you will then see the Actions.

Possible outcomes—for example, crossing the street safely or being hit by a truck—may occur in another universe. This leads to the theory of multiple universes where all outcomes occur, the first in one universe, while the other in another. An outcome occurs if probabilities are realised. Ibn ʿArabi's system was able to decipher the connection between the essential *Nafas ur-Raḥmān* (Breath of the Merciful) and the concept of *tarjīḥ* or preference or preponderance, where Allāh in His Might tips possible condition-dependent existents into actual existence. The whole system of the great master is the realisation that existence is a series of infinite possibilities brought into realisation by a Preponderating Being. The Infinite universes that are a possible outcome of quantum life are nothing more than the Qur'anic principle that all creation is a never-ending series of Divine Creative Acts that engender existence at each and every instant.

As the *Qurʾān* says: '*Kullu yawmin Huwa fī sha'an...*' 'At each Instant He Is Undertaking His Creative Act' كُلَّ يَوْمٍ هُوَ فِى شَأْنٍ (*Surat ar-Raḥmān: Aya* 29).

Thirty-Eighth Reflection Day: Schrödinger's Cat

In case you are more interested in the meaning of *al-waqt* or the Moment, this is an explication of Schrödinger's cat and the Qur'anic concept of *waqt*, time, or timing. Richard Feynman, the great physicist, said: 'I can safely say that nobody understands quantum mechanics.' Nevertheless, here goes: The paradox of Schrödinger's cat is to do with collapsing wave functions. Any particle, or anything for that matter, can be expressed both in terms of a mass and as a wave. De Broglie expresses it as: Wavelength (l) = h/p where h is Planck's constant, a universal number (such as pi) and p is momentum. So anything in motion can be expressed as a wave also. The essentials of Schrödinger's paradox are as follows:

1. Put an electron in an opaque box. The electron can be expressed as a wave and as a point mass as per de Broglie above.
2. Divide the box into two identical parts, both opaque, so that you as an observer don't know where the electron is for certain.
3. Logic would tell us that the wave function of the electron would be divided into two equal parts, and that the probability of finding the electron in either half is equal.
4. However, we cannot be certain where the electron is until we actually look and see. This is an axiom of quantum mechanics. You cannot make a claim as to where anything is until you observe it.
5. However, once we see and locate the electron, quantum mechanics tells us that the wave function associated with the other location, which existed before by necessity, is now collapsed to zero.
6. Ergo, the simple act of observing something causes the wave function associated with it, i.e. it is both here and everywhere, to collapse to zero when it is associated with 'elsewhere'. Quantum mechanically, we are both here and everywhere, while the here is established by observation and everywhere is an essential possibility.
7. Schrödinger postulated an experiment whereby he put his cat in an opaque box with an atom whose decay triggered a mechanism that would kill the cat.

The decaying atom has a wave function which, assuming a half-life of five minutes, would either kill the cat or not. Therefore the decaying atom's wave function for the first five minutes must include in its formulation a living cat. AND a dead cat. If we look into the box, then the wave function collapses into a dead cat or a live cat.

8. But how can a cat be both alive and dead? Can a cat, a non-rational being, be deemed an observer that can cause the wave function of the decaying atom associated with a dead cat to collapse? How can both states, which must by necessity exist, be negated by an act of observation?
9. According to Wigner, a contemporary of Schrödinger, a machine cannot make the observation that causes a wave function to collapse. This can only be done by a sentient conscious observer observing the machine.
10. If Wigner is right, there is no way that any wave function could collapse in the history of the universe before the rise of a conscious mind.
11. Therefore, if life is a molecular transaction based on an infinitely small probability of life actually occurring, then there is no possibility of life emerging from the dual wave function of life/non-life unless and until a conscious agent acts upon it, thereby collapsing the non-life wave function to zero.
12. Similarly, the rules apply to any system, including the universe in its entirety. If the universe in its entirety can be expressed as a wave function—and it can, theoretically—then for the universe to exist (A + wave function) or not exist (A - wave function) it must have an external agent/observer to collapse the non-existence wave function.
13. There is no way out of this paradox unless the observer is part of the system which, when it collapses, leads to multiple universes where all possible outcomes emerge, a conscious observable universe and an unconscious unobserved universe, where the cat and I are alive (universe 1), where we are both dead (universe 2), or where one is dead and the other alive (universes 3).

14. Basically therefore, whenever an event occurs with possible outcomes, i.e. I cross the street safely or I may be hit by a truck, both outcomes occur, the first in one universe while the other outcome occurs in another universe. This leads to the theory of multiple universes where all probabilities are realised.

Formula *á* la de Broglie is: K= (Q+QM/A)/ P

Knowledge = *Qur'ān* plus quantum mechanics, mediated by Ibn 'Arabi, with the whole mediated by the Prophetic way.

Only Allāh Knows Best...

WEEK THIRTY-NINE

8.73. The Door of Purity (*Bāb as-Safā*) باب الصفاء

وَإِنَّهُمْ عِندَنَا لَمِنَ الْمُصْطَفَيْنَ الْأَخْيَارِ

Wa innahum 'indanā lamin al-muṣṭafīna al-akhyār

'With us they shall be among the virtuous of the elect.'

(*Qur'ān*, 38:47)

Whenever you interact with the Realm of the unseen, the less colouring you bring to it—the less of yourself—the more true and vital is the quality of your engagement. *Ṣafa'*, or Purity, is the perfection of sincerity. You can have a commanding self, *Nafs al-Ammara,* or worse, a demanding self, and still occasionally be sincere. If you are Inspired, your sincerity becomes that much more established. As you move on along the spectrum, you become increasingly attuned to vibrations coming from the realms of the unseen. Purity becomes the distillation of sincerity and your sincerity is polished and reflected in a mirror that has little rust. At this Stage the self has progressed to remove all of the colourings that would affect the way it engages. In his famous poem, Rumi talks about a vessel taking on the colour of the fluid held within it. The vessel here is a metaphor for the Purified Self, and whatever is imparted to it affects its colour.

Anṣārī: Purity is the name given to the denial of guile, and in this doorway it means the disappearance of any colouring to one's self. It has three degrees:

1. The Purity of one's knowledge on the path, which focuses on the purpose of one's striving and regulates the concern of the wayfarer.
2. The Purity of one's state in which one witnesses the effects of verification, tastes the delights of supplications and erases the outer world.
3. The Purity of connectedness which merges with the triumph of the wayfarer in immersion in the Truth of Lordship, drowns the end in the beginnings of seeing essences, and folds the burden of obligations into the Might of the Eternal.

Purity is the perfection of sincerity. One can be sincere in one's purpose and efforts but sincerity still has to be filtered through the nature of the self. Sincerity of the commanding self is an occasional state; the inspired self a more established state and so on. At this stage of the wayfarer's evolution, the self has progressed along the spectra of conditions, and would have progressively lost not only its wiles and guiles about any colouring it might have taken. It becomes like Rumi's vessel. It will take the colouring of whatever is poured into it. Its reflective powers become unsullied, pure and clear. What is poured into it is the Light of the Eternal, and it will begin to reflect the qualities that point to oneness. Past and future merge; hardships vanish; and the eye of certainty becomes keener to the truth of certainty. This, of course, gives you a sense of great joy and rejoicing, which is the Fourth Door.

8.74. The Door of Rejoicing (*Bāb as-Surūr*) باب السرور

قُلْ بِفَضْلِ اللّهِ وَبِرَحْمَتِهِ فَبِذَٰلِكَ فَلْيَفْرَحُوا

Qul bifaḍlillāhi wa biraḥmatihi fabidhālika falyafraḥū

'Say: This is through God's bounty and Mercy. At this let them rejoice'. (*Qur'ān*, 10:58)

Once you are in this stage, you know that this is the best possible journey. There is no other effort that is worth it. Everything else is reduced to pettiness, given the immensity and significance of this path.

Anṣārī: Rejoicing is the apogee of good news. It has three degrees:

1. The Rejoicing of tasting, tempered by three sorrows: a sorrow derived from concern of being cut off; a sorrow driven by the darkness of ignorance; and a sorrow that comes from the possibility of separation.
2. The Rejoicing of witnessing, removing the veils of knowledge, the bonds of obligations and the pettiness of other choices.
3. The Rejoicing that comes from hearing the response. It removes the traces of loneliness, knocks on the door of seeing, and delights the soul.

Rejoicing is a form of exalted joy. It is the self that is righteously triumphant, not because it has conquered the outer world, but the triumph of having navigated the valleys and peaks of the journey. The goal is in sight. The cascade of openings is continuous and the soul, seeing in the self an ever clearer reflection, begins to take delight in the purified self. The soul is ever perfect but once it sees itself reflected, the soul that is more perfected, keeps the devoted joy of the realised self, which is merely a reflection of the Rejoicing soul that has within it all the Attributes, albeit in limited form, of Allāh. It guards the seeker, the servant, and the mirror of the self is now clear and the vision it presents is extremely pleasing and a cause of Rejoicing.

Thirty-Ninth Reflection Day:

Listen to Bach's Kantata 'Jauchzet Gott in Allen Landen'.
Dhikr: O Creator, O Shaper— *Yā Khāliq Yā Muṣawwir* يا خالق يا مصور

WEEK FORTY
8.75. The Door of Secrecy (*Bāb as-Sirr*) باب السِّر

اللَّهُ أَعْلَمُ بِمَا فِي أَنفُسِهِمْ

Allah a'lamu bimā fī anfusihim

'Allāh knows best what is in their hearts....' (*Qur'ān*, 11:31)

If you zero in on the heart, not its shape, its form or the body in which it comes, you go immediately to the Secret. Although the journey from periphery to centre involves working on the body, and maintaining its health and balance as much as possible is a prerequisite, it is its inner dimension, that of the soul, which is the true aim. The body is made and maintained by the most exalted spiritual forces of the purity of creative Love, and this work should include the stretching of the physical body as well as the expansion of the physical heart, the spiritual reality of which contains the whole universe. Allāh Says in a *Ḥadith Qudsi* that the whole universe cannot contain Him but the heart of a believer can.

Anṣārī: The Secret is the inner meaning of what is experienced. It has three degrees exemplified by three groups:

1. A group who had exalted their concerns, purified their intentions and righted their actions. They did not hesitate over forms, nor did they attach meaning to names...These are God's instruments wherever they are.
2. A group who dealt with those whose States were lower than their own; who revealed less of what they had seen; and spoke of affairs that were below what they had experienced. They are in guidance and have the right courtesy and integrity.
3. A group whom the Truth Has Made them unaware of themselves, oblivious to their state, and assured them with visions of the inviolability of their state. This is the condition of the saintly ones.

The Secrecy of the wayfarer is the inner knowledge and certainty of the veracity of the path and the truth of the states that one traverses. In the First Degree, those who hold their Secret do so by a single-minded focus on their journey, indifferent to the calls of the material world and to its vanities. They preserve their Secret by avoiding all forms of outer contaminants—power and authority, reputation and prestige; wealth and accumulation. Their Secret is safe mainly because of the ignorance of people of their true states. They walk in the world, avoiding things and deflecting people; they do not see any difference between themselves and others because their Secret is safe. Your Secret is safe because people generally do not know or understand your states and conditions.

At the Second Degree, they preserve their Secret by dealing with people within their capacities to understand and comprehend. Be cautious when you talk to or deal with people whom you do not know, as you can only guess at their *maqām*. When dealing with people whom you know are also on the path and may have reached the levels that you have, or even levels you have not yet achieved, you can talk to them with the knowledge or understanding of the degree to which they have reached. Do not speak to them of your level, speak to them at their level. There is interaction, engagement, perhaps an element of mentoring involved here. You do not open up your true state to avoid being misunderstood. Those who are more advanced necessarily cannot reflect their experiences onto those who have not had similar experiences. This goes back to the prophetic saying that you should deal with people according to their level of knowledge and realisation.

Do not deal with people to show where you are or point out to them realities you have reached, if they have not reached them yet and cannot understand. If you obey this injunction, you will be safe, and your Secret, in the sense of your ability to see from the outer shell to the inner reality, is safe because you are revealing only an aspect of your State. Dissimulation is often necessary, as what is not understood can be threatening and even frightening to others. 'Deal with people according to their capacities to comprehend,' said the Prophet (S). In this stage, it is Allāh Who Protects the wayfarer's Secret by making them oblivious to any other reality. At the Third Degree they have already surrendered and are not in the business of protecting their Secret. You are surrendered and your Secret is safe, protected by the Protector.

8.76. The Door of Breath (*Bāb an-Nafas*) باب النفس

فَلَمَّا أَفَاقَ قَالَ سُبْحَانَكَ

Falammā afāqa qāla subḥānak

'And when he came to, he said: Glory be to You!.' (*Qur'ān*, 7:143)

The Sixth doorway or landing is the Door of Breath, or *nafas*. Breath here is not the physical breath, it is the breeze that carries with it the signals and signs from the unseen. That is why Anṣārī says: 'Breath energises the breather.' It may sound trite to say that breath energises—of course it does in the physical sense. In the inner sense, however, the Breath which carries the signs, symbols and promises also has this effect on the aspirant, but it is a spiritual energising quality. Visualise yourself in a condition where the Breath that you are drawing in is, in fact, a breeze from the unseen. You will see what happens when you constrict. When you are not able to draw that oxygen, it may sometimes cause you to feel angry, at an early stage, if you do not have access to what gives you vitality. Spiritual vitality is also maintained by this *nafas*, which has three degrees:

Anṣārī: The First type of Breath is a beacon for the wayfarer; the Second type is an ascension for the wayfarer; the Third is the crowning glory of the verifier:

1. A Breath that constricts the wayfarer in the absence of the Beloved, in the knowledge that patience will rectify the condition. It can be accompanied by anger at the loss of direct experience.
2. A Breath that appears with the manifestation of the Real. It is a breeze that emanates from the doorway of rejoicing, full of the light of existence, and pointing to the realm where there are no more signs and symbols, the realm of the essence.
3. A Breath that is sanctified by the fire of the sacred, continuous with the signs of eternity. It is the Breath that is known as 'the Pearls of Light'.

The root of the word *nafas* are the three letters: n,f,s, *nūn, fā, sīn* (ن ف س), from which derive the words for self (*nafs*), Breath (*nafas*), Breathing (*tanaffus*,) myself (*nafsi*), population (*nufūs*), and the same or similarity (*nafsuhā*). It is one of the key words in the science of *taṣawwuf*, drawing in and connecting the self and other selves and finally connecting all selves with the universal self, the Breath of Life, rooting them in the same Source and confirming the essential identicalness of the universal self. The universal self of God's manifestations of *Ar-Raḥman* (The Merciful), the Breath of Mercy, emanates from Him and cascades down to creation. In the *Qur'ān* we are all drawn from a universal pattern but as you come down through the layers to the multiplicity of individuation, the universal self begins to take on the colouring and the shapes and contours of the individual. It is as if the universal self Breathes into the individuated self the universal pattern, confirming both its essential similarity and simultaneous difference: multiplicity within unity.

The quality and character of the Breath itself therefore varies according to the condition of the self and its degree of accomplishment within the journey. For the wayfarer in the early stages, the Breath of the Merciful is a potent reminder of the wonders of drawing near. Its absence generates a longing that is constricting, but still bears the promise of what is to come. The West Wind or the *Zephyr* that clears the storms and promises the arrival of spring. The second group of stages is the wind that accompanies the coming of the spring and points to the wonders yet to come. In the third group of stages the wind carries the wayfarer. There are no more harbingers of what is to come. The wayfarer becomes a verifier, *muḥaqqiq,* riding on the Pearls of Light. Anṣārī says that this is the Breath that carries Saints, *awliya',* the great beings, the Prophets, bringing with it knowledge of the unseen from the Source of all Being.

Fortieth Reflection Day:

O Loosener of the tongues speaking intimate sayings!
O Diffuser of intimacy in the retreats of Your invokers!
You permeate the breathing of the knowers of secrets!
We have no companion but Your Name's remembrance!
We have no provision but Your enduring recollection!
We have no guide other than You leading us to You!
O God! Look after the need of the one who only needs You!
[Anṣārī's *Munājāt**]

WEEK FORTY-ONE

8.77. The Door of Exile (*Bāb al-Ghūrba*) باب الغربة

فَلَوْلَا كَانَ مِنَ الْقُرُونِ مِن قَبْلِكُمْ أُولُو بَقِيَّةٍ يَنْهَوْنَ عَنِ الْفَسَادِ فِي الْأَرْضِ إِلَّا قَلِيلًا مِّمَّنْ أَنجَيْنَا مِنْهُمْ ۗ وَاتَّبَعَ الَّذِينَ ظَلَمُوا مَا أُتْرِفُوا فِيهِ وَكَانُوا مُجْرِمِينَ

Falawlā kāna min al-qurūni min qablikum ūlū baqiyyatin yanhawna ʿan il-fasādi fil-ardi illā qalīlā mimmān anjaynā minhum wattabaʿa alladhīnā ẓalamū mā atrifū fīhī wakānū mujrimīn

*Maybudī, A. F., Rashīd al-Dīn, Anṣārī al-Harawī, ʿA. M., Ḥikmat, ʿA. A. (1960) *Kashf al-asrār va ʿuddat al-abrār: maʿrūf bi-Tafsīr-i Khvajah ʿAbd Allāh Anṣārī.* Tehrān: Intishārāt-i Dānishgāh-i. Dual Volume, Book I, p. 574.

'Would that in ages past before you, there had been a group, a remnant, who forbade corruption on earth! Except for a few, and these We saved.' (*Qur'ān*, 11:116)

Exile is of three kinds: Exile from home—here it does not mean exile from your country, but an Exile from your True Home, the Abode of Eternity. If you are in that state, if you feel that you are in an environment where you are surrounded by people who are unable to relate to your condition—a corrupt age of corrupt people—then you are in Exile. Knowledgeable ones are few, ignorance is prevalent. If it seems there is no true person amongst enemies, many of us do feel Exiled. This Second kind is an Exile which has in it the seeds of rejoicing, because you are Promised the Abode. The Third kind, the Exile of the gnostic is in itself strange, and what they are witnessing is strange. It is not something that is immediately recognisable. You see different worlds, not the rewards of the known worlds. It is not the reward you are seeking, it is proximity to the Divine.

Anṣārī: Exile is a name given to the solitary withdrawal from others. It has three degrees:

1. Exile from homelands. The death of such an Exile is a form of witnessing, in the grave their measure would be light and on the Day of Reckoning they will be joined with Jesus, son of Mary, *'Issa ibn Mariam*.
2. Exile in their state, and these are the Exiles who will receive good news. They are the goodly ones caught in a corrupt age with corrupt people, knowledgeable ones surrounded by ignorance or a true person amongst hypocrites.
3. The Exile of concern, which is an Exile that seeks the Truth. It is the Exile of the gnostic because their witnessing is in itself strange and what they see is also strange. The Exile of the gnostic is the Exile of strangeness; for they are also strangers in this world and the next.

The Prophet (Pbuh) said: 'Islam entered the world a stranger; and will return as a stranger. So give the good news to the strangers.' Being in a State of *ghurba,* which means both Exile and strangeness, does not carry the same negative connotation as worldly exiles. On the contrary, it contains all the hallmarks of success and victory. Being in Exile as a stranger in a world which has in it the seeds of corruption is easily understood. Exile from one's homeland in the way of the Truth carries its own reward, as does the Exile of one who is already a stranger amongst their own people, as they seek what others cannot understand or appreciate. The most acute kind is the Exile of the one who has achieved openings and stages that put them beyond the measure of material or even spiritual concerns. Indifference to what others avidly seek is the mark of the Exile of the gnostic (*al-ʿārif*). It is the Exile of the stranger from what is most familiar and comprehensible; but it is an Exile rendered pure by choosing the road towards the Truth. It is the road of strangers and the solitary ones, girdled by witnessing of the Truth.

8.78. The Door of Drowning (*Bāb al-Gharq*) باب الغرق

فَلَمَّا أَسْلَمَا وَتَلَّهُ لِلْجَبِينِ

Falammā aslamā wa tallahu lil-jabīn

'When both submitted to the Will of God, he bent down his head and on its side.' (*Qur'ān*, 37:103)

Drowning, *gharq,* is to do with the Prophet Ibrahim and his visions. Both Ibrahim and his son Ismaʿil were at the stage of complete loss of volition, when you are sunk and you know that you have no ability to counter the forces. To be in the company of Abraham and Ishmael you have to have the absolute certainty they had. If you look at it from a rational, or even a spiritual perspective, why would a man be prepared to willingly slaughter his own son, a person most dear to him? If someone did that now it would be classified as murder. You have to be in such an exalted state of being. It is not limited to the prophets but potentially of all those who can only act according to Allāh—the condition of absolute obedience—in a state of Absolute Exaltation, the State of Drowning, because between the Prophet, or exalted being, and the Divine Presence there are no more veils. An instruction, command or signal that comes is not filtered through any medium. It comes to that person as is, not subject to reason or to any further qualifications.

Anṣārī: Drowning is the name given to one who is in the midst of this station and has gone beyond the bounds of separation. It has three degrees:

1. The Drowning of knowledge in the eye of one's state. This is the person who has won by uprightness, and verified the signs, and thus earned the right to be called a drowning person.
2. The Drowning of signs in unveiling. It is the person who speaks from one's state and moves according to what the person has seen, and is indifferent to the forms that the person passes by.
3. The Drowning of the multiplicities that one sees in gatheredness. This is the person who is enveloped in the lights of the saintly ones. They open their eyes, contemplating the Eternal Light, leaving behind all cares and concerns of this world.

The Qur'anic *āya* refers to the absolute certainty of Abraham and his son, Ishmael, preparing to lay down his life according to the Commands of Allāh. The Drowning of Abraham is the complete disappearance of the veil of separation, so that the Command is not from the other but from the One. There is no questioning its veracity because it emanates from the One Source to a receptacle that sees no duality. The degrees of Drowning in this Stage is the submersion of what is lower into what is higher, removing any trace of the lower condition. At its highest level, it is the light of prophecy and sainthood, which brooks no other source of Truth. At that point the individuality of the self becomes disconnected from any other source of authority and disappears.

Forty-First Reflection Day:

Now listen to this reed-flute's deep lament—About the heartache being apart has meant:

Since from the reedbed they uprooted me—My songs expressed each human's agony,

A breast which separation's split in two—Is what I seek, to share this pain with you:

When kept from their true origin, all yearn—For union on the day they can return.

Among the crown, alone I mourn my fate,—With good and bad I've learnt to integrate,

That we were friends each one was satisfied—But none sought out my secrets from inside;

My deepest secret's in the song I wail—But eyes and ears can't penetrate the veil:

Body and soul are joined to form one whole—But no one is allowed to see the soul.

It's fire, not just hot air, the reed-flute's cry—If you don't have this fire then you should die!

Love's fire is what makes every reed-flute pine, Love's ferment thus lends potency to wine;

The reed consoles those forced to be apart,—Its notes will lift the veil upon your heart,

Where's antidote or poison like its song,—Or confident, or one who's pined so long?

The reed relates a tortuous path ahead, Recalls the love with which Majnūn's heart bled: The few who hear the truths the reed has sung—Have lost their wits, so can speak this tongue.

The day is wasted if it's spent in grief—Consumed by burning aches without relief.

Good times have long passed, but we couldn't care When you're with us, our friend beyond compare!

While ordinary men on drops can thrive A fish needs oceans daily to survive:

The way the ripe must feel the raw can't tell My speech must be concise, and so farewell.*

* Rūmī, M. J. (2008) *The Masnavi*. Translated with an introduction and notes by Jawid A. Mojaddedi. Oxford: Oxford University Press.

WEEK FORTY-TWO

8.79. The Door of Detachment (*Bāb al-Ghayba*) باب الغيبة

وَتَوَلَّى عَنْهُمْ وَقَالَ يَا أَسَفَى عَلَى يُوسُفَ

Wa tawallā ʾanhum wa qāla yā asafā ʿalā Yūsuf

'So he turned his face away from them, saying "How I mourn Joseph".' (*Qurʾān*, 12:84)

Anṣārī: Detachment or turning away is of three degrees:

1. The Detachment of the wayfarer from the grip of what is familiar and the strewn obstacles, so that the wayfarer touches the realities.
2. The Detachment of the wayfarer from the outer forms of knowledge and seeking the causes of one's actions.
3. The Detachment of the gnostic from states, visions and stages by entering the fortress of gatheredness.

Turning away from what is familiar to what is real, from form to meaning and from multiplicity to unity is the hallmark of the process by which the wayfarer establishes their station on the path. The more one is disconnected from the commonplace, material and mundane and the more one's vision is focused on what is alive and true, the greater is the degree of accomplishment. Detachment requires a degree of discernment and discrimination—or *furqān* as the *Qurʾān* calls it. It is the discernment that comes from assigning the appropriate values and worth to phenomena, acknowledging and then verifying the realms of the unseen, and then disconnecting even from them towards the single Source of the One behind all the forms and meanings.

8.80. The Door of Capability (*Bāb at-Tamakkun*) باب التمكّن

ففا أصبر إِنَّ وَعْدَ اللَّهِ حَقٌّ وَلَا يَسْتَخِفَّنَّكَ الَّذِينَ لَا يُوقِنُونَ

Fa aṣbir inna waʿd Allāhi ḥaqqun wa lā yastakhiffannak alladhīna lā yūqinūna

And persevere, for God's promise is true and be not disheartened by those who have no conviction.' (*Qurʾān*, 30:60)

Anṣārī: The Station of Capability is higher than that of tranquillity. It is a sign of the permanence of one's stable state. It has three degrees:

1. The Capability of the adept. This requires that the adept is driven by a sound purpose, a shining vision, and a broad pathway that eases their Journey.
2. The Capability of the wayfarer in whom will be combined the firmness of their detachment, the bright lights of unveiling and the purity of their State.
3. The Capability of the gnostic in reaching the Divine Presence wearing the mantle of pure being.

The Door of Capability is the potential to achieve ends and can be brought into being by an act of volition. Having the potential guarantees the wayfarer that when the time comes to exert the final push, the reserves of power are there to thrust the wayfarer upwards on the Journey. The degree of potential spiritual focus one has is thus an accumulation of power that is kept until it is needed. It is what is deployed when one seeks to move from one stable or tranquil state to the next. Hence Anṣārī rightly accords it a higher value than the State of Capability. An outer metaphor for Capability is the concept of energy, latent energy, and kinetic energy. Every entity body has within it energetic capacity. Once that is manifested, it becomes an active kinetic energy. The expression of action is embedded in the object itself. A table, for example, has within it huge amounts of kinetic energy that could be derived from this potential energy. It is locked up in matter. It contains the potential of generating heat and light, if you set fire to it. Within the inner soul, the Capability of a person on the path is critical. Without that, your power may be exhausted at any stage.

Having a latent reservoir of power Capability allows you to realise your potential, which is a very important condition to be in. Now you can build up these reserves gradually, the more you progress. It is like a geometric progression. The higher you are on the scale, the greater are your reserves of energy for you to go to the next Stage. It has a built-in compensatory factor. If you burn this table, the energy locked up in it cannot be augmented. In the inner world, it can and it multiples and continues to create, recreate and transform. At this level of *Wilaya*, Guardianship, the latent capacity to generate insights, conditions and states that are exalted exist there in reserve. It is not always manifested.

Sometimes, if you read stories about the great ones, they do not always come up with whistles and bangs, but there is the potential for realising whatever needs to be realised at that point, in order to express or reflect what is in their hearts.

Tamakkun is to have within you the potential of expressing conditions as well as pushing you to the next level and it is a very significant halting point on the path. The more accomplished one is, the more all these reserves of Capability build up. They do not need to manifest themselves but you know that they are there as a reserve for you to draw on. These are for those who have gone beyond that stage and are attracted to the next stages, which become even more luminous and subtle and may be even harder to express, because they begin to deal with states that are extremely difficult to reflect, experientially. Perhaps there is the potential to realise what can be achieved by courtesy and desire.

Forty-Second Reflection Day:

Suggested *Dhikr* for the Stage of Guardianship:

Al-Wālī (The Guardian) *Al-Wārith* (The Inheritor) *Ar-Rāfi'* (The Uplifter)
Yā Wālī ~ Yā Wārith ~ Ya Rāfi' يا والي ~ يا وارِث ~ يا رافع

WEEK FORTY-THREE
The Final Doorways (*Abwāb al-Ākhira*) أبواب الآخِرة

We have now reached the final two stages—the last twenty doorways—of Anṣārī's *Manāzil.* At these levels of accomplishment, the wayfarer has gradually dissolved the glues that have given an autonomous reality to their existence and can now see the Presence from which true existence is derived. It might be a good point here to reflect on how practical and useful it is for those on the spiritual path, for wayfarers, not as a formalistic programme which has a definite beginning and end, but rather to do with changing your perceptions and ultimately having the awareness to be able to acknowledge that inner realities are subject to and determined by a different set of forces and rules to the outer world. Even learning an outer artform, skilled trade or sport is an ongoing process with an inner aspect involving some disciplining of the *nafs* to enable the outer discipline to develop and improve the level of skill.

Because we are and have been immersed in the outer world from the day that we were born until the day that we depart, it is natural that the stimuli of the material world, the physical, mental and psychic world prevail and, through a process of repetition and continuous immersion, one becomes established in a way of looking at things which may even be unconscious. We may strive not to give it exclusivity but it can easily become the way that we determine what reality is. Training in a creative art can certainly help by imbuing our work with more consciousness, a greater awareness of our environment at many levels as well as a deliberate use of the breath and more global activation of the mind. Performing arts tend to involve the whole being, including the subtle bodies, thus increasing general integration.

These stages are designed to create the circumstances where you can unpackage yourself, to go into the basic components of self and then reassemble them in ways that are more conducive to dealing with reality. The process is not one of simply confirming and verifying, it is also a process where we disconnect and unlearn. This is not done by abandoning all pursuit of knowledge regarding the way in which outer physical realities order themselves—if we do that then we become unbalanced and are not able to deal with outer realities properly—rather it is through an inner preference for a different set of rules. Inner perceptions do not necessarily give you the tools to interact in the outer world. Arts mediate the integration of inner and outer realities by dealing with the meanings and spiritual reality behind physical manifestations. This is why spiritual development is a creative process.

The unlearning and disconnecting part of the process is only for you to be allowed to confirm and verify and then to reach a certain equilibrium between the two. It is also unlearning habitual thinking and behaviours in favour of conscious choices. It is essential that the basic components of the inner realities are unbundled, recognised and then reassembled in an internally consistent way in which you can perceive and relate to them. That is when the real gains and successes would come, from this and other spiritual insights. This certainly applies to the works of, for example, Ibn ʿAṭa' Allāh, the maxims and in the case of the writings of Ibn ʿArabi and nearly all the spiritual masters of the great period of Islamic spiritual effulgence. They require that you develop these subtle senses of inner perception in order to make maximum practical use of them, in order to understand spiritual forces.

The forces that hold sway in the spiritual realm are analogous to the forces that hold the outer world together. In the physical, material world, the component building blocks of the cosmos are held together by four fundamental forces of nature: gravity, electro-magnetism, the weak nuclear force and the strong nuclear force. A researcher has to unravel the play of these forces to observe the actions of bodies and particles. The inverse forces that create the circumstances whereby we perceive subtler realms also need to be unbundled, which can be extremely powerful, as powerful as the strong nuclear force that keeps the electrons, protons and neutrons together. There is also an analogy for this in the spiritual realm. The forces that maintain the independent identity of self-consciousness, individuation, mind, intellect and so on, have to be unpacked and replaced with another experience of reality and existence.

These inner forces keep your sense of identity together, and therefore, when you have to unbundle and unpack them you run a very serious risk. You have to exert a huge amount of energy to split an atom. Similarly, you have to exert a great deal of energy to unbundle the components of the individuated self-consciousness. You have to overcome the understanding of consciousness that is rooted in the material and go beyond the personal mind, through which we filter all experiences, often with an internal running commentary. You have to go beyond this, beyond analytical intellect, and beyond your own sense of individual autonomy. The entire process of the *Manāzil,* seen in contemporary terms, is to do with that—how to quieten the personal mind and release perception and knowledge from the limitations of the material and mental, thus opening it to the subtler universe of the experience of unity. That is why the last doorway of the *Manāzil* is the Door of Unity or *tawḥīd.*

In these final stages, it is difficult to relay the experience of unity to those who have not tasted its reality. The description of a new continent is not the same as the experience of witnessing it. Language is inadequate for this purpose and when it has to be employed, its effects are often uneven. If one is to summarise the entire effect of the *Manāzil,* it is the acquiring of new ways of perception and experience that are in accordance with the subtler realities. The tools that we have developed and honed to experience and deal with the material and psychic worlds are inappropriate, in fact quite useless, when dealing with the realm of the unseen, *Al-Ghāyb*. Although we experience it in some form, it is often not fully consciously and we may try to rationalise it and explain it away by using the constructs of the material, measurable worlds, instead of paying closer attention to our inner faculties in order to unravel the mysteries of the unseen realms.

The process of ungluing the bonds that appear to give reality to a person is not easy; in fact it can be quite harrowing if it is not properly conducted and carefully supervised. The temptation is always to use one standard and if what is familiar and instinctive is replaced by what is uncertain and unstable, the effects can be disastrous—both for the inner and outer journey. If you are not very careful about it, if it is not done through a form or structure, with guidance, direction and orientation, you can end up questioning the most basic elements of your identity. If you are not properly equipped by both having the inner and outer senses in balance, as well as approaching it in a measured, directed way, you may end up with an internal chain reaction that goes wrong, like an uncontrolled nuclear reaction. It is as simple and as complex, but it requires the acquisition of a new way of perceiving and experiencing that is in accordance with the subtler realities.

That is why it has these gradations of the three degrees of each of the doors. It is really to do with the gradations that the wayfarer experiences in the true and genuine quest for the realm of the unseen. It is a realm that is awaiting your discovery. It is not something that you have to put on the right filters in order to perceive. It is a realm that is there, it is a real realm, but it is mainly absent from daily experience and is referred to in Arabic by the word *ghayb*, meaning absent or detached, but is frequently translated as 'unseen'. It has a reality, but its potential only becomes real if you realise it in yourself. Its reality comes into existence, as you approach it. Then it approaches you. It is a process of the ungluing of the bonds that give you a certain external reality, allowing you to go inward and examine its reflection on the soul, which is not only our subjective personal experience of reality but also our perception of universal reality.

The key is to maintain a proper balance between the material and the spiritual realities, of reconciling inside with out, so to speak, and to use the correct mechanisms of perception where and when appropriate. The mark of the true wayfarer is the ease and effortlessness by which they deal with the material and subtler worlds, using the right methods and tools in the correct context. Inner fleeing and absolute freedom joined with determined outer action and ethical conduct. These last stages do not require the customary detailed description, as they are the condition of a realised master from whom all veils have been lifted. Whether they are instantaneous flashes rendered comprehensively or a measured reflection of a person established in their station is something that cannot be determined. The writings of Ibn ʿArabi, Ibn ʿAṭa' Allāh and other masters, exhibit the same ambiguity. They are probably both. Flashes that were recorded at the time and then reproduced textually later after reflection.

There are some people who are not able to translate their experiences into comprehensible language—ʿAbdul-Jabbār Niffari, for example, one of the greatest spiritual masters in *Islām* whose flashes are challenging. A lot of what was written down from him by his students comes across as a contorted spiritual state, because he was trying to describe a continent that others have not seen. When Columbus returned, he tried to describe to Queen Isabella what was going on there, and people could not quite relate to it—different birds, fauna and flora. In the case of Anṣārī, his Flashes and Ecstasies were then filtered through a Sobriety, which he rendered in an organised, accessible, doctrinal way. They are, in both cases, flashes, therefore they have to be real, not a theoretical statement by a professor, but the experiences of a true master that are then rendered in ways that are more or less accessible and comprehensible.

9. The Stage of Realities (*Manzal al-Ḥaqā'iq*)

Overarching Names: The Teacher *al-Rashīd* الرشيد

The Witness *ash-Shahīd* الشهيد

These are established states, stations of people who are at the highest levels. The First Door of Stage of Realities, *Ḥaqā'iq*, is the Door of Unveiling or *Mukāshafa*.

9.81. The Door of Unveiling (*Bāb al-Mukāshafa*) باب المكاشفة

فَأَوْحَىٰ إِلَىٰ عَبْدِهِ مَا أَوْحَىٰ

Fa awḥā ilā 'abdihi mā awḥā

'And He revealed to His servant what He revealed.' (*Qur'ān*, 53:10)

Unveiling is knowledge that is implanted in the wayfarer's heart that shows the wayfarer the wonders of what is being witnessed. When you remove the veil, what you see behind it, the Truth and Reality is so powerful, so true, it is an astonishing sight. Unveiling is when what is seen astonishes continuously, because it shows the Bounties and Gifts of *Al-Wahhāb,* of Allāh and His Commands. It shows the perfection of everything; you see things in terms of instants, (*laḥdh*), and the past—the entire experience of the universe from pre-time to now—and what is going to emerge from this moment in the future unveiled in front of you. It reveals the multilayered, multifaceted Beauty of Allāh through inspiration and astonishment. It moves from flashes to a sustained observation, and finally to seeing only the essence of things. In *Sūrat an-Najm*, the highest form of Unveiling is experienced by the Prophet as he nears the Lote Tree of the Furthest Point (*sidrat al-muntaha* سدرة المنتهى).

Anṣārī: *Mukāshafa* or Unveiling is the flow of the secrets between two hidden realities. In this door, it is to reach what actually exists beyond the veils in three degrees:

1. The First Degree is the Unveiling that points to the correct verification, and it is impermanent. When it is sporadic and is not blocked by dispersion, even as a haze might have blurred their station, the seeker has nevertheless achieved a degree which no force could block, and no

cause could divert, and no ill-fortune could cut. This is the Degree of the determined one.

2. If this continues, then it becomes the Second Degree, in which the state becomes more permanent.
3. The Third Degree is the Unveiling of essence, which is not the Unveiling of knowledge, nor the Unveiling of a spiritual condition. It is an Unveiling that leaves no trace that might indicate satiety, nor one that causes a pause, nor one that resorts to figurativeness.

The purpose of this Unveiling is towards witnessing, which is the next Door.

9.82. The Door of Witnessing (*Bāb al-Mushāhada*) باب المشاهدة

إِنَّ فِي ذَٰلِكَ لَذِكْرَىٰ لِمَن كَانَ لَهُ قَلْبٌ أَوْ أَلْقَى السَّمْعَ وَهُوَ شَهِيدٌ

Inna fī dhālika ladhikrā liman kāna lahu qalbun aw alqā as-samʿa wa huwa shahīdun

'In this is a reminder to one possessed of heart, or one who hears attentively, and bears Witness.' (*Qurʾān*, 50:37)

Beyond that unveiling, the autonomy of the individual disintegrates. You have no reality, even your shadow disappears. This is that extremely high and very rare form of unveiling, and it is unclear whether any normal human beings are capable of reaching this level—apart from the Prophets, Imams and Saints—and of experiencing this kind of instantaneous recognition of reality and entirely unveiled witnessing as a continuous state, and be in continuous astonishment. From Unveiling you go beyond sight into *mushāhada*, a very high form of seeing, which is the realisation of Witnessing a matter, an event, or a state, and understanding the forms in which realities are manifested—knowledge whose purposefulness is achieved by unveiling.

In some ways, therefore, seeing could precede total unveiling. Witnessing in this sense, however, is that you witness the reality of the matter, rather than the apparent unfolding of the event. You see not only the forms in which events or realities are manifested, but you bore into them. There is a difference between confirming reality and understanding its meaning and witnessing the spiritual reality behind it and everything, the whole chain of realities and events that brought it into being.

When you see something with this kind of laser vision, you see into its meaning and purpose, rather than just its momentary appearance. It is necessary to get the full import and reason, without feeling the need to ask why, and when that happens, you start pondering or reflecting in a prescient way.

Anṣārī: Witnessing is the complete dropping of the veil, and it is superior in rank to unveiling, as unveiling still has elements of the Attributes and of images; while Witnessing is purely that of the Essence of the Real. Witnessing is of three degrees.

1. The First Degree is to see certainty beyond the boundaries of knowledge, in the tablets of the light of existence, bowing to the obliteration of multiplicity.
2. The Second Degree is an ocular Witnessing that cuts the ropes of indications, wearing the robes of sanctity, and silences allusions.
3. The Third Degree is Witnessing the many while drawn to the essence of multiplicity, certain of its Onrushes, and sailing the ocean of existences.

> Forty-Third Reflection Day:
>
> Ponder on the words of Sayyida Zaynab, the granddaughter of the Prophet, after seeing her family martyred on the battlefield of Karbalā and standing up to the tyrannical emperor responsible for the massacre: 'I saw nothing but beauty (*mā ra'aytu ilā jamīlā* ما رأيتُ إلا جميلة).' She witnessed the spiritual reality behind the events which unfolded in horrific scenes on the physical plane, and beheld in astonishment the beauty and perfection of their higher meaning.

WEEK FORTY-FOUR

9.83. The Door of Pondering (*Bāb al-Mu'āyāna*) باب المعاينة

أَلَمْ تَرَ إِلَىٰ رَبِّكَ كَيْفَ مَدَّ الظِّلَّ

Alam tara ilā rabbika kayfa maddaẓ-ẓilla

'Have you not seen how your Lord has stretched the shadow.'

(*Qur'ān*, 25:45)

Pondering is to verify the actions of Allāh *Al-Qadīr*, The Enabler, when one has had the veils removed and sees with inner sight. Shadows have no reality, except as they reflect the light of being. Pondering is to peel away the illusory layers and cacophonies that surround manifestations and to see in them only the 'Hand' of Allāh. It is understood to be when the stretching of the shadows occurs with the sinking of the sun at *maghreb* time, because of the movement of the earth, when the shadow the sun's light casts stretches. Ultimately it is this apparent change in length and the manifestation, when you ponder it is really nothing but the sun experienced in different ways, filtered through the turbid medium of the atmosphere* at an acute angle to the earth. Pondering is to relate whatever one witnesses in this state to reality, to the Light, the Source of all lights, consciousness and life.**

Ponderings are of three types:

1. The First is the Pondering of vision.
2. The Second is the Pondering of the eye of the heart, which is to know a matter by its attributes in a manner that brooks no perplexity nor doubt. This is Pondering on the aspects of knowledge.
3. The Third is to ponder on the heart of spirit. Pondering on reality with absolute clarity, spirits are thus purified and honoured by ongoingness, resonating with the splendour of the Divine Presence. They see the Might and are drawn irresistibly to annihilation in the Divine Presence.

Suhrawardi mused that light is the clearest of all Divine manifestations and that Allāh Is the Primordial Light from which all light stems, with various degrees of intensity depending on their proximity or distance. That Light calls us to draw near, like the cliché of moths to a flame. The sun itself has its own power to attract, as it gradually orbits the central sun, or galactic centre. These are physical lights, although itself invisible; its sources appear bright and it illuminates gross matter when reflected by it, but there is also an internal light whose beams shine in parallel and guide us spiritually. Physical light can seem to overpower

*One of Goethe's colour experiments described in his *Farbenlehre* involves holding a glass jar of cloudy water to the light and see it take on a reddish hue, while turning blue with the light in front of it.

** Suhrawardī, Y. ibn Ḥabash & Ziai, H. (1998) *The book of radiance. Partaw'nāmah: a parallel English-Persian text*. Costa Mesa, Calif: Mazda Publishers.

solid matter, rendering it visible or invisible. Internal Light can be seen without eyes. The Divine Light is invisible to physical eyes but can be witnessed by the spiritual eye of the heart.*

9.84. The Door of Life (*Bāb al-Hayāt*) باب الحياة

أَوَمَن كَانَ مَيْتًا فَأَحْيَيْنَاهُ

Awman kāna mayitan fa aḥyaināhu

'Or he who had been dead and We brought him into Life.' (*Qur'ān*, 6:122)

This is the Door of Life itself, *ḥayāt*, bringing the human being and spiritual potential back to Life in the sense of developing the faculties, the spirit and the breath that allow you to deal with it. This is what is meant by Life here. It is a Life that comes about as you unbundle your self and reconfigure—a different kind of Life. The breath of the outer life comes when you are born and departs when you physically die, but the breath of inner Life is when you unglue the components of a constructed 'reality' that has blocked your true vision. Once these are unglued and reconfigured, then Life comes into being anew. This is the kind of Life you do not want to lose. You do not want to see the capacities inherent in that Life dissipate from you. In the initial phases, there is a fear that you might lose the possibility of experiencing this powerful inner sight. Then, as you establish yourself in this condition, it becomes the Life of seeing unity, seeing gatheredness all around you. Then, ultimately, in the final stages of the Life of sheer existence, not just the spiritual breath, it gives you this sheer knowledge that you are only a reflection of true being, which is Life of truth.

Anṣārī talks of three kinds of Life:

1. The First Life is Life that arises from the death of ignorance. It has three breaths: the breath of fear; the breath of hope; the breath of Love.
2. The Second Life is the Life of gatheredness from the death of separation. It has three breaths: the breath of necessity; the breath of impoverishment; the breath of pride.

---

*As Imam 'Ali said that he could not worship a God he did not see, meaning he could see Him with his inner eyes, his mind's eye, or the eye of his pure heart.

3. The Third Life is the Life existent which is Life in the Truth. It has three breaths: the breath of Awe as it slays illnesses (of the heart); the breath of Existence as it banishes separation; the breath of individuation which ignites attachment.

There is nothing beyond this for observers nor any power for allusion.

Forty-Fourth Reflection Day:

Who Are You and What Do You Want?

He said, 'Who is at my door?' I said, 'Your humble slave.'
He said, 'Why have you come?' I said, 'To offer salaams.'
He said, 'How long will you wait?' I said, 'Until you call.'
He said, 'How long will you boil?' I said, 'Until you resurrect me.'
I laid claim to love, swore oaths of love, and told how I lost all power and position for love.
He said, 'The judge asks to see your witness.' 'These tears, these pale cheeks.'
'Your witness has bloodshot eyes and cannot be trusted.'
I said, 'By your high justice, they are just and true.'
He said, 'Who was your companion?' 'Your gift of imaginal vision.'
'What called you here?' 'The fragrance of your cup.'
'What do you want?' 'Faithfulness and intimacy.'
'What do you want from me?' He said. 'Your subtle grace,' I said.
'Where is the greatest pleasure?' 'In Caesar's palace,' I said.
'And what did you see there? ' A hundred fascinations.'
He said, 'Then why is it so desolate?' 'For fear of thieves.'
'Who is the thief?' He said, 'Whatever challenges our vanity,' I said.
'Where is safety?' He said, 'In abstinence and pure consciousness of God.'
'What is abstinence?' I said, 'The way of peace.'
'Where is catastrophe?' 'In the street of Your love.'
'How do you travel there?' He asked. 'With integrity,' I said.
Silence. If I were to utter more, you would be completely gone, left without a door or roof.
[By *Mawlana* Muḥammad Jalāl ud-Dīn Rūmī*]

*Jalāl al-Dīn Rūmī & Helminski, K. E. (2008) *The pocket Rumi*. Boston, Mass: Shambhala.

WEEK FORTY-FIVE

9.85. The Door of Constrictiveness (*Bāb al-Qabḍ*) باب القبض

قَبَضْنَاهُ إِلَيْنَا قَبْضًا يَسِيرًا

Qabaḍnāhu ilaynā qabḍayyasīrā

'Then We Drew it unto Ourselves, a little at a time.' (*Qur'ān*, 25:46)

Then we move on to the Door of Constrictiveness, *Qabḍ.* We have experienced that before, but in a different stage. At this stage of highest realisation, the kind of Constrictiveness that comes is actually the force of being drawn to Divine Presence. It pulls you. It is not so much a kind of pulverising force, but more akin to being covered, protected by your knowledge for your knowledge, by God's Might, rather than a force that crushes or smothers you. God's Covering, through the manifestation of His Name *As-Sattār,* can be to protect the wayfarer from the malice of others; or to protect one from revealing their true condition. It is a way of protecting the realised wayfarer from others, not physically, but by not letting others become aware of their state or condition because they will either resent it or not understand it. It could cause great friction. It is a form by which your true condition, by God's Mercy, is Covered from others. With Constrictiveness, another Door opens, that of Expansiveness.

Constrictiveness in this Door is the station of the selected ones, which Allāh the Truth has Kept for Himself. They are of three groups.

1. A Group whom He Drew Close by the grip of death, keeping them from the eyes of the multitudes.
2. A Group whom He Covered with a disguising cloak, draping them with forms, and hiding them from the eyes of the multitudes.
3. And a Group whom He Drew Closely to Himself, Gathering them secretly into His Presence, and sparing them from their selves.

9.86. The Door of Expansiveness (*Bāb al-Basṭ*) باب البسط

يَذْرَؤُكُمْ فِيهِ

Yadhra'ūkum fīhi

'Wherewith you multiply.' (*Qur'ān*, 42:11)

The Door of Expansiveness has other features. You become immersed in a sense of unlimited potential. Again, in the physical world, there are similar states and conditions, some of them chemically induced, some by hypnotism or other forms of influence or persuasion where you feel that you are unlimited. But it is an impermanent or even a false expansiveness. The enormous potential that is open to you is a state (*ḥāl*) that can also be confirmed as a permanent feature. It allows you to constantly be in a state of great optimism and see vistas opening up in front of you, continuously unfolding. At the final stage it is the permanent State of Expansiveness, of seeing only the good, seeing only the true manifestations of the Names as they unfold, and the knowledge of the enormous potential. This can cause you great elation, and opens up the Door of Intoxication.

Expansiveness is when He Attaches to the traits of the bondsperson the grades of knowledge, and when He Covers the hidden nature of the bondsperson with the garments of devotion. These are the folk of disguises or ruses and form three groups under each of the three degrees of Expansiveness.

Each of the three groupings have spread onto the field of Expansiveness for one of the three purposes, and each of the three degrees fulfils a particular purpose:

1. Expansiveness for the elevation of creation. They mingle with creation and are considered of it. Creation is illumined by their light, realities are gathered and secrets are safeguarded.
2. Expansiveness by the power of their purposefulness and the strength of their vision. They are a group whose insights are not clouded by what they observe, for their Expansiveness is due to the grip of constrictiveness.
3. The Third Group expanded their milestones on the path, for they are the leaders of guidance and lanterns for the seekers.

Expansiveness is an increase in the knowledge and elated state of the wayfarer. It can come about by keeping the companionship of the learned ones and other adepts; or by immersing oneself in reflection and contemplation as do wayfarers; or by aiding and assisting other adepts or wayfarers on their Journey. This is the Expansive state of the gnostics, *al-ʿarifīn*, but it is Allāh Who Is the Origin of the Expansive Powers. This is clearly exemplified by (Rumi—Shaykh Muḥammad

Jalāl ad-Dīn al-Balkhi)—and in more recent times by Hazrat Inayat Khān, in their inclusivity and universality, accepting followers and students from all faiths, backgrounds and walks of life on the basis of their potential for total transformation. This is a blossoming of the unconditional Love (*mawadda*) of earlier stages and constitutes radical acceptance, forgiveness and, for want of a better word, tolerance (*tasāmuḥ*) in action.

قُلْ إِنَّ رَبِّي يَبْسُطُ الرِّزْقَ لِمَن يَشَاءُ مِنْ عِبَادِهِ وَيَقْدِرُ لَهُ

Qul inna Rabbī yabsiṭu ar-rizqa liman yashā'u min 'ibādihi waya-qdiru lahu

'Say my Lord increases knowledge and provision to whomever He wants of His servants, in due measure.' (*Qur'ān*, 34:38)

Forty-Fifth Reflection Day:

Ibn 'Ata' Allah al-Iskandarī from the Book of Wisdom, *Ḥikām*

Ḥikma 81

He expanded you so as not to keep you in constriction, and constricted you so as not to keep you in expansion, and He took you out of both states so that you do not belong to anything apart from Him.

Ḥikma 82

The gnostics are more fearful when in expansion than when in constriction, for very few can maintain the boundaries of courtesy to Allāh in the state of Expansion.*

WEEK FORTY-SIX

9.87. The Door of Intoxication (*Bāb as-Sukr*) باب السكر

قَالَ رَبِّ أَرِنِي أَنظُرْ إِلَيْكَ

Qāla Rabbi arinī anẓur ilayka

'He said, "My Lord, let me see You."' (*Qur'ān*, 7:143)

The Door of Intoxication is obviously alluding to spiritual Intoxication, where the bounds appear to dissolve, and you can become ecstatic.

*From Haeri, F. (2001) *The Wisdom of Ibn Ata'Allah.* A Translation and commentary. London: Zahra Trust. See also Al-Iskandarī, A. & Anṣārī, A. (1979) *Ibn 'Ata' Illah: The book of Wisdom; Khwaja Abdullah Anṣārī: Intimate conversations.* Translations & notes by Victor Danner & Wheeler Thackston, New York: Paulist Press.

Everything around you becomes unbounded. Everything is immersed in the ocean of potential. All potentials can happen. It becomes like an ocean of delight; your patience, constrictiveness, everything is forgotten in the joy of wonder, but this is also a dangerous state. Anṣārī guards against it and those who have had these glimpses advise regarding it. It can lead to unbounded utterances, *shatḥāt*—ecstatic statements that sometimes go beyond the realm of the permissible from a *Shara'i* perspective and can lead to terrible things. It is very rare these days, as there are not very many people at this stage. Intoxication in this Door is the loss of control whilst in a state of ecstasy. This is the Station of the Lovers especially. The innermost point of annihilation does not accept them, and the gradations of knowledge do not reach to them.

There are three signs of Intoxication:

1. Reluctance to indulge in events when The Mighty is Present.
2. Coursing through the ripples of yearning, while empowerment is established.
3. And drowning in the sea of joy, with patience wandering.

Anything apart from this is perplexity, mistakenly referring to it as Intoxication or a thirst that carries the same name in error. All else is an inadequacy in inner sight, such as the intoxication of miserliness, or the intoxication of ignorance, or the intoxication of desire.

1,000 years ago there were people like Ḥallāj, Sahravārdi *al-Maqtūl**, who made statements and comments that appeared profoundly antithetical to the *sharīʿa.* They were tried by *sharīʿa*, found guilty, and in some cases they had sentences passed, and therefore, when you are in a State of Intoxication, you have to bound yourself, otherwise you may cause harm to yourself or others if you start uttering outrageous statements or making inappropriate claims, creating confusion and mayhem. Intoxication is a state where ecstasy is nearly unbounded. The heart is immersed in the ocean of delight and all struggles are

*Suhrawardi is also known as *ash-Shaykh al-Maqtūl,* or the Murdered Master, having been executed by order of *Sahaḥ ad-Dīn al-Ayūbi,* perhaps for his esoteric ideas, including reincarnation, drawing from different ancient scriptures, as well as his powerful influence on Ṣahaḥ ad-Dīn's son.

forgotten in the joy of wandering. Nevertheless the wayfarer must guard against utterances that are discourteous and from revealing the secrets which have been revealed to them. Overstepping the bounds can lead to righteous application of the limits of the law, as had happened to al-Ḥussayn ibn Mansūr al-Ḥallāj or Shihāb ad-Dīn Yeḥya ibn Ḥabash Suhrawārdī.

9.88. The Door of Sobriety *(Bāb aṣ-Ṣaḥw)* باب الصحو

حَتَّىٰٓ إِذَا فُزِّعَ عَن قُلُوبِهِمۡ قَالُواْ مَاذَا قَالَ رَبُّكُمۡۖ قَالُواْ ٱلۡحَقَّ

Ḥattā idhā fuzza' 'an qulūbihim qālu mādhā qāla Rabbukum qālu al-ḥaq

'Until, when terror is removed from their hearts, they shall ask: "What did your Lord say?" and they shall answer "The Truth".' (*Qur'ān*, 34:22)

Intoxication on the journey is towards the Truth. Sobriety on the other hand, is by the Truth. Sobriety is parallel with the state of expansiveness as intoxication is with the state of constrictiveness. The latter is still perplexed, awaiting the realisation of the purpose; the sober one is not perplexed by shadows. The sober wayfarer travels by the knowledge of the One but is still dazzled by the Light of Power and Might. This drunkenness on the journey is towards it as you are approaching *al-Ḥaqq* and you see all the constraints dissolve, and you reach this ecstatic state. You are going towards a goal. Once you reach the goal, you cannot just stop. Another state kicks in, which is the state of Sobriety, or *ṣaḥu*, in which your actions, states and conditions are not towards the Truth, but are now by the Truth. Sobriety, *ṣaḥu* is to expansiveness what intoxication is to constrictiveness.

Sobriety is a station higher than intoxication, and it corresponds with the station of expansiveness. Sobriety is a station that is above awaiting, has no need of demanding, devoid of any embarrassment. Intoxication is within Truth, while Sobriety is by Truth. And all that is in the eye of truth is not free from perplexity, the perplexity of bewilderment, or rather the perplexity of seeing the Light of Might. Whatever is by the Truth is whole, and has no impairment, and is not harmed by any deficiency. Sobriety is one of the stations of life, the valleys of gatheredness, and the tablets of existence. That sometimes brings you to the next stage, which is a state in which the veils are removed and the bounds are dissolved. You may reach a state where there is a certain connectedness.

Forty-Sixth Reflection Day: Poem by Al-Ḥussayn ibn Manṣūr al-Ḥallāj (d. 922):	
I am astonished by you and by me, O You Who Are the devout wish of all who wish	عَجِبتُ مِنكَ وَمِنّـي يا مُنيَـةَ المُتَمَنّي
You drew me near You until I thought You were me	أدنَيتَني مِنكَ حَتّى ظَنُنتُ أنَّكَ أنّـي
Annihilated in ecstasy until You Erased me from myself in You	وَغبتُ في الوَجدِ حَتّى أفنَيتَني بِكَ عَنّـي
O my Grace in life and my comfort after my burial	يا نعمَتي في حَياتـي وَراحَتي بَعدَ دَفنـي
I have no intimacy with anyone but You, where Is my fear and my safety	ما لي بِغَيرَكَ أُنسٌ مِن حَيثَ خَوفي وأمني
O You, the Gardens of Meanings that surround all my Art	يا مِن رياض معانيهْ قَد حَّوَيْت كُلَ فَنّي
And if ever I wished for anything, You Are my every wish	وإن تَمَنَيْتُ شَيْئًا فأنتَ كُلَ التَمنّـي

WEEK FORTY-SEVEN

9.89. The Door of Connection (*Bāb al-It'tiṣāl*) باب الإتّصال

فكَانَ قَابَ قَوْسَيْنِ أَوْ أَدْنَىٰ

Fakāna qāba qawsayni aw adnā

'And was two bows' lengths or nearer.' (*Qur'ān*, 53:9)

Connection to the Divine Presence starts with perseverance in one's purpose, moves to a Connection drawn from witnessing, and finally the Connection is established by the Eternal Presence of Being. This is the presence of proximity. But this is also a very dangerous state. You think that you are now within the Divine Presence and, because you are there, you think you are now in the circle of proximity, but you have to be on guard. Allāh Warns you in the *Qur'ān* of Himself and that you had better be careful you do not make any attributions to yourself.

No matter how realised, how many of these veils have lifted, there is still transcendence. There remains a state of exaltation which does not belong to you. There are states, Names that belong Only to Allāh like The One. We cannot be The One, *Al-Waḥid* or The Eternal *Aṣ-Ṣamad.* It is not something that you can aspire to. On the other hand you can be the one for another person and, therefore, reflect that Divine Reality in limited human form.

We are also eternal in the One and our soul is immortal, as our spirit is part of His Spirit.

Connection is of three degrees: the First Degree is the Connection of perseverance, the Second, the Connection of witnessing, and the Third is the Connection of existence:

1. The Connection of perseverance is to rectify the intent, then to purify the will, then to verify the state.
2. The Connection of witnessing is to be free of deficiencies, free of justifications, and the collapse of myriad thoughts.
3. The Third Degree is the Connection with existence, which cannot be measured or described. It can only be indicated by signs and borrowed Names.

9.90. The Door of Disconnection (*Bāb al-Infiṣāl*) باب الإنفصال

وَيُحَذِّرُكُمُ اللَّهُ نَفْسَهُ

Wa yuḥadhdhirukum Allāhu nafsahu

'And Allāh cautions you regarding Himself.' (*Qur'ān*, 3:28)

Disconnection is an essential element of the journey at the final stages, for as Allāh Is Proximate, so Is He Ever Exalted. 'None can be compared to Him' as the *Qur'ān* says. The wayfarer, having achieved the further reaches of the journey, must be alert to God's Incomparability, and not indulge in dangerous fantasies of conjoining with the Creator by completely dissolving the veils and boundaries. The pulsating states of nearness and farness; proximity and exaltedness; similarity and incomparability must always be kept in balance. Do not go beyond the Lote Tree of the limit, even if you think you have reached that State. It is the highest, most exalted state, being the prophetic ascent, bringing proof. Disconnection is a door of the highest quality, because one's instinct is to move forward. Caution here is absolutely essential. This applies at various degrees to all of us on this path.

There are no Stations that are more expansive than the State of Disconnection. It has three aspects:

1. The First Aspect is the Disconnection that is a condition of attachment. It is to be detached from the Two worlds (of witnessing and the unseen), by disconnecting your vision of them, your concern for them, and your care about them.
2. The Second Aspect is to disconnect from the Disconnection that we mentioned, so that nought can distract you from witnessing verification, even by the act of Disconnection.
3. The Third Aspect is to disconnect from connection, that is a Disconnection from witnessing the complexities that preceded connection, for disconnecting and connecting, despite their differences in name and form, share the same measure of defects.

All of these doors have their reality at other stages, but they are put in this order because that is where the sequencing might be most pertinent, although elements of them exist everywhere throughout the structure. The Door of Disconnection, that is pulling back in order to maintain the balance, is essential at all levels of this journey. Again, many people on this path in the past have found themselves in the unenviable position of making statements and utterances which are borderline. This is a jsourney of not either or, but both. You are near and far, you are proximate, but you recognise the Exaltedness of Allāh. There are many similarities. He is as close to you as your jugular vein, but at the same time, there is nothing that can be compared to Him *layssa kamithlihi shay'* لَيْسَ كَمِثْلِهِ شَيْءٌ (*Qur'ān*, 42:11). This constant balancing act of equilibrium, knowing the intermediary path, *al-ummat al-wasata,* is the pathway of true wayfaring.

Forty-Seventh Reflection Day:

Recommended Dhikr for the Stage of Realities:

Al-Ḥayy (The Alive/Living) *Al-Qābiḍ* (The Constrictor) *Al-Bāsiṭ* (The Expander)

Ya Ḥayy ~ Ya Qābiḍ ~ Ya Bāsiṭ يا حي ~ يا قابض ~ يا باسط

10. The Stage of the Endings (*Manzal an-Nihāyāt*)

منزل النهايات

Overarching Names: The First *al-Awal* الاول

The Last *al-Aākhir* الاخر

WEEK FORTY-EIGHT

This last stage is a stage of realised people and when we bandy about the words like *m'ārifa*, gnosis, and *fanā'*, annihilation, we should be very careful when we use them as they refer to the most exalted, elevated states and we must exercise extreme caution when claiming these states and conditions. The Stage of the Endings, *an-nihāyāt* begins with the Door of Gnosis or *m'ārifa.* All the āyāt that Anṣārī chooses are very apt as they are Qur'anic descriptions of these states. It also confirms and roots the entire journey in the highest form of knowledge, which is embedded in the *Qur'ān*. Many who read the *Qur'ān* will try to disconnect this path from either *Islām* or the *Qur'ān* as if it somehow sprung on its own and has its own reality, and its own rules, and is only tangentially concerned with Revelation Theology. This is certainly not the case amongst the people like Ibn 'Arabī and 'Aṭa Allāh al-Iskanderī and it is definitely not the case with Anṣārī. They were all extremely high level Islamic scholars and their thought, works and practice are all *Qur'ān* based.

The Stage of the Endings had ten Doors:

10.91 The Door of Gnosis (*Bāb al-Ma'ārifa*) باب المعرفة

وَإِذَا سَمِعُوا مَا أُنزِلَ إِلَى الرَّسُولِ تَرَىٰ أَعْيُنَهُمْ تَفِيضُ مِنَ الدَّمْعِ مِمَّا عَرَفُوا مِنَ الْحَقِّ

Wa idhā sami'ū mā anzila ilā Rasūli tarā a'iunahum tafīḍu min ad-dumū' mimmā 'arfū min al-ḥaqqi

'And if they listen to what had been revealed to the Messenger you will see their eyes overflowing with tears from the truth they recognise.' (*Qur'ān*, 5:83)

The kind of states and stations that Anṣārī describes are all inferred from Quranic expositions of these states. So when he says here, 'and if they listen to what has been revealed, 'He revealed to the messenger, you will see their eyes overflowing with tears.' They cry because they are overwhelmed by the Power of this Truth and the Knowledge that they have not heard of or known before. They see with the inner eye that drills into the reality of things, and what they think of as knowledge, which is the accumulation of facts, is not necessarily the same as this kind of Knowledge, and certainly in terms of its scope, its symbolism, its importance, that was an entirely inferior form of knowledge. Realising that it is an inferior form of knowledge is not to deny its reality, but rather to recognise that there are higher forms of Knowledge.

It is an axiom that the lower cannot understand the higher. For example, an insect cannot understand the reality of a human being. On the hierarchical scale of existence, this form of Knowledge, which is Knowledge of the unseen, by its very nature is greater and more encompassing than a lower form of knowledge, which has its reality, but is dimensionally on a different plane. They weep because they are overwhelmed by the scale of openings that emerge from this Gnosis. The Prophet asked Allāh many times to show him things as they really are. To Know things as they are is to Know their essence, their meaning, and the highest form of it is to relate what you see to the powers given you, that is the Attributes, then relating the Attributes to the Source, keeping in mind all the while the unknowability of the Essence and the heart of the matter, the impossibility of independent Knowledge outside the Knowledge given.

Gnosis is to encompass Knowledge of the essence of things as they are. It is of three degrees and those with Gnosis of it are in three groups:

1. The First Degree is to Know the Divine Qualities and Attributes. Further conditions are required for certainty. These rest on three pillars:
   The First is to confirm the Attribute and its true Name with no similitude.
   The Second is to reject any similitude without simultaneously denying it in totality.
   The Third is despairing of truly Knowing its essence and refraining from trying to interpret its subtleties.

2. The Second Degree is to recognise the essence by denying the contradistinctions between Essence and Attribute. This arises from the Knowledge of gatheredness, is purified in the realm of annihilation and reaches fulfilment in the Knowledge of ongoingness, as it approaches the essence of gatheredness. These rest on three pillars:

   Allowing the Reality of the Attributes to prevail over their appearances.
   Allowing the reality of the Stations to prevail over the ways to them.
   Allowing the realities to prevail over their expressions.

This is the Gnosis of the selected ones, which rests on the horizons of reality.

3. The Third Degree is Gnosis that is drowning in the Divine Precepts. It is not reached by ratiocination, neither by indications, nor by any other means. It rests on three pillars:

   Witnessing Proximity.
   Transcending Knowledge.
   Contemplating Gatheredness.

Some of their Names have appeared in this text and their signs have manifested in creation. This has been affected by seeing the light that emanates from their innermost, the enlivening of the intellect that plants the seeds of reflection, and the re-enlivening of the heart that engenders appropriate Inquiry through glorification and contemplation. You may talk about it, but if you realise it, you have to then efface yourself and remove from your self any traces of independent power, which includes Knowledge. The last Stage of true Gnosis is to drop any claim to Gnosis. When that happens, then you reach the Door of Annihilation, *fanā'*.

10.92. The Door of Annihilation (*Bāb al-Fanā'*) باب الفناء

كُلُّ مَنْ عَلَيْهَا فَانٍ وَيَبْقَى وَجْهُ رَبِّكَ ذُو الْجَلَالِ وَالْإِكْرَام

Kullu man ʿalayhā fānin wa yabqā wajhu Rabbika dhul-Jalāli wal-Ikrām

'All who are upon her [earth] are ephemeral, and there remains the Face of your Lord, Majestic and Noble.' (*Qur'ān*, 55:26-27)

Annihilation is the effacement, gradually or abruptly, suddenly, catastrophically, or incrementally, of any reality except the 'Face' or the Aspect of the One. Passing through the Valley of Annihilation, of which many have experienced flashes during heightened *adhkār*, a kind of dissolution, it is not something that is difficult to achieve, but it is frenzied. At this final stage, Annihilation means the affirmation of reality only to the One, first by knowledge and exertion and then by immersion in its reality. There is no true knowledge that is not rooted in the One Reality. The wayfarer then becomes oblivious to any assertions of Truth other than with and by Allāh. You are oblivious to the ersatz knowledge that comes from the self or from others. All manifestations of existence vanish as they are drawn back into the One and become merely aspects of Allāh. As the *Qur'ān* says, 'Kill your selves [the lower self/ego] for that is better for you with your Lord...'

Annihilation is the fading away of all except reality, in terms of knowledge, its denial, or its affirmation. It is of three degrees:

1. The First Degree is the Annihilation of knowledge in the Knower. This is the Annihilation of knowledge. Then the Annihilation of the seen in the Seer. This is the Annihilation of denial. Then the Annihilation of the desire for separate existence. This is the true Annihilation.
2. The Second Degree is the Annihilation of the quest of demands, so as to eliminate it; the Annihilation of the witnessing of knowledge, so as to eliminate it; and the Annihilation of the desire for witnessing, so as to eliminate it.
3. The Third Degree is the Annihilation of the witnessing of Annihilation. This is true Annihilation, glimpsing the lightning of the essence, sailing the ocean of gatheredness, and seeking the path of eternity.

The objective in *taṣawwuf* is not to stop there, but to pass through *fanā'* to the next stage, which is the Door of Eternity, *Baqā'*.

Forty-Eighth Reflection Day:

ʿIraqi's Divine Flashes *Lamahāt*

[From Flash VI]

On the fact that the lover is the mirror of the Beloved, and vice versa, each appears in the stage of the other and is not delimited by its own peculiarities.

The end of the affair: The lover sees the Beloved as his own mirror, and himself as the mirror of the Beloved.

Without cease
gazing into the purity
of the Friend's face, he sees the universe
Imaged in his own reality
And if he once looks back
Into the chamber of his heart
He finds there like a blazing sun
The sweet face of his heart-thief.

Sometimes one is a witness, the other is witnessed, sometimes the reverse. Sometimes one appears in the other's tints; sometimes one is perfumed with the other's fragrance.

Now Love tailors the lover a cloak of radiance and perfection, adorning him with the accoutrements of exquisite grace: he looks at himself and sees only the colour of the Beloved, sees himself all HIM. He shouts, 'Glory be to me, how exalted is my state! Who is like me? Or is there ought but me in the two worlds?' (Bayazid).

Or again, Love drapes the Beloved in the robes of the lover, that the Beloved might climb down from the Station of Majesty and Self-Sufficiency and plead thus with His lover:

'I Swear by My Right
I Love you
So to love Me in return
Is your responsibility.'

Sometimes the Beloved's quest grasps the skirt of the lover, saying, 'Is not the desire of the pious drowned out endlessly by their desire to Me?' And sometimes the lover's desire raises its head from the neck of the Beloved's cloak and declares, 'Verily I desire them more than they desire Me!' Sometimes the Beloved Himself becomes the lover's sight, that He might say, 'I saw my Lord with the eye of the Lord. I asked, "Who art Thou?" and He answered, "Thou." Sometimes the lover becomes the Beloved's voice and says, '*Grant him protection until he hears the words of God.*'

In Love alone

Can such wonders be.

[From Flash VII]

On the Self-Manifestation of Love
Through its Non-delimitation in all the loci-of-manifestation
And its appearance in the clothing of Belovedness
For all kinds of perception and cognition.

Love courses through all things....No, it is all things. How deny it when nothing else exists? What has appeared—if not for Love—would not have been. All has appeared from Love, through Love, and Love courses through it... No, all of it is Love.*

WEEK FORTY-NINE

10.93. The Door of Eternity (*Bāb al-Baqā'*) باب البقاء

وَاللَّهُ خَيْرٌ وَأَبْقَى

Wa Allāhu khayrun wa abqā

'Allāh is better and more abiding.' (*Qur'ān*, 20:73)

Eternity is what remains after annihilation is transcended. Knowledge is replaced with the knowledge of the Source of Knowledge; similarly for Power, Life, and all the Names and Attributes. The wayfarer is effaced by the inimitability of the Essence, only to be reconfirmed in existence by Essence's Abiding. Then your *baqā'* comes when you return back to 'physical reality', you snap out of it. The Eternity of the spiritual wayfarer is of a different kind. It is a condition

*From 28 Flashes by the thirteenth-century Persian mystic from Hamadān, Fakhruddin 'Irāqī, F. al-D. I. (1982) *Divine Flashes*. Translation and Introduction by William Chittick and Peter Lamborn Wilson, Preface by Seyyed Hussein Nasr. New York: Paulist Press.

that stays indefinitely. It is a reflection of an infinite condition, of the Name *Al-Bāqi*, The Eternal, The Everlasting. Nothingness is nothing more than the absence of everything. Allāh tells you that you may pass through the Door of Annihilation, but you should move on because 'I Am *al-Bāqi*,' The Everlasting, The Eternal. You are effaced, removed, humbled, pulverised by inevitability, only to be reconfirmed by the abidingness of The Abiding, which then makes you a verifier. You become a *muḥaqqiq* in a Doorway of Verification.

Everlastingness is the Name that remains after the collapse and annihilation of the pointers to reality. It is of three degrees:

1. The First Degree is Eternity of the Knower after the collapse of the known, in actuality and not merely in being known.
2. The Second Degree is the Eternity of the Witnessed after the collapse of the witness, in actuality and not merely in expression.
3. The Third Degree is the Eternity of that which has not vanished in reality, by erasing what never had existed in any case.

10.94. The Door of Verification (*Bāb at-Taḥqīq*) باب التحقيق

قَالَ أَوَلَمْ تُؤْمِن ۖ قَالَ بَلَىٰ وَلَٰكِن لِّيَطْمَئِنَّ قَلْبِي

Qāla awalam tu'min qāla balā walākil liyaṭma'inna qalbī

'Have you not believed?' And he said, 'Yes, but so that my heart can be at peace.'

(*Qur'ān*, 2:260)

The Door of Verification is the door of seeing only from Truth. That is, you have come to Reality, *al-ḥaqq* and you emerge from it but then you see by it, and then you see in it. You see with the Eyes of the One, your hands become the Hands of the One, your feet the Feet of the One. You have become a repository of the Attributes and you verify them by carrying them. You verify by your actions, states and conditions, that ultimately whatever you witness cannot rival His Vision, your knowledge cannot compare to His Knowledge. Your states, degrees of realisation, whatever you think of yourself, is nothing compared to God's Reality. Verification is to move from Truth, by Truth and then in Truth as a Verifier, *muḥaqqiq*.

Verification is to remove your desires from Reality, then by Reality; and then in Reality.

These Names have three degrees:

1. The First Degree is the removal of your desires from His Reality; it is to know that your knowledge cannot contend with His.
2. The Second Degree is that your witnessing cannot compete with His Witnessing.
3. As for the Third Degree, it is that your form cannot precede His Ancientness. Testimonies collapse, expressions are vacuous, and signs are obliterated.

> Forty-Ninth Reflection Day:
>
> God is the Most High and, over time, all attachments will end, means will vanish, customs will be voided, limits with be broken, understandings will be eliminated, history will fade away, allusions are transient, expressions are negated, information will be wiped out, but God eternally exists, and He exists in His ultimate Unity.*

WEEK FIFTY

10.95. The Door of Ruses (*Bāb at-Telbīs*) باب التلبس

وَلَلَبَسْنَا عَلَيْهِم مَّا يَلْبِسُونَ

Wa lalabasnā ʿalayhim mā yalbisūn

'And confused them even more than they are already confused.'

(*Qurʾān*, 6:9)

Then comes the Door of Ruses, *telbīs*, which means to dress, clothe or cover. *Libās* in Arabic means clothing. It can also mean a Ruse, something that creates a different impression. It is here translated thus as the *aya* that Anṣārī uses tends to confirm the use of the term Ruses: 'And confuse them even more than they are already confused.' So why do we need this door? Why do you need to have Ruses after all this?

*From Anṣārī's *Sad Maydan* in *Farsi* 30 years prior to *Manāzil,* Anṣārī al-Harawī, A. M., ʿA & Angha, N. (2010) *Stations of the Sufi path: the one hundred fields Sad Maydān of ʿAbdullāh Anṣārī of Herat*. Cambridge: Archetype.

The answer becomes quite clear: it is, again, a form of protection. It is to acquire the condition of *telbīs* or being in a position where you confuse the enemy of your intentions and your reality, mainly to protect yourself. You want to guard your time with Allāh and you do not want it to be affected by being drawn back into the physical, mental or psychic realms. To prevent that, you hide your true reality.

Ruses are to disguise an existing being with a camouflage.

It is a name with three meanings:

1. The First is to disguise the Truth by the outer forms of the cosmos, for those who see only multiplicity.
2. The Second Ruse is the disguise of the people of safe-guardedness. They cover up their times with Reality. They keep silent about their extraordinary gifts.
3. The Third Ruse is the disguise of those who hold sway over the world. They show mercy to people by seeming to engage with causes, not for their own sake, but to bring ease to the world. This is the station of Prophets and then of teaching masters, who have emerged from the Valley of Gatheredness and point to its Essence.

These Ruses are created by connecting existing entities to causes, places and events and by attributing knowledge to the means of gaining it, and issues to their justifications, judgements by their evidences, retributions for crimes, and rewards for obedience. Thus contentedness is disguised as contentment and displeasure that warrant connection and separation, and that reveal joy and wretchedness. The Truth is disguised as the truth of matters by reference to causes and material gains. Phenomena are linked to their apparent causes and advantages. Employing such Ruses for feeble eyes and minds, while they perfect their verifications and their practice, they are people who are a mercy from Allāh The Exalted, The Mighty for those people with whom they mingle, who see only multiplicity and seek causes.

There is an entire group called *Melāmatīya* who are in this state. They draw blame and condemnation on themselves, deliberately, so that people do not suspect them of being what they really are. It is a group that has practically disappeared. It is a licence given for advanced wayfarers to put on this cover, this Ruse, to deflect people from knowing their reality, so that they themselves are not deflected from their engagement with the One. The people of Mecca said, 'What kind of prophet are you? You walk in the marketplace, you go and shop and carry your groceries home. You do what normal people do.' They wanted some kind of affirmation of his prophethood by a physical and emotional dimension. The Ruse was that he was exactly that: his prophetic status was hidden or camouflaged by God's Permission, both to protect the Prophet as well as to allow him the necessary essential time to be with the One.

Permission is given to those who are so engrossed in absorption into the One that they need to be protected from being dragged into people's conflicts and dramas and other, less noble distractions, entertainments, practices and activities. The wayfarer seeks ways to disguise their true condition from all other than Allāh, by using Ruses that hide their true spiritual condition. Wayfarers jealously guard their time with their Creator from the eyes and reach of others. This is the way of Prophets who walk in the markets as if they are one with the common folk, eating of their food, and being concerned with their concerns; all the while immersed in an inner Intoxication that is boundless.

10.96. The Door of Existence (*Bāb al-Wujūd*) باب الوجود

يَجِدِ اللَّهَ غَفُورًا رَّحِيمًا

Yajid Illāha ghafūrar-raḥīmā

'He will find Allāh All-Forgiving, All-Merciful.' (*Qur'ān*, 4:110)

لَوَجَدُوا اللَّهَ تَوَّابًا رَّحِيمًا

Lawajadū Allāha tawwābar-raḥīmā

'They would have found Allāh the Turner, the Most Merciful...' (*Qur'ān*, 4:64)

Qaribullah & Darwish translation ~

وَوَجَدَ اللَّهَ

Wa wajad Allāha

'and he found Allāh.' (*Qur'ān*, 24:39)

Wujūd can mean more than three things. It can mean existence, being or finding. *wajd*, for example, means ecstatic state, but its root is 'to find', from the Divine Name *Al-Wājid*. The Qur'anic term for Existence is Finding. The discovery or finding of the unseen is Existence. The limited existence that we see is infinitesimal compared to the Existence of true *wujūd*. Here for the first time, Anṣārī quotes three *āyāt* for one door. At every other door he quoted only one. It is probably for emphasis. *Wujūd*, Existence, the reality of Existence is a form of discovery, and when you know that the reality of any matter comes from Allāh, this gives that matter Existence. Existence emerges from a process of seeking and finding. It is not something that is earned, but something that is Bestowed. You cannot expect to experience Existence except by seeking and yet many people seek and do not find. Finding is a Bestowal from Allāh and is the success that comes from knowing the reality of a matter. It is a Knowledge from the subtler realms that is hurled into the wayfarer's heart. It is higher than any other type of knowledge for it comes by the grace of the All-Knower, displacing and superseding all other forms of knowledge.

Allāh Exalted Most High Is He, has uttered the word Existence in many instances in the *Qur'ān*. Finding is the Name for success in locating the reality of a matter. It is a Name with three meanings:

1. The first is finding Divine Inimitable Knowledge, that undercuts demonstrable knowledge by true disclosure from the Real.
2. The second is finding Reality incontrovertibly, shorn of any signs or indicators.
3. The third is finding the station of the fading away of the forms of existence as one is overwhelmed by the beginnings of the matter of Existence.

Fiftieth Reflection Day:

Give me the flute and sing ~ Gibran Khalil Gibran	اعطني الناي وغنّي ~ جبران خليل جبران
Give me the flute and sing, as singing is the secret of eternity	أعطنى النايَ وغنّ فالغناء سر الخلود
And the cry of the flute remains after existence is annihilated.	و أنين الناي يبقى بعد أن يفنى الوجود
Did you take the forest as a home, as I did, without the castles	هل تخذتَ الغابَ مثلي منزلاً دونَ القصور
Following the streamlets and climbing the rocks?	فتتبّعتَ السواقي و تسلّقتَ الصخور ؟
Did you bathe in perfume and dry yourself with light?	هل تحمّمتَ بعطرٍ و تنشّفتَ بنور
And drink the dawn as wine from ethereal goblets?	و شربتَ الفجر خمرا في كؤوسٍ من أثير ؟
Give me the flute and sing, for singing is the best of prayers	أعطنى الناي وغنّ فالغناء خير الصلاة
And the cry of the flute lingers after the annihilation of life.	و أنين الناي يبقى بعد أن تفنى الحياة
Did you sit in the afternoon, like me, between heavy eyelids the Grapes hanging in sunlit clusters, like golden chandeliers?	هل جلست العصر مثلي بين جفنات العنب
Was the grass as your bed and starry space for your quilt?	هل فرشت العُشبَ ليلاً وتلحّفتَ الفضاء
Ascetic to what will come, forgetful of what is past	زاهداً في ما سيأتي ناسياً ما قد مضى ؟
Give me the flute and sing, for singing is the justice of hearts	أعطني الناي وغنّ فالغنا عدل القلوب
And the cry of flute continues after the perishing of sins.	و أنينُ الناي يبقى بعد أن تفنى الذنوب
Give me the flute and sing, and forget illness and cure	أعطني الناي وغنّ و انسَ داءً ودوا
For human beings are but lines written in water.	إنما الناس سطورٌ كُتِبت لكن بما

WEEK FIFTY-ONE

10.97. The Door of Divestment (*Bāb at-Tajrīd*) باب التجريد

فَاخْلَعْ نَعْلَيْكَ

Fa akhla‘ na‘layk

'Remove your sandals.' (*Qur'ān*, 20:12)

Then we move to the Door of *tajrīd,* translated as Divestment. Here the most apt metaphor from the *Qur'ān* is Allāh addressing Moses when he comes to the most sacred valley and is entering, allegorically, into the Divine Presence, the realm of proximity. There an element of Divestment is required, and the most obvious form of Divestment, the least pure of a person's outer form or attire is shoes and feet, because they walk on all kinds of terrain. Taking off your sandals is a metaphor for divesting yourself from your lower qualities. This is when you are then allowed to enter the realm of purity, or pure existence. Here Divestment is a kind of shedding away: you shed all your preconceptions, acquired knowledge, acquired consciousness, and try as much as possible to be in a transparent state where the light just flows through without meeting any obstacles or blocks, and without casting a shadow. When Moses entered this valley, he entered it in the condition of Divestment—shedding or removing all the cloaks of materiality, physicality and even, in the end, spirituality. You take that mantle off too. That opens to you the Door of Singularity or *tafrīd.*

Divestment is the erasure of seeing the signs, and it is of three degrees:

1. The First Degree is the Divestment of the heart of unveiling from acquired certainty. Divestment is to stop seeing what appears to be seen; in other words, not to confuse the form of a matter with its essence.
2. The Second Degree is the Divestment of the heart of gatheredness from the understanding of knowledge. In many instances, a glimpse of what is desired (for example, certainty) is confused with the absolute certainty that brings no questioning.
3. The Third Degree is the Divestment of the kernel from witnessing Divestment. The wayfarer even needs to be divested from the need for Divestment.

10.98. The Door of Singularity (*Bāb at-Tafrīd*) باب التفريد

وَيَعْلَمُونَ أَنَّ اللَّهَ هُوَ الْحَقُّ الْمُبِينُ

Wa ya'lamūna ann Allāha hūwa al-ḥaqq al-mubīn

'And they know that Allāh is the manifest Truth.' (*Qur'ān*, 24:25)

The Stage of Singularity is comparable to a road with one signpost, whichever way you turn points to the same direction, like a compass that has gone wild, it has, in essence, only one orientation. The orientation is towards the One Truth—*ila al-Ḥaqq*. Then at a higher level it is by the Truth, *bil-ḥaqq*, by the vision of the Reality of the One and finally, it becomes of the Truth, *ma'al-Ḥaqq*. Your experiences, whichever signs you see, take you round a circling, spiralling current, as the dervishes (*darawīsh*) turn and whirl around and around, mirroring the spiral of the galaxy and movement of the whole universe. It is a form of *tafrīd,* an axial connection with the One. You use the cardinal points of the compass in quick succession until you seem to bend space and time to continually confirm the Truth, *al-Ḥaqq,* in a perpetual terrestrial and celestial dance.

Singularity becomes the necessary conclusion and is thus of three degrees:

1. Singularity is the signpost to the One Truth. Whenever the wayfarer experiences and sees an inner reality they first see in it the pointer to the One.
2. Singularity of journeying by way of the Truth. Then the wayfarer experiences all realities with the Eye of the One.
3. Singularity of seeing all realities as emanating from the One and being of that One Truth.

When the constant and continuous affirmation of the One becomes an established station, then the Door of Singularity has been opened. Then comes the second to last stage, that of *Jāmi',* gatheredness and Allāh is The Gatherer, *Al-Jāmi'*. Singularity is the word that refers to the signs to the Real, which has the following three degrees, then by the Real, which has the final three degrees, and from or of the Real, which has the preceding three degrees. All of these are still part of Singularity and are to be contemplated as facets of an holistic unity, rather than compartmentalised as three separate entities—somewhat reminiscent of the much misunderstood mystery of the Trinity.

As for the Singular reference of the signs to the Real, it is of these three degrees:

1. The Singular devotion to the purpose because of yearning.
2. Then the Singular devotion to Love, even to destruction.
3. Then the Singular devotion to witnessing, for the sake of connectedness.

As for the singular reference of the signs by the Real, this is of three degrees:

1. Referring to the Singularity of the signs with pride.
2. Acting on the Singularity of the signs with good conduct.
3. Protecting the Singularity of the signs with constrictiveness

It is of outer expansiveness that encompasses a pure constrictiveness, to guide towards the Real and to call on Him.

Fifty-First Reflection Day:

O God!
If another found You through Inquiry, I found You by fleeing from me.
If another found You through invocation, I found You through self-forgetting.
If another found You by seeking, It's from You I found the seeking!
O God!
You are Yourself the *means* to Yourself, You were the First and are also the Last.
To say any more would be meaningless.*

WEEK FIFTY-TWO

10.99. The Door of Gatheredness (*Bāb al-Jāmiʿ*) باب الجامع

وَمَا رَمَيْتَ إِذْ رَمَيْتَ وَلَكِنَّ اللَّهَ

Wamā ramayta idh ramayta wa lākinna Allāh

'And you did not throw when you threw; but it was Allāh Who Threw.' (*Qur'ān*, 8:17)

The *aya* descended during a battle in which the early Muslims were supported by Angelic Forces so, even greatly outnumbered, they won,

*Al-Iskandarī, A. & Anṣārī, A. (1979) *Ibn 'Ata' Illah: The book of Wisdom; Kwaja Abdullah Anṣārī: Intimate conversations*. Translations & notes by Victor Danner & Wheeler Thackston, New York: Paulist Press. P. 248.

and were very pleased with themselves. This *aya* reminds them that it was not them who won, and they should not give themselves too much credit, as it was Allāh Who Helped them. Gatheredness (*jāmi'*) is a condition of the wayfarer: by referring the entire circumstance back to Allāh, all of creation and existence is gathered in His Hand. It is not to deny the limited truth of causality, but it is just that—limited and conditional. To have any reality all conditioned forms of existence and casualties have to flow back to their Source, and the wayfarer knows that the unfolding of events in time and space are moved by the Ultimate Cause. They occur the way they do because of the Actions of Allāh Who tips them into existence. This is called *tarjiḥ* (ترجيح) and there are infinite potentials of things to come into being, but only one comes into being because of the One Who Tips it into existence, from the realms of the unseen into being as we experience it.

Gatheredness is what demolishes multiplicity, cuts allusions, and moves beyond water and clay after being truly established, free of any colourings and dualities, ceasing to be aware of causality and ceasing to witness its features. It is of three degrees:

1. The Gatheredness of knowledge is the dissolution of the knowledge of proofs in pure Divine Knowledge.
2. The Gatheredness of existence is the dissolution of the terminus of connectivity in the Essence of Existence.
3. The Gatheredness of essences is the dissolution of all the pointers of allusions into the Essence of the Real.

Gatheredness is the purpose of all the Stations of Wayfarers. It is the shoreline of the Ocean of Unicity.

10.100. The Door of Unity (*Bāb at-Tawḥīd*) باب التوحيد

شَهِدَ اللَّهُ أَنَّهُ لَا إِلَٰهَ إِلَّا هُو

Shahid Allāhu lā ilāha illā Hū

'Allāh bears witness that there is no god but He.' (*Qur'ān*, 3:18)

This gives you the last door, the Door of Unity. It is not the oft expressed and discussed *tawḥīd*, which is the *tawḥīd* of two, i.e. confirmation of the Unity of the One by another party. It is the *tawḥīd* of Allāh referring to Himself in the *Qur'ān*, Bearing Witness that there is no god but He—it is the *tawḥīd* of the One—Uniting all in His Oneness. This is the highest form. It is not the *tawḥīd* of human beings, trying to draw everything back into a singular Source: that is a great *tawḥīd* of sorts, that of the previous station, but it is the *tawḥīd* of the One by the One and all we can do is to acknowledge that. It is the knowledge of our affirmation, our confirmation, that Unity itself is what Allāh has Ordained. That is what He Says in the *Qur'ān*. This must be the highest station of the wayfarer. We experienced *tawḥīd* in many limited ways, the adjective *tawḥīdi* has become a kind of shorthand, but the Truth of *Tawḥīd* is God's *Tawḥīd,* not our *tawḥīd.*

There is no higher knowledge possible at all levels of spiritual accomplishment and it has three degrees:

1. The First Aspect is the Unicity of the beginner. This is corrected by the signs. It is the affirmation that there is no deity but Allāh.
2. The Second Aspect is the Unicity of the wayfarer. This is confirmed by realities, and it is the assertion that the entire circumstance of existence and creation emanates from and returns to Him.
3. The Third Aspect is the Unicity born of eternity. For the final stages of the journey, it is the knowledge that Unity Itself is what Allāh has ordained upon Himself. Here the Stations of the *Manāzil* end.

Unicity is the Sanctification of Allāh above all originated matters. For the scholars spoke of what they spoke, and the verifiers indicated what they indicated in this way, for the purpose of correcting Unicity. And anything else from state or station, all carry defects.

The First Unicity is the testimony that there is no deity but God, Alone with no partners, the singular, The Eternal who was neither born nor gave birth, with no likening unto Him. This is the clear and apparent Unicity, which negates the major error of association. On Unicity was the direction of prayer set, and to It is allegiance due; on It life and property were guarded, and the lands of *Islām* were separate from the lands of unbelief. On It the faith of common folk was validated, even if they were unable to prove its tenets after they had freed themselves from misconceptions, confusion, and doubt, and even after they had, nevertheless, established Its Truth through an accepting heart, and the signs are the message and the existent things. It is binding by Listening to the message. It is found by seeing the Splendour of the Real and grows on seeing the signs.

The Second Unicity, which is confirmed by witnessing the reality of things, is Unicity based on dropping of apparent causes, transcending the disputations of the intellect and ceasing from clinging to the visible signs. It is not to seek proofs for Unicity nor to find justifications in reliance, nor to find the means in salvation. Rather, the seeker sees the ancientness of the Real in His Wisdom and Knowledge and His Justice in placing of matters in their appropriate positions, all the while binding them inside their true measure and covering their nature in their outer form. The seeker would have perfected his understanding of the defects in knowledge and progressed on the path of seeing beyond originated things. This is the Unicity which is refined by the knowledge of annihilation, and purified by the knowledge of gatheredness. This Unicity is irresistibly attracted to the Unicity of the masters of Unity.

As for the Third Unicity, it is the Unicity that the Real has kept for Himself and He alone is Entitled to it as He is the Most Powerful. He Revealed Flashes of it to the inner secrets of His Chosen ones. They are as if mute in their incapacity to describe it, unable to relay it to others— and this is what is meant when the tongues of the guides on the path speak of fleeing from, or abandoning the originated things, affirming only the Eternal beyond time. However, this symbol of Unicity is inherently flawed and ought to be dropped. This is the kernel of the symbols used by scholars on this path but irrespective of how superlative they are in describing and classifying this Unicity, it becomes ever more concealed when attempts are made to explain it, more elusive when classified and more difficult when described.

It is this Unicity to which people of spiritual excellence and refined states strive. It is this Unicity which is the purpose of those who glorify The Almighty, and those who speak of the essence of gatheredness. Upon this Unicity crash all symbols and metaphors. No tongue could ever speak about it, nor any sign point to it. Unicity is beyond the capacities of originated things, nor is it apprehended in certain ages or explained by causes. The Unicity of the Sufis could be described in these three verses:

No one singled out the One...for everyone who did so denied Him.

The Unicity of one who speaks of His Essence...is merely a borrowing cancelled by the One.

His Unicity of Himself is His Unicity...other descriptions by His describers are false.

Fifty-Second Reflection Day:

Recommended *Dhikr* for the Stage of the Endings:

Al-Bāqī (The Eternally Remaining) *Al-Wāḥid* (The One) *Al-Jāmi'* (The Gatherer)

Yā Bāqī ~ Yā Wāḥid ~ Yā Jāmi' يا باقي ~ يا واحد ~ يا جامع

Appendix 1
Dhikr for all Stages of *Shaykh* ʾAbdullah al-Anṣārī's *Manāzil is-Sā'irīn*

Each Stage has an overarching pair of Divine Names which hold sway over its contents and context. Some pairs are polarities (i.e. opposites), while other reaffirm the former.

Each Name in the suggested *Dhikr* (e.g. *Yā Mujīb ~ Yā Laṭīf ~ Yā Karīm*) is to be recited 33 times, 99 for each Stage + 1 *Yā Allāh* per Stage to confirm *Tawḥīd* = 1,133 in total.

1 Dhikr for the Preliminary Stage of Stirrings (Taḥrikāt/Tamḥīdiyāt):

Overarching Names: *Al-Bāṭin* (The Hidden) *Aẓ-Ẓāhir* (The Manifest) الباطن الظاهر

Al-Fattāḥ (The Opener) *Al-Qādir* (The Enabler) *Al-Muqaddim* (The Advancer) *Al-Mu'akhkhir* (The Delayer)

Yā Fattāḥ ~ Yā Qādir ~ Yā Muqaddim ~ Yā Mu'ākhir يا فتاح ~ يا قادر ~ يا مقدم ~ يا مؤخر

2 Dhikr for the Stage 1 of Beginnings (al-Bidāyāt) :

Overarching Names: *Al-Muḥyī* (The Lifegiver) *Al-Mumīt* (The Lifetaker) المحيي المميت

Al-Mubdi' (The Originator) *At-Tawwāb* (The All-Forgiver) *As-Samī*ʿ (The All-Hearer)

*Yā Mubdi' ~ Yā Tawwāb ~ Yā Samī*ʿ يا مبدئ ~ يا تواب ~ يا سميع

3 Dhikr for the Stage 2 of Gateways (al-Abwāb):

Overarching Names: *Al-Muʿiz* (The Ennobler) *Al-Mudhil* (The Humiliator) المعز المذل

Al-Mujīb (The One Who Responds) *Al-Laṭīf* (The Most Subtle) *Al-Karīm* (The Most Generous)

Yā Mujīb ~ Yā Laṭīf ~ Yā Karīm يا مجيب ~ يا لطيف ~ يا كريم

4 Dhikr for the Stage 3 of Deeds (al-Muʿamalāt):

Overarching Names: *Al-Qawī* (The All-Powerful) *Al-Muntaqim* (The Rectifier) القوي المنتقم

Al-Raqīb (The Vigilant) *Al-Wakīl* (The Trustee) *Al-Nāfi'* (The Bestower of Benefits)

Yā Raqīb ~ Yā Wakīl ~ Yā Nāfi' يا رقيب ~ يا وكيل ~ يا نافع

5 Dhikr for the Stage 4 of Ethics (al-Akhlāq):

Overarching Names: *Al-Muqīṭ* (The Nourisher) *Al-Muqsiṭ* (The Equitable) المقيط المقسط

Aṣ-Ṣabūr (The Ever-Patient) *Ash-Shakūr* (The Ever-Grateful) *Al-Ḥalim* (The Ever-Clement/Forbearing)

Yā Ṣabūr ~ Yā Shakūr ~ Yā Ḥalīm يا صبور ~ يا شكور ~ يا حليم

6 Dhikr for the Stage 5 of Roots (al-ʾUṣūl):

Overarching Names: *Al-Bāʾith* (The Resurrector) *Al–ʿAẓīm* (The Mighty) الباعث العظيم

Al-Muqtadir (The Source of All Power) *Al-Mu'min* (The Inspirer of Faith) *Al-Mughnī* (The Bestower of Wealth)

Yā Muqtadir ~ Yā Mu'min ~ Yā Mughnī يا مقتدر ~ يا مؤمن ~ يا مغني

7 Dhikr for the Stage 6 of Valleys (al-Awdiya):

Overarching Names: *Al-Khabīr* (The All-Aware) *Al-Baṣīr* (The All-Seeing) الخبير البصير

Al-ʿAlī (The Most High) *Al-ʿAlīm* (The All-Knower) *Al-Ḥakīm* (The All-Wise)

Yā ʿAlī ~ Yā ʿAlīm ~ Yā Hakīm يا علي ~ يا عليم ~ يا حكيم

8 Dhikr for the Stage 7 of the States (al-Ahwal):

Overarching Names: *Al-ʾAdl* (The Just) *Al-Ḥafiẓ* (The Sustainer) العدل الحفيظ

Al-Wudūd (The Beloved) *Al-Matīn* (The Existent) *Al-Muhaymin* (The Protector)

Yā Wudūd ~ Yā Matīn ~ Yā Muhaymin يا ودود ~ يا متين ~ يا مهيمن

9 Dhikr for the Stage 8 of Guardianship (al-Walāyāt):

Overarching Names: *Al-Wāli* (The Guardian) *Al-Walī* (The Close Friend) الوالي الوليي

Al-Walī (The Friend) *Al-Wārith* (The Inheritor) *Ar-Rāfiʾ* (The Uplifter)

Yā Walī ~ Yā Wārith ~ Yā Rāfiʾ يا والي ~ يا وارث ~ يا رافع

10 Dhikr for the Stage 9 of Realities (al-Ḥaqā'iq):

Overarching Names: *Al-Rashīd* (The Teacher) *Ash-Shahīd* (The Witness) الرشيد الشهيد

Al-Ḥayy (The Ever-Living) *Al-Qābidh* (The Constrictor) *Al-Bāsiṭ* (The Expander)

Yā Ḥayy ~ Yā Qābiḍ ~ Yā Bāsiṭ يا حي ~ يا قابض ~ يا باسط

11 Dhikr for the Stage 10 of the Endings (al-Nihayāt):

Overarching Names: *Al-Awwal* (The First) *Al-Ākhir* (The Last) الأول الآخر

Al-Bāqi (The Eternally Remaining) *Al-Wāḥid* (The One) *Al-Jāmiʿ* (The Gatherer)

Yā Bāqī ~ Yā Wāḥid ~ Yā Jāmiʿ يا باقي ~ يا واحد ~ يا جامع

Appendix 2
Twenty-Eight Stages of Being and Consciousness in Ibn ʾArabi's Seals of Wisdom

Self *Nafs*	Prophet	Soul Level	Form	Wisdom *Ḥikma*	Planet
1	Adam	*Ammāra*	Tetrahedron	Speech	Mars
2	Seth	*Lawwāma*	Cube/Hexahedron	Angelic Inspiration	Jupiter
3	Noaḥ/Nuḥ	*Mulhama*	Octahedron	Divine Inspiration	Saturn
4	Enoch/Idrīs	*Muṭma'inna*	Dodecahedron	Sanctification	Venus
5	Abraham	*Rāḍiya*	16-point star	Being lost in Love	Mercury
6	Isaac/Isḥāq	*Marḍīya*	Icosahedron	The Real in Word	Neptune
7	Ishmael/ Ismāʿīl	*Insān al-Kamil*	24-point star	Elevation in the Word of *Ismāʿīl*	Earth/moon /Uranus

Heart *Qalb*	Prophet Nabī	Level	Element	Wisdom *Ḥikma*	Planet
8	Jacob/Yaʿqūb	*Al-Fu'ād*	Fire	*Ruḥ* in the Word	Mars
9	Joseph/Yūsuf	*Al-Lubb*	Water	Light in the Word	Jupiter
10	Eber/Hūd	*Al-Fu'ād*	Earth	Unity in the Word	Saturn
11	Shelah/Sāleḥ	*Al-Lubb*	Air	Revelation in Word	Mercury
12	Jethro/Shuʿāyb	*Al-Lubb*	Earth	Heart in the Word	Venus
13	Lot/Lūṭ	*Al-Qalb*	Water	Power in the Word	Neptune
14	Ezra/ʿUzāyr	*Al-Qalb*	Water	Decree in the Word	Uranus

soul *Rūḥ*	Prophet Nabī	Wisdom *Ḥikma*	Soul Level
15	Jesus/ʿIsa	Prophecy in the Word	*Ammāra*
16	Solomon/Sulaymān	Mercy in the Word	*Lawwāma*
17	David/Dāwūd	Existence in the Word	*Mulhama*
18	Jonas/Yūnus	Breath in the Word	*Muṭma'inna*
19	Job/Ayyūb	The unseen in the Word	*Rāḍiya*
20	John/Yeḥya	Majesty in the Word	*Marḍīya*
21	Zakarīya	Sovereignty in the Word	*Insān al-Kāmil*

spirit *Rūḥ*	Prophet Nabī	Wisdom *Ḥikma*	Geographical Area
22	Elijah/Eliās	Intimacy in the Word	Palestine/Syria
23	Luqmān	*Iḥsān* in the Word	Nubia/Sudān
24	Aaron/Harūn	Imamate in the Word	Palestine/Egypt
25	Moses/Mūsa	Sublimity in the Word	Palestine/Egypt
26	Khālid	*Aṣ-Ṣamad* in the Word	Arabia/Interspace
27	Muḥammad	Unique Wisdom in the Word	Arabia/Ḥijāz
28	God Allāh	Creation in The Word	Everywhere

Glossary of Arabic Terms

Adab – Courtesy, manners, politeness
Akhlāq – Ethics, morals, good conduct
Allāh – God, The Absolute
Anṣār – Prophet's Helpers
'Aql / 'uqūl – Intellect(s), mind(s)
'Aṣl / 'Uṣūl – Origin(s), root(s)
Asmā' al-Ḥusna – Divine Names
Asnām – Idols
'Atash – Thirst
Āya / ayāt – Verse(s)
'Ayn – Eye, wellspring
Barzakh – Interspace, hereafter italicise and correct Iman
'Azm – Determination
Bāb / Abwāb – Door(s), gate(s)
Baqā' – Eternity
Baraka – Blessing
Barq – Lightning Flashes
Bashā'ir – Stirrings
Baṣīra – Inner Sight
Basṭ – Expansiveness, expansion
Bidāyā – Beginning
Dahshe – Astonishment
Dhawq – Taste
Dhikr / adhkār – Remembrance, litanies
Dīn / adyān – Religion(s), reconnection, return
Du'ā – Supplication
Dunya – Earthly life
Fajr – Dawn
Fanā' – Annihilation
Faqr – Poverty
Firār – Abandonment, Fleeing
Firāṣa – Clairvoyance
Fu'ād – Spiritual heart
Futtūwwa – Nobility, chivalry
Ghaflah – Heedlessness, oblivion
Gharq – Drowning
Ghāyba – Detachment
Ghinā' – Wealth
Ghīra – Vigilance, jealousy
Ghūrba – Exile, absence, strangeness
Ḥadīth – Prophetic saying(s)
Ḥajj – Pilgrimage
Ḥāl / aḥwāl – Spiritual state(s), condition(s)
Hanīf – Universal monotheism
Ḥaqīqa / Ḥaqā'iq – Reality, realities
Ḥaqq – Truth, right
Ḥawza – Circle of knowledge, seminary
Ḥayā – Life, Modesty
Hayaman – Overwhelm
Ḥayra – Confusion, Perplexity
Hidāya – Guidance
Hijri – Islamic lunar calendar
Ḥikma – Wisdom
Ḥimma – Resolve
Ḥobb / maḥbūb – Love, beloved
Ḥūrma – Sanctuary
Ḥuzn – Sorrow
'Ibādāt – Acts of worship
Idrāk – Realisation
Iḍṭirāb – Agitation
Iftirāḍāt – Assumptions
Iḥsān – Goodness, improvement
Ikhbāt – Quietening
Ikhlāṣ – Sincerity
Ikhtiār – Selection
Iktisāb – That which is earned
Ilā – towards
Ilhām / Mulhama -Inspiration, inspired
Illa – Except, with the exception of
'Ilm – Knowledge, science
Īmān / mu'min – Faith, believer
Ināba – Delegation
Inbisāṭ – Exuberance

Infiṣāl – Disconnection, separation
Insān(a) – Human being
Inziʿāj – Agitation, disturbance
Irada – Will, wilfulness
ʿIrfān(i) – Mysticism, esoteric, mystical
Ishfāq – Concern
Islām / Istislām – Yielding, submission, surrender
Istiqām – Uprightness
Ithār – Preference
It'tiṣāl – Connection
Iʿtiṣām – Steadfastness
Jalālī – Majestic
Jamālī – Beautiful
Jāmiʿ – Gatheredness
Kahf – Cave
Kāmāl / Kāmil – Complete, Perfect(ion)
Khabr / akhbār – News, report(s)
Khalaqa / Khalq / Khallaq – Creation, innovator
Khalīfa / khulafaʾ – Caliph(s)
Khāliṣ – Unadulterated
Khawf – Apprehensiveness, fear
Khulūq – Good Character
Khushūʿ – Reverence
Khwāja – Venerable
Kufr / kāfir – Disbelief, unbeliever
Kun fa yakūn – Be and it is
Lahdh – Instant Recognition
Lā ilāha illa Allāh – No god but God
Lawm / Lawwāma – Reproach, blaming
Libās – Dress, clothing
Lubb – Core, kernel
Lumaʿ – Shining jewels
Maʿārifa / ʿArif(īn) – Gnosis, gnostic(s)
Malāmatiya – Blame-seekers
Maghreb – Sunset prayer
Maḥabba – Love, care
Majdhūb – Irresistibly attracted, drawn
Malik / Mamlaka – King, kingdom
Manṭaq – Conference, logic
Manzal / Manāzil – Stage(s), halting points, landings
Maqām – State, condition, standpoint
Maraj al-baḥrayn – Confluence of the two seas
Marāyāt – Mirrors
Mathal / amthāl – Parable(s), proverb(s), example(s)
Mawadda – Love, affection
Mawjūd – Present, extant
Muʿamal / Muʿamalāt – Deeds, dealings
Muʿāyāna – Pondering, wondering
Muhājirūn – Migrants from Mecca
Muḥarram – First month of the Islamic year
Muḥāssaba – Accountability
Mukāshifa – Unveiling
Munājāt – Adorations, Exhortations
Murād – Desired, wanted
Murāqaba – Watchfulness, vigilance
Murīd – Adept, disciple, follower, novice,
Mushāhada – Witnessing
Muthābara – Perseverance
Naʾām – Bounties
Nabi – Prophet
Nafas – Breath, breathing
Nafs / nufūs – Ego, personal self, selves
Nāsi / nisyān – Forgetful one(s)
Nihāya / Nihāyāt – Ending(s)
Nūr / Anwār – Light(s)
Qabḍ – Constrictiveness, constriction, contraction
Qalb – Physical heart
Qalaq – Anxiety
Qamar – Moon
Qaṣd – Purposefulness
Qisim – Part, section
Qudsi – Holy
Qurʾān – That which is recited

Raghba – Inclination
Raḥma – Compassion, Mercy
Rajā' – Confident Expectancy
Ri'āya – Protection
Riḍa / Rāḍia / Murḍiya) – Contentment, content, contented with
Riyāḍa – Spiritual Exercises
Rifqa – Companionship
Ṣabr – Patience
Ṣafā'a – Purity
Safar – Travelling
Saḥw – Sobriety
Sā'ir / Sā'ira / Sā'irīn – Wayfarer(s)
Sakīna – Serenity
Salāh – Prayer
Samā' – Sky, heavens
Sama*'* – Audition, listening
Ṣidq – Truthfulness
Silsila / silsilāt – Chain(s)
Sirr – Secrecy, secret
Sukr – Intoxication, drunkenness
Sunnah – Prophetic deeds
Sūra / sūrāt – Chapter(s)
Surūr – Rejoicing
Shadda – Strong, double weight letter
Shahada – Witnessing, testimony
Shams – Sun
Sharī'a / shara'i – Law, legal, path
Shawq – Longing, yearning
Shaykh – Spiritual Leader, Teacher
Shukr – Gratitude
Tabaṭṭul – Devotion
Ṭabaqāt – Classes, grades, levels, stages
Tadhakkur – Reflection
Tafakkur – Reflection
Tafrīd – Singularity
Tafwīḍ – Delegation
Taḥaddi – Challenge
Tahdhīb – Refinement
Taḥqīq – Inquiry, confirmation, Verification
Tajrīd – Divestment
Tajwīd – Rules of recitation
Talbis – Clothing, dressing, Ruses
Tamakkun – Capability, capacity
Ṭama'nīna / Mutma'inna – Assured/ness
Tamhīdiyāt – Preliminaries
Tarjiḥ – Preference
Tartīb – Ordering, organising, tidying
Ṭarīqa / ṭuruq – Path, Sufi group, way
Taṣawwuf – Sufism, esoteric *Islām*
Taslīm – Surrender
Tawāḍu' – Diffidence
Tawakkul – Reliance
Tawba – Recognition of Error
Tawḥīd – Unity, unicity
Ṭayr – Flying bird
Ta'ẓīm – Exaltation
Thiqa – Confidence
Uns – Intimacy
Wādī / Awdiyā' – Valley(s)
Wā'y – Awareness, Consciousness
Wajd – Ecstasy
Waqt – Moment, time, momentousness
Warā' – Self-discipline
Wilāya – Guardianship, intimate friendship
Wujūd – Being, Existence, Presence
Yaqḍa – Awakening
Yaqīn – Certainty, Certitude
Zuhd – Asceticism

Bibliography

Al-Ghazali, A.H.M. (1924). *Mishkāt Al-Anwār. 'The Niche for Lights.' A translation with introduction by W. H. T. Gairdner.* (Asiatic Society Monographs. vol. 19.).

Al-Iskandarī, A. & Anṣārī, A. (1979) *Ibn 'Ata' Illah: The Book of Wisdom ; Kwaja Abdullah Anṣārī : Intimate conversations*. Translations & notes by Victor Danner & Wheeler Thackston, New York: Paulist Press.

Al-Rawi, R-F., (2015) *Divine Names: 99 Healing Names of the One Love.* Calligraphy by Maje Seif, translation by Monique Arav. Northampton MA: Interlink Books.

Al-Rawi, R-F., (2017) *Göttliche Namen: Die 99 Heilenden Namen der Einen Liebe*. Kalligraphie von Majed Seif. Neu Isenburg: Cosmics Verlag.

Al-Shabrāwī, 'A. K. (1997) *The Degrees of the Soul: spiritual Stations on the Sufi path*. London: Quilliam Press.

Anṣārī al-Harāwī, 'A. M. & Rifâ'î, H. (2011) *Stations of the Wayfarers*. Paris: Albouraq.

Anṣārī al-Harāwī, 'A. M. (1976) *Manāzil al-sāyirīn*. Ravan Farhadi, A. G. ed. Kābul: Bayhaqī Kitāb Khparawulo Mu'assasah.

Anṣārī al-Harawī, A. M., 'A & Angha, N. (2010) *Stations of the Sufi Path: the one hundred fields Sad maydān of 'Abdu"llāh Anṣārī of Herat*. Cambridge: Archetype.

Anṣārī al-Harawī, A. M., 'A. & Singh, J. (1939) *The Persian Mystics: The Invocations of Shaykh 'Abdullāh Anṣārī of Herat, A.D. 1005-1090*. [1st ed.]. London: J. Murray.

'Aṭṭār, F. al-D. (1974) *The Conference of the Birds: Mantiq Ut-tair : a philosophical religious poem in prose*. London: Routledge and Kegan Paul.

Ghazzālī, A. (1986) *Sawāniḥ: Inspirations from the world of Pure Spirits. The Oldest Persian Sufi treatise on Love.* KPI.

Goethe, J. W. von (1967) *Goethe's Theory of colours. Translated by Charles Lock Eastlake.* London: Frank Cass & C.o.

Haeri, F. (2008) *Witnessing Perfection*. Ropley: O Books.

Haeri, F. (2001) *The Wisdom of Ibn Ata'Allah.* A Translation and Commentary. London: Zahra Trust.

Ibn Arabi, M. (2014). *The Four Pillars of Spiritual Transformation.* Trans. Stephen Hirtenstein. Oxford: Anqa Publishing.

Ibn al-'Arabī (1980) *The Seals of Wisdom*. Norwich: Diwan.

'Irāqī, F. al-D. I. et al. (1982) *Divine Flashes*. Translation and Introduction by William Chittick and Peter Lamborn Wolson, Preface by Seyyed Hussein Nasr. New York: Paulist Press.

Jabbar, A., Jabbar J. (2012) *Abdullah Al-Anṣārī and his work*. England: [publisher not identified].

Jalāl al-Dīn Rūmī & Helminski, K. E. (2008) *The Pocket Rumi*. Boston, Mass: Shambhala.

Katz, S. T. (2013) *Comparative mysticism: an anthology of original sources*. Oxford: Oxford University Press.

Khalidi, T. (2008) *The Qur'ān*. London: Penguin Classics.

Quṭb al-Jīlī, ʿA.K.I. & Burckhardt, T. (1983) *Universal man*. Sherborne: Beshara.

Maybudī, A. F., Rashīd al-Dīn, Anṣārī al-Harawī, ʿA. M., Ḥikmat, ʿA. A. (1960) *Kashf al-asrār va ʿuddat al-abrār: maʿrūf bi-Tafsīr-i Khvajah ʿAbd Allāh Anṣārī*. Tehrān: Intishārāt-i Dānishgāh-i.

Milani, S. F. H. (2011) *Prayer*. London: Islam English Press.

Milani, S. F. H. & Hegedüs, A. (2004) *The source of Islamic spirituality: comment on Surah 17 The Night Journey—Surah Isrāʾ / Bani Isra'il*. London: Islam in English Press.

Newton, I. (2003) *Opticks*. Amherst, N.Y.; Prometheus Books.

Niffarī , M. A. J. (1935) *The Mawāqif and Mukhātabāt of Muhammad Ibn ʿAbd ʿL-Jabbār Al-Niffarī: with other fragments*. Ed. Trans. Arthur John Arbery. Cambridge University Press for the Trustees of the 'E.: J. W. Gibb Memorial'; London, Luzac & co.

Ṣadr al-Dīn Shīrāzī, M. ibn I. & Peerwani, L.P. (2008) *spiritual psychology: the fourth intellectual journey in transcendent philosophy: volumes VIII & IX of the Asfar*. London: ICAS.

Regin, D. & Schiller, F. (1965) *Freedom and dignity. The historical and philosophical thought of Schiller.* The Hague: Martinus Nijhoff.

Shah-Kazemi, H.R. (2019). *Imam ʿAli: From Concise History to Timeless Mystery.* London: The Matheson Trust for the Study of Comparative Religion.

Steiner, R. (2011) *The Philosophy of Freedom (the Philosophy of Spiritual Activity): the Basis for a Modern world Conception*. Special ed. Forest Row: Rudolf Steiner Press.

Steiner, R. H. (1937) *Knowledge of the Higher Worlds and Its Attainment: a Revised and Enlarged Edition of 'The way of Initiation' with 'Initiation and its Results'*. 3rd. ed. / Authorised English translation by G. Metaxa / Edited by H. Collison. S.l: Rudolf Steiner Publishing Co.

Suhrawardī, Y. ibn Ḥabash & Ziai, H. (1998) *The Book of Radiance: Partaw'nāmah : a parallel English-Persian text*. Costa Mesa, Calif: Mazda Publishers.

Ṭāhā, M. M. (1987) *The Second Message of Islam.* 1st ed. Trans. A. A. An-Na'im. Syracuse, New York: Syracuse University Press.

Zajonc, A. (1993). *Catching the light: The Entwined History of Light and Mind.* Oxford University Press.

About the Authors

'ABDULLAH AL-ANṢĀRĪ (1006–1089), also known as Pir-i Herat, was a Sufi saint who lived in Herat, Ghaznavid Empire (modern-day Afghanistan). Ansari was a commentator on the Qur'an, scholar of the Hanbali school of thought (madhhab), traditionalist, polemicist and spiritual master, known for his oratory and poetic talents in the Persian language.

ALI ALLAWI is an economist, historian–biographer and award-winning author. His works include *The Occupation of Iraq: Winning the War, Losing the Peace* (2007), *The Crisis of Islamic Civilisation (2009), Faisal I of Iraq* (2014), *The Spiritual Path: Conversation with a Sufi Master* (2017) and *Rich World, Poor World* (2024). He has served in government in the Republic of Iraq as Minister of Finance and Deputy Prime Minister, and has followed the Sufi path for the past 50 years.

JULIA KATARINA is a trained mezzo-soprano, multi-instrumentalist and accomplished performer of both Arabic and European classical repertoire, cellist in three orchestras and solo oud song recitalist. She holds an MSc in Applied Music Psychology and an MA in Islamic Studies. Having made the ultimate Christian pilgrimage to Jerusalem in 2008, she embraced Islam in Al-Aqsa mosque while living and teaching at music schools in Palestine, where she also learned fluent Arabic. Her musical journey is intertwined with her spiritual path having performed Qawwali and Persian Ṣūfī music.